MW00579352

"This book offers tremendous encouragem
in worship. John Rempel takes his readers beyond words to gestures, beyond preaching to sacraments. Rightly convinced that heavenly things are mediated by earthly things, he challenges us to leave behind the rationalism of the Enlightenment's disenchanted universe and to take seriously the truth that the incarnation places us in a sacramental universe."

Hans Boersma, Saint Benedict Servants of Christ Chair in Ascetical Theology, Nashotah House Theological Seminary

"Though this book will be valuable to worship planners and leaders of all traditions, *Recapturing an Enchanted World* is an especially rich resource for liturgically lean traditions. Offering astute guidance through the thickets of sacramental history and theology, this book illuminates what was lost by dissenters and Free Churches in the Reformation and invites rediscovery of 'the bounty of a sacramental universe.' What makes the book stand apart is Rempel's gift for felicitous language, well-considered examples, and abiding passion for wholehearted worship embodied in word and deed—a true treasure for all who care about worship."

Marlene Kropf, professor emerita in spiritual formation and worship, Anabaptist Mennonite Biblical Seminary, Elkhart, Indiana

"Rempel contrasts today's 'disenchanted' world, where the material realm is self-sufficient and empty of Spirit, with the 'enchanted' world, where Spirit shapes matter through colors, shapes, and movements. Sacraments mediate Spirit through common physical actions and elements: eating (bread), drinking (wine), and washing (baptism). Sacraments celebrate Spirit and matter's most intense interaction: God's incarnation in creaturely fragility. God's Spirit continues creation's transformation by renewing individuals, uniting them, and enabling them everywhere to further shape the world."

Thomas Finger, author of *A Contemporary Anabaptist Theology: Biblical, Historical, Constructive*

"John Rempel in *Recapturing an Enchanted World* has masterfully examined and argued for the centrality of meaningful sacrament and ritual within the Body of Christ. His book persuasively invites the reader to embrace the mystery of Christ in how we shape our worship."

Bruxy Cavey, teaching pastor of the Meeting House, Ontario, Canada, and author of *The End of Religion*

"John Rempel gently leads the reader on an intimate journey through the middle ground between history's excesses concerning 'sacrament.' His simple, gentle persuasion nurtures a renewed appreciation for the significance of our corporate actions and should facilitate understanding and promote conversation within and across Christian traditions, helping us fulfill Jesus' prayer that we 'may be one.' I intend to require my students to become his companions."

Timothy Ralston, professor of pastoral ministry, Dallas Theological Seminary

"The incarnation of our Lord is a minor doctrine for many, but John Rempel recounts its significance for worship, doctrine, and practice. *Recapturing an Enchanted World* orients us historically within time and place, but only to remind us spiritually of our transcendent end. This gentle and pious scholar wants us to see the full spiritual reality of our incarnate Lord Jesus through word and sacrament—wisdom calls us to hear him."
Malcolm B. Yarnell III, author of *God the Trinity* and *The Formation of Christian Doctrine*

"John Rempel draws on decades of ministry and study to offer a welcome alternative to the 'lean,' disenchanted liturgical traditions that leave us in unbridgeable isolation and thicker, enchanted traditions that have lost an ethical component and, therefore, relevance to our neighbors. He fleshes out a free-church notion of the transformative sacramentality of congregational life that bears the love of God to the world."
Stephen B. Boyd, J. Allen Easley Professor for the Study of Religions, Wake Forest University

DYNAMICS OF CHRISTIAN WORSHIP

RECAPTURING AN ENCHANTED WORLD

RITUAL AND SACRAMENT IN THE FREE CHURCH TRADITION

JOHN D. REMPEL

Foreword by GORDON T. SMITH

Academic

An imprint of InterVarsity Press
Downers Grove, Illinois

InterVarsity Press
P.O. Box 1400, Downers Grove, IL 60515-1426
ivpress.com
email@ivpress.com

InterVarsity Press® is the book-publishing division of InterVarsity Christian Fellowship/USA®, a movement of students and faculty active on campus at hundreds of universities, colleges, and schools of nursing in the United States of America, and a member movement of the International Fellowship of Evangelical Students. For information about local and regional activities, visit intervarsity.org.

Cover design and image composite: David Fassett
Interior design: Jeanna Wiggins
Images: trees in forest: © Alexander Schitschka / EyeEm / Getty Images Plus
         white wall background: © Nadine Westveer / EyeEm / Getty Images

ISBN 978-0-8308-4929-1 (print)
ISBN 978-0-8308-5117-1 (digital)

Printed in the United States of America ∞

InterVarsity Press is committed to ecological stewardship and to the conservation of natural resources in all our operations. This book was printed using sustainably sourced paper.

Library of Congress Cataloging-in-Publication Data
A catalog record for this book is available from the Library of Congress

P	24	23	22	21	20	19	18	17	16	15	14	13	12	11	10	9	8	7	6	5	4	3	2	1
Y	40	39	38	37	36	35	34	33	32	31	30	29	28	27	26	25	24	23	22	21	20

IN GRATITUDE TO MY FRIENDS

in East and West Berlin (1971–1973)

and in New York City (1989–2003)

who opened brave, new, and beguiling worlds to me

CONTENTS

Foreword by Gordon T. Smith   ix

Preface   xi

Acknowledgments   xvii

1 An Enchanted World?   1
Surrender to the Water

2 Embodiment, Language, and Sacrament   11

3 Ritual, Sacrament, and Spirit   30
Incarnating the Transcendent

4 The Sacramentality of Time   55

5 Baptism   66
The Art of Rising from the Dead

6 The Meal Jesus Gave Us   100
New Testament and Patristic Era

7 The Meal Jesus Gave Us   122
Middle Ages and Reformation

8 The Meal Jesus Gave Us   141
Anabaptism, Free Churches, and Peace Churches

9 The Meal of Covenant   163

10 Service of the Lord's Supper   174

Afterword   183

Appendix 1 An Order of Service for the Lord's Supper | 193

Appendix 2 Liturgy for Footwashing and Agape Meal (Love Feast) | 199

Appendix 3 Emmaus Communion | 202

Bibliography | 205

Name Index | 213

Subject Index | 215

Scripture Index | 220

FOREWORD

GORDON T. SMITH

THIS IS A TERRIBLY IMPORTANT BOOK; and it is timely. You are holding in your hands a fine piece of accessible scholarship and a gift to the whole church, not merely those within the Free Church tradition. It is a terrific contribution to the current ecumenical conversations because of the way this project proceeds: John Rempel speaks to his own tradition but does so in dialogue with other traditions.

The approach taken to the important topic, the sacraments, is so very appropriate—as he frames it: to provide a correction to an overcorrection. This is a brilliant tactic or posture to take in addressing this topic that has been so divisive at key points in the history of the church, notably the sixteenth century. What he does is demonstrate than an overcorrection is really, in the end, no correction at all. And in this case, the overcorrection meant that those within Free Church and Evangelical Christian communities have as much as anything missed out on the beauty and power of the sacramental life of the church.

Related to this is the overall tone of the manuscript: non-defensive and attentive to the insights of others with whom he may well differ. And this tone allows him to demonstrate that we may well have more in common with other traditions than points of difference. Rempel's work is a fine example of what is now called "receptive ecumenism."

Rempel's historical overview is worth the price of admission. This is superbly well done. He has detailed what needs to be mentioned without being onerously focused on the particulars: just as much detail as one needs to be "in the know" and able to understand the issue or issues at hand. And by the historical overview, I include the work that Rempel does on the book of Acts and the experience of the early church. In this book you will be introduced to patristic sources, the voices and perspectives from the Reformers, as well as contemporary sources.

The particular relevance of Rempel's work is that he speaks to what he calls "liturgically lean churches" in a manner that frees them and opens them to learn from the more liturgical or historical traditions. In the process, he helps those within the Free Church and evangelical world to come to a much greater appreciation of the critical and essential place of ritual in the life and witness of the church. Naturally and appropriately, this call to a renewal in sacramental theology and practice is grounded in a renewed appreciation of the incarnation.

PREFACE

IN WORSHIP WE ARE "lost in wonder, love, and praise"[1] of the God who created all things out of love and watches over all of creation. This God is not only the Source of life, but also the Incarnate One, and the One who indwells all that is. The psalmists, those balladeers of ancient Israel, poured out their yearning for God's presence.

> My soul longs, indeed it faints
>> for the courts of the LORD;
> my heart and my flesh sing for joy
>> to the living God. (Ps 84:2)

Simply opening ourselves to the One who is "unresting, unhasting and silent as light"[2] reorders our lives; we leave the Presence changed.

In traditional societies the forms in which life is lived change slowly: children learn how to worship by imitating the adults around them. New designs are woven in the cloth we call ritual, but slowly enough that its overall pattern remains intact. People are guided into unselfconscious habits of worship. Living, as we do now, in societies of constant, creative, chaotic change, we long for a spirit of worship and forms of worship that will set us free to come before God authentically, with mind and heart and song—that is, with all that we are and make.

In order to find words and acts that have integrity, people of our time in Western societies need to self-consciously appropriate the practices and patterns of historic Christian worship and give them genuine form for the ever-shifting, pluralist culture of which we are a part. To do that we need to know both our own denominational tradition and that of other parts of the body of Christ so that we arrive at a way of worshiping that makes a new whole of

---

[1]Charles Wesley, "Love Divine, All Loves Excelling," in *Hymnal: A Worship Book* (Elgin, IL: Brethren Press; Newton, KS: Faith and Life Press; Scottdale, PA: Herald Press, 1992), #592.
[2]Walter Smith, "Immortal, Invisible, God Only Wise," in *Hymnal*, #70.

all its parts. Although this book focuses on one particular part of the body of Christ, it aspires to be ecumenical in spirit and method.

It is intended as a guide for those who wonder why their church has certain habits of worship and not others, for those who feel that something is missing when they come to church but they don't know what it is, and for those who want to take into account how the church has worshiped through the ages. I hope it will be of service specifically to those who plan and lead worship.

To embark on this journey we need a road map. There are many good books that take the main pilgrimage route. We will start there as well by talking about the meaning of the incarnation and how ritual expresses the incarnation. Then we will take back roads that crisscross the main route. Since this is a book on ritual and sacrament, we will focus primarily on baptism and what we call the Lord's Supper, the Eucharist, or Holy Communion and secondarily on the sacramental nature of time. As we travel, we will see that the dominant tradition (established churches, called mainline churches in North America) preserved some of the habits of the earliest Christian generations but also lost many of them, like the art of improvisation on an agreed-upon liturgical pattern. This rhythm of preservation and loss and improvisation is true also of the dissident tradition, the movements that took back roads through church history. We will pay special attention to the kind of church that arose at the Reformation in Europe (Anabaptist and its Mennonite offspring) and in the seventeenth century in Britain (Baptist). They were radical and nonconformist in their dissent from the union of church and state. Yet they remained tied to the long Christian tradition by their trinitarianism. They and communities like them are called Free churches because they claimed freedom from the state in matters of belief, worship, and discipleship. They arose to champion a kind of church one becomes part of by a personal confession of faith and whose worship arises from this intense and intimate community. They had much in common with kindred movements of reform within mainline churches, known as pietists or evangelicals. But in their attempt to correct what had gone wrong, they often overcorrected: they not only put aside abuses of word and sacrament but gave up some of the principles and practices behind them. This ultimately impoverished their worship.

What I have just written locates the two types of church in historic Christianity. They remain valuable for the typology they provide. At the same time, these two historic types do not adequately describe the shifting expressions of denominational and postdenominational church life today. The implication of my approach is that both types of church can arrive at greater wholeness in their liturgical life by learning from each other, especially in a world where one-time established churches are becoming gathered churches, somewhat like the historic Free churches. My goal is to correct the overcorrection that dissenting movements made in reaction to established Catholic and Protestant churches. To do so I want to sketch out some high points in the development of sacramental worship among trinitarian communions in the Western Christian tradition, placing nonconformist churches and minority understandings of sacraments alongside established churches and dominant understandings of sacraments.

Everyone who proposes an interpretation of a subject does so from a particular vantage point. The quest to praise God with "clean hands and pure hearts" (Ps 24:4) has many aspects to it. There is a growing body of literature, for example, that reflects on Christian worship on the basis of the new engagement between science and religion concerning the unfolding vastness of the universe. Similarly, there is an emerging perspective on worship based on the peaceful encounter among world religions. I write from the vantage point of the colossal moral tragedies of the twentieth century. I lived and traveled in Eastern Europe during the late 1960s and 1970s. I stood frozen to the ground at the intake hall in Auschwitz; I sat speechless next to a survivor of the massive bombing of civilians in Dresden. Never had such horrible wars been fought, such remorseless slaughters undertaken. That the chief antagonists were Christian nations, bloodying the body of Christ on the basis of their higher loyalty to a nation, is one deliberately ignored aspect of this carnage. What does this say about human nature? What does it say about the church's misunderstanding of the gospel? Even more, what does this say about God? Where was God when innocent children were being slaughtered?

No one who wants "to do justice, and to love kindness, and to walk humbly with . . . God" (Mic 6:8) can escape these questions. We need to heed them, not only because people who have given up on faith press them upon us but because we cannot worship God with integrity until we have grappled with them. There is no clear-cut answer to these harrowing questions. In the end, the Christian response is simply to confess, to lament, to plead with the God who made us, who came to our side to die with us and for us, and in whom we can never be lost. Even in the midst of our suffering and our questions we are called to praise God. The God of the Bible and our willingness to be changed by his presence is where true worship begins.

That is why I spend time early in the book calling for two responses. One of them is a purgation of religious language. The other is the realization that words alone are inadequate to our encounter with the Holy One. Our nature as beings with a body as well as a soul speaks and listens through gestures and signs as well as words. We speak two languages. That is one of the first implications of Christ's incarnation for worship. Just as a word is lit up in meaning by a gesture, so also a gesture calls for a word of assurance about what it has led us into. Sermon and sacrament belong together.

I grew up in the Mennonite church, a Free Church, with both an evangelical dimension and lingering fragments of liturgical form. We observed the church year from Advent to Pentecost with the partial exception of Lent. Instead of using traditional Lenten practices to guide people in following Jesus as he prepares to accept the cross, we had a week of evangelistic services in which we tried to do something similar. But the two seldom came together. As long as I can remember I have yearned for authentic and life-giving rituals wedded to an evangelical spirit, gestures that go beyond words and words that unlock the actions we perform. The meaning of the term *evangelical* is so fiercely disputed in our day that I need to say what I mean by it. I understand it as referring to the believer's participation in Christ. Paul says it best: "It is no longer I who live, but it is Christ who lives in me. And the life I now live in the flesh I live by faith in the Son of God, who loved me and gave himself for me" (Gal 2:20). I use *evangelical* as an adjective and not a noun; it is one aspect of a larger reality. It is that part of a much larger gospel of God's kingdom that grounds us in God experientially.

The purpose of this book is threefold. Its first intention is to describe the barren landscape of many Christians and churches whose worship and spirituality lack ritual and sacrament. The second purpose is to present Christ's incarnation as the door to a universe in which matter mediates spirit and allows us to "touch and handle things unseen."[3] The third purpose is to propose an interpretation of the sacramental—particularly the Lord's Supper and baptism—that is life-giving for worshipers and leaders of worship, especially those from liturgically lean traditions.

Let me say more about each of these purposes. What about the barren landscape I have hinted at above? In many churches there is a longstanding wariness of signs and symbols. This wariness goes back to the sixteenth-century Reformation. Ritual acts had lost their life-giving power for some people because they were severed from their roots in the gospel. For them, touching the relic of a saint, for instance, was no longer a door to God but an earthbound object that had innate power. Then came the Enlightenment. Some of its early thinkers strove to find complementary roles for religion and science. But increasingly the thrust of the Enlightenment was to confine religion within the bounds of reason. Other philosophers of science concluded that there was no evidence in the material world for God. With the flowering of modern science, the physical and spiritual worlds were increasingly separated. In the wake of this separation, sacraments were denigrated in two ways. They were disparaged by skeptics as part of a primitive stage of human development. Ironically, they were also disparaged by some believers, who taught that the spiritual path transcended matter and had no need for its mediating role.

Second, for all of its good intentions, this attempt at transcendence forsook the way in which God had chosen to come to us when the "Word became flesh and lived among us" (Jn 1:14). The stupendous assertion of the New Testament is that God encountered us on our terms, taking on our body and blood. To put it another way, Jesus is the human face of God: the fullness of God indwelled him (Col 1:15-20). This reality is the ultimate grounding for the realm of symbol and sacrament. It makes transcendence tangible. The incarnation is the other "language" the gospel speaks; it choreographs the mystery of existence in sounds and silences and gestures. The chapters of this book trace the church's pilgrimage across the centuries in enacting this elusive reality.

Third, this book is a proposal to reclaim the enchanted world of God's nearness in worship and discipleship. My proposal drinks deeply from Scripture

---

[3]"Here, O My Lord, I See Thee," *Hymnal: A Worship Book* (Elgin: Brethren, 1992), #465.

and the long Christian tradition in the West. It also pays attention to dissenting streams of church history that sought a way between (1) sacramentalism (objects and actions that mediate grace) that became preoccupied with objects and (2) spiritualism (the higher path to God is unmediated) that trivialized the incarnation. In crafting the vision for this book I went in search of a seamless way of worshiping and living that held together evangelical spirit, liturgical form, and incarnational mission. At the heart of that project was a way of loving God that turned me toward my neighbor—and my enemy. This happens most profoundly in receiving the bread of forgiveness, which Christ becomes for us, and turning it into the bread of justice and peace.

I have written this volume for people seeking a greater portion of the transforming presence of God in worship and mission. It is not a theologian's book for other theologians. Among others, I had three seemingly opposing groups of people in mind as I wrote. First, I wanted to fire the imagination of people who help shape their congregation's worship. Second, I wanted to lure people who find themselves in barren spiritual landscapes back into the bounty of a sacramental universe. Third, I wanted to give people resources to expand the horizon of the denomination they are part of and encourage them to stay there rather than to leave for some "more perfect" form of worship.

As I wrote, my mind often turned to churches—both liberal and conservative—that are ritually "lean." They like to keep it simple so they can take home from worship a chunk of truth that they can live out and speak out during the week to come. At the same time, many people from those communities feel increasingly earthbound, without a sense that God has met them and changed them when they gather. Church ends up being all about them and their commitments. Others are trying to find the transcendent by reinventing worship every Sunday. And they wear out doing so. Still others are ready to borrow awareness and patterns from ritually "fat" traditions but want to recast what they borrow to express their own "lean" church's character. They are looking for help in doing so.

To sum up, I'm looking for partners on a journey toward worship expressed in sacrament as well as word, a kind of worship that transforms everyone who risks entering its orbit.

ACKNOWLEDGMENTS

THE INKLINGS THAT MADE ME receptive to the enchanted world go back to my undergraduate years. Hearing the Anglican minister John Stott preach in an evangelical spirit seamlessly joined to a liturgical form convinced me that the two could belong together. In his meticulously written *Baptism in the New Testament,* the Baptist New Testament scholar G. R. Beasley-Murray, concluded that in Paul's writings believer's baptism is a sacramental act. This realization set me free to rethink the interpretation I had grown up with. My mentor and then colleague at Conrad Grebel College and the University of Waterloo, Walter Klaassen, modeled a liturgical sensibility in a Free Church key for me. My colleagues in the Ecumenical Chaplaincy Group at Waterloo, especially David Hartry, agreed to preach in one another's chapels in the hope that we could enter into the words and gestures of each other's traditions. These encounters left a lasting mark on my ministry.

During my doctrinal studies at the Toronto School of Theology I discovered a provocative essay by the Reformed theologian F. J. Leenhardt in which he modeled how Protestants might think through Catholic eucharistic theology free from their inherited biases.[4] Later in my studies I read Edward Schillebeeckx's *The Eucharist.* He claimed Leenhardt's essay as one of the influences on his own reconceptualization of the Eucharist. Schillebeeckx's injection of the concept "transignification" into the ecumenical debate was of groundbreaking significance to me. In the course of my doctrinal work, the Anabaptist theologian Pilgram Marpeck became more and more crucial to my academic and pastoral ministry, most importantly because of his far-reaching theology of the incarnation.

I came to my ministry in the Manhattan Mennonite Fellowship with this background. I remain grateful to the elders at MMF, Suzanne Kreps and Virgil Wiebe, as well as others in the congregation, who trusted me in leading

---

[4]F. J. Leenhardt, "This Is My Body" in *Essays on the Lord's Supper* (Atlanta: John Knox, 1958), 24-85.

them into more liturgical and sacramental worship. Participation in the Eucharistic Prayer Seminar of the North American Academy of Liturgy broadened and deepened my grasp of the subject. I thank my colleagues at Anabaptist Mennonite Biblical Seminary, especially Marlene Kropf and Alan Kreider. All of them welcomed my convictions concerning the Lord's Supper and challenged them in helpful ways. I am grateful to Thomas Finger and Neal Blough for their fresh elucidations of Marpeck's thought. Finally, I am indebted to Hans-Jürgen Goertz of the University of Hamburg for years of conversation and correspondence on doing theology in general and Anabaptist studies in particular with integrity.

A new generation of scholars of the ancient liturgies demonstrated the diversity of early developments and the complementarity of structure and improvisation. For the first time I saw the potential of the convergence of historically separate ways of praising God: liturgical worship, which had preserved the charism of structure, and Free Church worship, which had preserved the charism of improvisation. At about the same time "Baptist sacramentarianism" came to my awareness. Historians and theologians, some of them influenced by the above ecumenical convergence, reappraised early Baptist identity and saw in it a sacramental dimension that had later been lost. It confirmed my hunches and expanded my frame of reference for Free Church worship.

I owe a debt of gratitude to my editor at InterVarsity Press, David McNutt. He has the talent of sensing the author's intentions and is devoted to their realization. Every detail matters to him. His collegial approach to getting a manuscript ready for publication always took my concerns into account. I am honored to have my book chosen by InterVarsity Press as the first one in the Dynamics of Christian Worship series.

I am indebted to Rachel Hartzler for her expertise as a copy editor and an index and bibliography maker as well as her steady support of my project. Finally, I want to thank my sister and housemate, Rita Brown, for her many gestures of solidarity as I toiled and for the joy each of us has had writing books that are the culmination of our careers.

1

AN ENCHANTED WORLD?

SURRENDER TO THE WATER

WHEN I WAS SEVENTEEN, I was baptized. I had great expectations as the Sunday of my initiation into the body of Christ approached. Finally it arrived. In the morning there was preaching on the meaning of conversion and discipleship, on belonging to the church. In the evening the twenty-one candidates entered the church in procession. After more preaching and praying, the candidates were called one by one into the baptistery and asked questions that would change our lives. When I had answered them all with "yes," the minister called out so everyone could hear, "On your confession of faith in Jesus Christ, I baptize you in the name of the Father, the Son, and the Holy Spirit." Then he put his arm behind my neck to support it. For a moment I was breathless; then I surrendered to the minister's outstretched arm and was lowered into the watery deep where I was buried with Christ.

Something happened in that surrender to the water for which I had no words. On the one hand, everything had been in place before my baptism: God calling me to Christ, me answering with a trembling faith, the church confirming that God had acted in my life. What had happened, I came to understand later, was that God's inward work in me and my inward journey to God were condensed into a moment and enacted outwardly in baptism. It was a tangible actualization of my conversion, both as a comfort and a challenge. The pastor's invocation of the Trinity was a confirmation that God had been involved in everything that had brought me to faith. Baptism was the sealing of my faith, the outward echo of the Holy Spirit's inward witness with my spirit. This echo confirmed two realities. One of them was that I belonged to Christ and the church. The other reality was that God had said yes to me and I had said yes to God before a host of witnesses: now there was no turning back! "Do you not know," writes Paul, "that all of us who have been baptized into Christ Jesus were baptized into his death?" (Rom 6:3). At the hands of the church, God the Holy Spirit reenacted all the aspects of my inward conversion outwardly. The Spirit took me to my death and brought me back to life.

You might have noticed that I've already been speaking the two languages required to grasp encounters with the divine: the language of words and the language of gestures. We speak both of them without noticing it. When I suddenly encounter a long-lost friend, I begin by putting into words how happy I am to see an old friend. But both of us realize that words aren't adequate to express the bond between us so we reach out and embrace each other.

This simple and familiar exchange between me and my friend sets the stage for what will be talked about in the chapters that follow, the inseparability of word and gesture to manifest the gospel. When actions are stylized and given communal expression, we call them *ritual*. For example, many churches include "the passing of the peace," in which worshipers wish one another the peace of Christ, in their Sunday liturgy. This greeting is not an occasion for getting caught up with each other but a refined gesture that passes on the peace Christ has brought. The intention of a ritual like this one is for it to be habit-forming. I practice passing the peace of Christ in church. Gradually, I gain the confidence and conviction to pass Christ's peace to people in my daily life as well.

Traditionally, ritual is one of the ways in which religion is made tangible. This is a paradox because the realm of the sacred and mysterious is vaster than our grasp. Take for example the foundational stories in the Bible about creation and exodus. The creation accounts of the book of Genesis (1:1–2:25) describe realities for which literal words are too small. The people who first told these stories unselfconsciously turned to their divinely inspired imagination for pictures and images big enough for their subject. "Let there be a dome in the midst of the waters, and let it separate the waters from the waters" (Gen 1:6). Modern, Western, self-conscious people call these stories myths of origin and meaning. They are written in stylized language; that is, their words are close to poetry with its repetitive forms, like "on the first day," "on the second day," and so on. Such language is easy to memorize. What scientists tell us took millions of years is described in Genesis as taking place in six days. The original audience (and we ourselves) can grasp this human scale of language without losing the point of the narrative, that God is the author of the cosmos.

Reason is essential to human endeavors of all kinds, but on its own it can't comprehend the intersection of time and eternity, the numinous place where we encounter God.[1] Ritual is the language the community enacts when it gathers; ceremony consists of the flourishes we add to highlight it. The ritual of Holy Communion comprises the Breaking of Bread and the sharing of the cup as well as the words accompanying this act. The ceremony is how we carry out the act. For example, in some churches the bread and wine are held aloft before they are shared. In ritualized communication there is a reciprocal relationship between sound and gesture. Sound includes the reading and preaching of Scripture in the ordinary cadences of speech but also the musical settings we create for it. Words put to music transcend the earthbound nature of language. Gesture includes the passing of the peace, the giving of money in the offering, and most densely the sacraments, especially baptism and the Eucharist.

The drama of ritual is both more compact and more spacious than literal words and actions. It is more compact because it enacts the heart of human belief and belonging. When a sick person asks for the anointing of oil, there are many aspects of the event that need to be attended to. They are all gathered together in the bafflingly simple gesture of applying oil to the sick person's forehead in the name of the Trinity. But the drama of ritual is also more spacious in the sense of the range of meanings it can include or imply. When we break bread and share wine in the Lord's Supper, it is at once a remembrance of Christ's death for us, an encounter with the risen Lord, and the remaking of the church into the body of Christ. We need rational discourse to sort out what and why we believe. But such discourse can get lost in its own wordiness trying to give voice to the mysteries of the gospel. Ritual comes to life the moment we realize that more is going on here than we have words for.

By means of a repeated act that evokes belonging, memory, and promise, ritual places individual experience within collective identity. On that Sunday

---

[1]Alan Lightman, a theoretical physicist and a "materialist," nevertheless has a place for what can only be described as "spiritual" and "transcendent." See Alan Lightman, *Searching for Stars on an Island in Maine* (New York: Pantheon, 2018), 70.

when twenty other believers and I were baptized, each candidate came to that event with an intensely personal conversion from the world to Christ, unique to each of us. And the rite of baptism had room for all those experiences: it made our individual journeys a part of the church's journey across the centuries. All of us shared one baptism, one profoundly simple gesture by which our belonging to Christ and his body was sealed.

ENCHANTMENT AND DISENCHANTMENT

Since rituals like baptism enfold believers in a collective reality big enough for all of them, it is easy to forget that there is another side to repeatable forms. If they are broken from their source (the Holy Spirit) and their setting (a congregation), they can become idols—objects that magically give us what we want while keeping God at a distance. In fact, we are tempted to believe that we can control God by manipulating the signs we have of him.

This fear that outward rituals might take the place of inward faith has been of concern throughout the history of the church. Reform movements have arisen across the centuries to make clear that it is only by God's grace responded to in faith that symbolic words and forms mediate encounter with the divine. This concern played a role in the origin of monasticism and mysticism as well as the Protestant and Catholic reformations. More radical dissenters from medieval church life, like Waldensians in the twelfth century, Anabaptists in the sixteenth century, and Baptists in the seventeenth century, sought to solve the problem by giving words a higher place than gestures. They did so for two reasons. One was to counter the use of ritual in superstitious ways. The other was to emphasize the response of the individual believer before God. Ritual acts are admirably suited to express the shared faith of a community. They need to be complemented by the unique aspects of each individual's faith; a ritual needs to be inhabited by such faith to be authentic. During the late Middle Ages and the Reformation the individual's faith was a subset of the community's faith. This attitude was not yet the same as the later assertion of the individual's autonomy, but the seeds of that notion were being sown. A trend was set in motion by the culture of the elites of the fifteenth and sixteenth centuries. It ripened into a cultural shift we call the Renaissance. There was both an unparalleled curiosity about the world and humanity and an unparalleled cultural and intellectual creativity in exploring them. Leonardo da Vinci and Galileo were the embodiment of the early Renaissance just as Martin Luther was the embodiment of the early Reformation.

Our immediate interest, which will be expanded in the following chapters, is to sketch the overlapping paths taken by the Renaissance and post-Reformation Protestantism into modernity. Both of them chafed at the comprehensive structures of thought and authority represented by the Roman Catholic worldview. Its picture of the world was one in which everything physical and spiritual was part of a larger whole held together by God. The political and religious hierarchies of Christian civilization were seen to embody God's order. Sociologists call such seamless cohesion of mind and matter under God an "enchanted world." As the Renaissance spirit progressed, greater and greater weight was put on the human capacity to comprehend itself and the world on its own. Science concluded that it was no longer necessary to posit a God in order to understand existence. This was a sea change in Western civilization, the "enlightenment" of humanity. This intellectual foundation for finding one's way in the cosmos led to the "disenchantment" of the whole creation. Creation was seen as a material reality governed by observable mechanisms rather than as an encompassing organism in which all parts of reality are held together by God's providence.

The concepts *enchantment* and *disenchantment* were popularized by the sociologist Max Weber, especially in his book *The Sociology of Religion*. They are poetic terms that evocatively describe the shift of consciousness we are recounting here. They are also romantic in their depiction of enchantment as an unfallen world of mystery, myth, morality, and community in contrast to a world devoid of them. In this disenchanted world, science is exalted and belief dismissed; mystery is not something to stand in awe of but to explain; knowledge is fragmented, and its goal is the pursuit of efficiency. Weber describes such a world as an "iron cage."[2] I have found these concepts most helpful in illustrating the contrast between these two worlds as they bear on the sacramental universe Christianity has traditionally occupied.

---

[2]Max Weber, *The Sociology of Religion*, trans. Ephraim Fischoff, intro. Talcott Parson (Boston: Beacon, 1963), 272.

The term "sacramental universe," for which there are competing definitions, is essential to the case I am making in this book. Let me give you a number of definitions that express the interpretation I follow. The presupposition of the term is the incarnation: Paul declares that Christ "was in the form of God . . . but emptied himself, . . . being born in human likeness (Phil 2:5-7). The church has deduced from this claim that God reveals himself through the material world, that matter can mediate spirit, and that the numinous can be found in the created order. For our purposes, this means that bread broken in Jesus' name is not simply a chemical equation but a latent bearer of his presence. In short, *sacramentality* is the mediation of the heavenly by the earthly.

The reality of a sacramental or enchanted universe has been misused historically in two ways. One misuse has veered into magic, suggesting that humans can manipulate the spiritual realm. The other misuse of this reality is to empty the material world of its spiritual potential. Taking the example I have just used, this second view might perceive bread broken in Jesus' name as nothing but a human term of reference, a mere symbol.

Can the world be resacralized? Can we make ancient myths and mysteries come to life again? Or is that a colossal act of nostalgia that sequesters the gospel and keeps it from speaking to people of our time? Historians and sociologists have traced the "desacralization" and "resacralization" of the universe in various ways.[3]

Our stake in this vast and amazing phenomenon we call the Enlightenment is how it affected religion. The Enlightenment was not a single reality. It had traits in its Dutch-Anglo form that differed from those of its French form. This included a different attitude between the two regarding religion and its relation to science. Little by little God receded from Enlightenment worldviews. The Roman Catholic Church gradually accepted the shift to a new science but opposed autonomous individuality and inquiry into the nature of things ungoverned by Christian philosophy. The mainline Protestant churches were of two minds. On the one hand, their very identity was based on a providential God. On the other hand, the place of the individual, whose status before God the Protestant Reformation had exalted, appealed to them

---

[3]Alexandra Walsham, "The Reformation and the 'Disenchantment of the World' Reassessed," *Historical Journal* 31, no. 2 (2008): 497-528, https://doi.org/10.1017/S0018246X08006808.

as did the freedom of the mind to explore the world through the scientific method. For a time, Protestantism hovered between an enchanted and a disenchanted universe, but it increasingly belonged to the disenchanted world, one in which the material and spiritual realms were completely separate. The material realm was rational, objective, and governed by its own laws; the spiritual realm was nonrational, subjective, and unprovable. Because of that, its sacraments ended up as human projections rather than divine enactments.

This Enlightenment worldview, in a popularized form, was attractive to two surprising forms of church life. One of them was called pietism on the Continent and evangelicalism in Britain. These movements sought the nurturing of personal piety and discipleship within the structures of national churches (allied with the state in providing religious institutions for the whole population). The second form of church life to which the Enlightenment focus on the individual appealed was the Free Church movement. These were dissenting faith communities in Britain and on the Continent who freed themselves from an alliance with the state. Membership was by the confession of faith of the believer, whether by infant or believer's baptism. They included Mennonites, Separatist Puritans, Baptists, Methodists, and their offspring in North America. The place of individual faith and competence before God was central. Although the church as the body of Christ and the Holy Spirit as the giver of faith were still foundational for them, the Free churches discovered a kinship with the Enlightenment belief that human beings can come to God on their own, without the mediation of the institutional church. This notion tapped into the suspicion Free churches had had of Protestant and Catholic national churches all along and made them susceptible to ways of thinking that went against the grain of other assumptions they held.

Two illustrations of this Free Church susceptibility follow. Some strands of those denominations bought into the Enlightenment scientific assertion that ritual, in its broadest sense, belongs to a "primitive" stage of human understanding. This is how the argument went: before humanity had a rational grasp of nature, it resorted to practices like offering sacrifices to unknown gods to appease them. In the light of science and with the aid of philosophy, inhabitants of modernity have learned to think abstractly. More and more we can explain why the world functions as it does. Rationality has replaced the mythic potency of ritual as a way of coping with the immensity of the world and the depth of our experience.

Thus two very different and often hostile worldviews—the Free Church concern for the individual's inward decision in the light of revelation and the secular concern for the individual's action in the light of reason—came together in popular forms to push aside the world of symbols. Other Free Church thinkers went even further: they agreed with the rationalists that nothing of God could be found in the outward world of matter.[4] In so doing they crossed the final bridge from an enchanted to a disenchanted cosmos. "Nature" was no longer "creation." It became a place in which sacrament and mystery have no place. Rationalistic Bible exegetes went on to impose this modern worldview on the Bible. Of relevance to the pilgrimage onto which this book invites the reader is the logic according to which cardinal New Testament passages concerning sacraments were read after this shift in thinking. For example, in Romans 6 Paul is presumed to rule out the possibility that God could use elements of creation as a medium of grace. So the argument goes: in baptism believers declare their faith, making the ritual of baptism an entirely human undertaking. This does not reflect Paul's claim that God the Spirit acts in baptism: "all of us who have been baptized into Christ Jesus were baptized into his death" (Rom 6:3).

I mentioned earlier that post-Reformation mainline Protestantism hovered between an enchanted and a disenchanted world. It is evident in theology, worship, and piety that scholars and ordinary believers alike, both in national and Free churches, continued to believe in sacrament and mystery. Yet they were caught up in an intellectual and cultural shift we call *modernism*. It is a seldom-explored irony that the Enlightenment cosmology from which they had borrowed continued, decade after decade, to chip away at the foundations of Christian belief. This book makes the case that this sequence of shifts in worldview is a missing piece of the puzzle in understanding how those forms of Protestantism that unwittingly made common cause with rationalism abetted the subjectivizing of spiritual reality and its reduction to the private

---

[4]The Scottish philosophy of common-sense realism (crudely: what you see is what you get) became the basis for theological arguments against a sacramental universe. Sydney E. Ahlstrom, "The Scottish Philosophy and American Theology," in *Church History*, vol. 24, no. 3, (1955): 257–272, JSTOR, www.jstor.org/stable/3162115.

and personal realm. The consequences of this transposition are vast. To begin with, it means that the public, political, material world is a law unto itself rather than a realm in which God is at work accomplishing his will. A good example of an incarnational stance toward nature is environmental justice. If God has bound himself to the creation and intends to save it (the new heaven and new earth of Rev 21), it becomes part of the church's mission.

The most profound reason behind this separation of the sacred and the profane on the part of churches is their narrowing and sidelining of the doctrine of the incarnation. Teaching on the Word becoming flesh often limits itself to a doctrine that asks for assent without delving into its consequences. In other parts of the church the significance of the incarnation is limited to the earthly ministry of Jesus. In response to this state of affairs, Free churches (as well as other Protestant churches and the Catholic Church) have realized anew in our time that a robust theology of the incarnation is not possible as a stand-alone doctrine but only on the basis of an encompassing trinitarian theology.

At the heart of the New Testament's message is the dazzling assertion that "the Word became flesh and lived among us" (Jn 1:14). For people who are afraid to mix spirit and flesh, this presupposition is like saying a square peg can fit into a round hole! From the vantage point of the incarnation, the relationship between spirit and matter is profound yet easy to distort. One example that comes to mind is sex. When it's engaged in casually or abusively, all that exists is flesh pushing on flesh. But when our bodies become the medium of our spirits, the Bible says that we become "one flesh" (Gen 2:24; Mt 19:4-6). When flesh, and matter as a whole, is seen as nothing more than molecules, there's no room for the animation of spirit. But when spirit inhabits body, as happened at the creation, creation comes to life.

That is how God made the world and how he redeemed it. In the mystery that is God, the church believes there are three persons mutually related as one being. One of these persons, the Word, took on flesh to embody what God is like and what God intends for the creation. At the heart of God's self-disclosure is his boundless love for us, vast enough to lead the Maker of heaven and earth to become one with us. Paul declares that we see "the glory of God in the face of Jesus Christ" (2 Cor 4:6). John turns to paradoxical language to make the claim that no one has ever seen God in the fullness of God's being. Yet "it is God the only Son, who is close to the Father's heart, who has made him known" (Jn 1:18). Paul takes the meaning of the Word becoming flesh an astonishing step further. He asserts that the church is the body of Christ and the dwelling place of the Spirit (1 Cor 12); it prolongs Christ's presence as the coming of the kingdom on earth. Through the Holy Spirit the church enacts that presence symbolically in the Lord's Supper and other ceremonies, and literally in acts of witness and justice in the world.

In this book, I want to make the case that God comes to us through the creation, through our bodies, through our actions. They become signs that promise us God is near.[5]

---

[5]Dietrich Bonhoeffer has a precise and insightful description of this reality in his *Ethics*, trans. Neville Horton Smith (New York: Macmillan, 1960), 8-25.

2

EMBODIMENT, LANGUAGE, AND SACRAMENT

IN THE BEGINNING WAS THE WORD, and the Word was with God, and the Word was God. He was in the beginning with God. All things came into being through him. . . . And the Word became flesh and lived among us" (Jn 1:1-3, 14). This claim concerning God's embodiment is the most sublime mystery of the gospel. It is so dazzling that an irresistible question arises: how can Christ be both the agent of creation and a member of creation, like us? There is no rationally provable answer to this question, but there are images that slowly reveal its truth. As he contemplates the vastness of God's love embodied in Jesus' death on the cross, the hymn writer is at a loss for words. He interrupts his description with the question, "What language shall I borrow to thank thee, dearest friend?"[1] We do well to remember that the subject we are exploring will often leave us at a loss for words.

In his search for language adequate to the subject, Paul is drawn to an intimate image, that of seeing God in the face of Jesus. God's glory, that which radiates from God and fills the temple in Jerusalem, is ultimately found in Jesus' face, the most revealing part of our anatomy (2 Cor 4:6). When he writes to the believers in Colossae, Paul expands on this claim in language that rises to the poetic. Christ is "the image of the invisible God," "the head of the body, the church," the one in whom "the fullness of God was pleased to dwell" (Col 1:15-19). Paul's climactic and comprehensive declaration concerning the mystery of Christ is that Christ Jesus,

---

[1] "O Sacred Head Now Wounded," *Hymnal: A Worship Book* (Elgin, IL: Brethren Press; Newton, KS: Faith and Life Press; Scottdale, PA: Herald Press, 1992), #252.

who, though he was in the form of God,
> did not regard equality with God
> as something to be exploited,
but emptied himself,
>> taking the form of a slave,
>> being born in human likeness. (Phil 2:5-7)

The Scottish Reformed theologian T. F. Torrance recalls an encounter of his as a military chaplain. A nineteen-year-old soldier lay dying. His unrelenting question to Torrance was "Is God really like Jesus?" Torrance assured him that, indeed, "there is no unknown God behind the back of Jesus for us to fear; to see the Lord Jesus is to see the very face of God."[2]

Most of the time most of us are like the dying soldier: all that ultimately matters is to trust that seeing Christ is to encounter the Maker of heaven and earth. All the sweat and tears it took the early church to arrive at the claims of Nicaea and Chalcedon, the most authoritative articulations of our belief in God as Trinity, had the profoundly simple goal of answering the soldier's question.

Yet, because of intellectual restlessness or the raw experience of suffering, many people find this claim inaccessible or incredible. Because the mystery of the gospel is barely within our grasp, we have been given two kinds of signs to help us comprehend it. One of them is the word; the other one is the sacraments. Christ is the Word of God, the one who discloses God's love and will. In reading and proclaiming the Bible, we listen for the echo of God's Word in our words. Because the Word became flesh, we look for God's act in the midst of our acts. In their profound simplicity ritual gestures, especially those we call sacraments, add a concrete language to God's pursuit of us and our pursuit of God. Both languages are native to the church. There are seasons in a pilgrim's life and settings in different cultures in which one of these languages speaks truth more illuminatingly than the other, but the body of Christ needs both of them to fully perceive God's presence in the church and the world. The animator of Word and sacrament is the Holy Spirit. The Spirit makes our proclamation into God's Word and makes the baker's bread we bless into the bread of life.

---

[2]As quoted in William C. Placher, "Three in One: Believing in the Triune God," *Christian Century*, April 17, 2007, 28.

The mystery of the Word becoming flesh is so dazzling that we fumble for words to describe it.[3] Because poets are more at home with paradoxical thinking, they are better than academics at finding words for their subject. The poet W. H. Auden simply says, "How could the Eternal do a temporal act, the Infinite become a finite fact?"[4] At the same time our questions are irresistible. If the only begotten Son of the Father could take on a human nature—the particular identity of a Jewish teacher in ancient Palestine—how could he still remain God? If he took upon himself the conditions of sin, how could he, alone among humans, not rebel against God?[5] If the answer to questions like this is yes, both Jews and Christians have asked, was the God here referred to still the monotheistic God of Israel? After enormous theological (and political) struggle, patristic writers asserted that Jesus Christ as revealed in the New Testament shares in the very identity of the God of Israel. To safeguard this lynchpin of Christian belief, the church distilled the images and claims of the New Testament into the doctrine of the Trinity. Its goal in doing so was both to confess God's self-disclosure in the Bible and to preserve his mystery.[6]

A paradox appears in both testaments of the Bible: God is infinitely beyond our grasp, yet he lets himself be known. Moses meets God in the burning bush (Ex 3:1-6); Isaiah is overwhelmed by God's enveloping presence in the temple (Is 6:1-8). Athanasius, the fourth-century church father, heightens the paradoxical nature of what ultimately happened. "The incorporeal and incorruptible and immaterial Word of God entered our world . . . in a new way, stooping to our level."[7] God, who is spirit, takes on flesh in solidarity with his creatures, to teach them and save them. If Christ were only human, then he would have died

---

[3]Russell Foster Aldwinckle, *More than Man: A Study in Christology* (Grand Rapids: Eerdmans, 1976), 77-89; and Jon Sobrino, *Christology at the Crossroads: A Latin American Approach* (Maryknoll, NY: Orbis, 1985), 316-42; first published as *Cristologia desde américa latina (esbozo a partir del seguimiento del Jesús histórico)* (Río Hondo, Mex.: Centro de Reflexión Teológica, 1976).

[4]W. H. Auden, *For the Time Being: a Christmas Oratorio*, ed. Alan Jacobs (Princeton: Princeton University Press, 2013), 29.

[5]Joe Jones brings a chastened and insightful vocabulary to the topic. Joe R. Jones, *A Grammar of Christian Faith: Systematic Explorations in Christian Life and Doctrine*, vol. 2 (New York: Rowman & Littlefield, 2002), esp. 402-26.

[6]Catherine LaCugna distills these developments and how they affected the language of worship in Catherine Mowry LaCugna, *God for Us: The Trinity & Christian Life* (San Francisco: Harper, 1973), esp. 111-27.

[7]C. S. Lewis, Introduction to *On the Incarnation*, by St. Athanasius (London: Mowbray, 1975), 33.

as a martyr; it was only because he was both divine and human that he could be our Savior. Thus the incarnation reaches its fulfillment in the atonement.

Even while the first believers were grappling with the significance of Christ's historical embodiment in Palestine, they were beginning to see its far-reaching implications. The incarnation was not only the unique entrance of God into the limitations of time and space; this unmatched incursion revealed a pattern of how the Creator comes to us through creation. Already in the 50s of the first century Paul describes the community that emerged from the Lord's resurrection as "the body of Christ" (1 Cor 12). Paul recognized a correspondence between Christ's historical and his sacramental presence in the visible community that confessed him. We have a hint that Paul applied the same principle to the signs that accompanied the church's coming into being, baptism (Rom 6) and the Lord's Supper (1 Cor 11:23-26; see also 1 Cor 10:16-17). Another way of describing this incarnational reality is to say that Christ is the primal sacrament. Karl Barth speaks about the sacrament of the being of Jesus Christ. By this he means that "the Son of God becomes identical with the man Jesus of Nazareth and therefore unites human essence with his divine essence."[8] The body of Christ continues Christ's enfleshment in history. Signs like baptism and the Eucharist are "derived sacraments" that locate Christ's presence here and now.

THE SEARCH FOR ADEQUATE LANGUAGE

What kind of speech is being used to talk about the incarnation? It is literal to the extent that it refers to historical realities like Jesus of Nazareth and the church. It is metaphorical in its use of literal language to describe something that is more than that. This language is also mythical in its attempt to describe a realm beyond the historical. In its recurring search for adequate language, the early church began speaking about the "body of Christ" in three ways—Jesus in Palestine (the historical body), the church (the sacramental body), and the Eucharist (the mystical body).[9] By doing so, the church was not

---

[8]Karl Barth, *Church Dogmatics*, vol. 4, pt. 2, *The Doctrine of Reconciliation*, ed. G. W. Bromiley and T. F. Torrance (Edinburgh: T&T Clark, 1967), 107.

[9]Henri de Lubac traces how by the High Middle Ages the church became the mystical body and the Eucharist the sacramental body, with profound effects on ecclesiology and sacramentology. Henri de Lubac, *Corpus Mysticum: The Eucharist and the Church in the Middle Ages*, trans. Gemma Simonds (Notre Dame, IN: University of Notre Dame, 2006), 75-100. This shift will be addressed in chap. 7.

reducing one category of Christ's presence to another; they remain distinct but refer to a single reality.

In the first and second centuries, including in the words of the New Testament, the church spoke about the "mystery" of Christ as both his hiddenness and his self-disclosure (e.g., Eph 3:1-12). Soon the church talked about mysteries in the plural, broadly referring to elements of everyday life that are latent bearers of Christ. For example, human love can become the bearer of divine love (1 Jn 4:7-12). Similarly, bread—taken, blessed, broken, and shared—can become the bearer of divine presence. These examples make it clear that in the New Testament the cultic and the ethical are not neatly separated. Encountering God turns us toward encountering people and other aspects of creation. This has immediate implications for our subject that we will see as we go along.

Our concern in this chapter is to establish the sacramental as a manifestation of the incarnational. In Paul's understanding, which was foundational for the early church, the church as the body of Christ was the prolongation of the humanity of Christ through time.[10] As we have seen, the church is the original sacrament. Particular ritual acts—those we normally call sacraments or ordinances—are a further expression of Christ's incarnation and his presence in the church. In the third century, when Latin replaced Greek as the language of the Western church, *mystērion* was translated as *sacramentum*. A sacrament was originally an oath of loyalty by an inferior to a superior. As the term was applied to worship, a sacrament became the inverse: God is the one who makes an oath of loyalty to us. God promises to be present with the signs he has given us.

In Christian usage the term *mystery* in and of itself and "sacrament" as its translation is at the heart of worship and thus deserves further comment. Its origin lies in the New Testament notion of the hiddenness of Christ that is now being revealed. In the post-apostolic church this concept was broadly applied. Rites of the church, especially baptism and the Breaking of Bread, were called "mysteries."[11] For Ambrose of Milan, a mystery was also what we

---

[10]This crucial concept is elaborated upon by Pilgram Marpeck in, for example, *Later Writings by Pilgram Marpeck and His Circle*, vol. 1, *The Exposé, a Dialogue, and Marpeck's Response to Caspar Schwenckfeld*, trans. Walter Klaassen, Werner O. Packull, and John D. Rempel (Scottdale, PA: Herald Press, 1999), 84-85, 115-19.

[11]Justin Martyr, "First Apology," in R. C. D. Jasper and G. J. Cuming, *Prayers of the Eucharist: Early and Reformed*, 3rd ed. (Collegeville, MN: Liturgical Press, 1990), 29. To help his hearers understand

anticipate receiving when we read the Bible.[12] Later commentators on the
liturgy turn to Platonic concepts in applying the notion of mystery concretely
to sacraments. Enrico Mazzo, a Catholic scholar of patristic liturgies, both
affirms and cautions against aspects of this development.[13] Centuries later,
the Protestant Reformation saw this development in a wholly negative light,
asserting that alien thought patterns had displaced Biblical ones.

During and after the Reformation some radical voices made the case for
the term *ordinance* because of the magical connotation sacraments had
acquired in the Middle Ages. They wanted to place the emphasis on actions
Christ himself had ordained. Most of them held that only baptism and the
Lord's Supper were mandated by Christ but allowed for other rites of the
church that marked God's presence in blessing, like marriage and ordination,
confession and anointing.

SPIRIT AND MATTER

People who are in love know things the rest of the world has yet to discover:
"Soul and body have no bounds to lovers."[14] Most of us have known moments
of ecstasy in which all boundaries are transcended and we are one with the
beloved—spouse, friend, nature—and of course, ultimately, God. Ecstasy is
blissfully unselfconscious. It is only when we look in on the experience from
a distance that we get glimpses of how it happened. In an experience of ecstasy
everything that I am is vulnerable to everything the other is: it is by means
of our body that we give our spirit to someone we love and receive the spirit
of our beloved. Even when I kiss the beloved, I am, at least in a small measure,
giving myself to that person.

This reality is expressed in the strikingly simple words the bride and groom
speak to each other in the historical ring ceremony of the Anglican Church.
"With this ring I thee wed; with my body I thee worship; and with all my

the word "mysteries," Justin compares the Christian ones with those of Mithras, a contemporary
religion. Alfons Fuerst sees this parallel as the beginning of pagan influences on the Christian
concept of mystery: *Die Liturgie der Alten Kirche* (Muenster: Aschendorff Verlag, 2008), 16.
[12]Enrico Mazza, *Mystagogy: a Theology of Liturgy in the Patristic Age* (New York: Pueblo, 1989),
16-18.
[13]Mazza, 168-174.
[14]W. H. Auden, "Lullaby," in *Selected Poetry of W. H. Auden* (New York: Vintage, 1977), 27.

worldly goods I thee endow."[15] This action of giving someone my spirit by means of my body is an aspect of what the biblical creation story means when it speaks of husband and wife becoming "one flesh" (Gen 2:24). Paul quotes this line, describing the human bond as a "great mystery" and honoring it by applying it to the relationship between Christ and the church (Eph 5:31-32).

The narratives in the Bible take the embodied nature of human identity and experience for granted. The paradox of our being is that in this life body and soul are inseparable, but only in the moment of ecstasy are they are identical, whether that experience is religious or sexual. God made us as whole beings; we are "bodied souls." Yet body and soul can be pulled apart. If we live only for money, for instance, our bodies lose their bond with spirit and become dead matter. By the same token, if we live only for spirit, that is, striving to transcend our earthiness, we are no longer at home in ourselves or for our neighbors. In his letter to the church in Corinth, Paul provokes believers who are preoccupied with food and sex. "Or do you not know that your body is a temple of the Holy Spirit within you, which you have from God, and that you are not your own? For you were bought with a price; therefore glorify God in your body" (1 Cor 6:19-20). It is our embodied self that is called to holiness.

Sometimes we long for pure body; we call that lust. But we also have times of longing for pure soul, as if we need to escape the world of matter to find ourselves with the divine. This tendency to seek either pure body or pure soul is the case not only with our own being, individually or collectively, but with symbolic objects in general. For instance, a rationalistic mindset can reduce the Bible to mere human words; on the other hand, a spiritualistic mindset can exalt it so highly that it has no traces of human composition. A more embodied understanding would say that the Bible contains God's Word mediated to us through human thoughts and words. This mediation of the heavenly by the earthly is what we mean by the term *sacrament*. Take baptism. At the one extreme are people who think of sacraments as quasi-physical realities: in their belief the washing with water saves, in and of itself. At the other extreme are people for whom physical objects could not possibly bear spiritual reality: in their belief the water of baptism is no different from water anywhere.

---

[15]Mark Searle and Kenneth W. Stevenson, *Documents of the Marriage Liturgy* (Collegeville, MN: Liturgical Press, 1992), 219.

My approach to overcoming these extremes is to assert that the material world has the potential to mediate spirit, but it always remains the medium and not the reality itself. When spiritual realities are reduced to things, objects that humans can manipulate rather than means of divine grace, they become obstacles on our path to God. The solution to this problem is not to put the world aside so we can ascend to the realm of pure spirit. Because we are made up of body and soul, these extremes of succumbing to spiritless matter or escaping into matterless spirit turn out to be false dichotomies. For example, I remember holy moments in my life when all obstacles were out of the way and I was alone with God, sitting on a rock as the sun arose over a breathtakingly still lake. Heart spoke unto heart. Yes, I was alone with God in the sense that no distraction, no divided loyalty, kept me from him. This did not happen, however, because I had been admitted into the realm of pure spirit. Quite the opposite: it was me in my wholeness, with my panting heart, me with the words of Scripture in my awareness, me at one with the palpable morning stillness of the lake that met God.

The apostle Paul was at home in the embodied nature of being because it was part of the Jewish understanding of creation. According to Christian interpreters, who carried aspects of Jewish thought concerning God's intention in creation forward, it culminated in the Word becoming flesh (Jn 1:14). In his incarnation Christ became one of us: God let himself be most fully known through the person of Jesus. It was by aspects of his embodied being, like his voice, that the disciples recognized Jesus after he had been raised from the dead (Jn 20:16, 20; 21:7, 12). In his reflection on the reality of Christ's embodiment, Paul promises that everyone who has become one with Christ will share in his wholeness of identity when the fullness of God's reign comes (1 Cor 15).

Human nature is made up of body and soul together; spirit is mediated by matter. So I have argued. Yet what about the raw fact that in death our being is torn from our body? In death we become naked souls (2 Cor 5:1-9). We relinquish our bodies and with them the wholeness of our created being. We are promised that, when time shall be no more, we, and all that was made, will be reclothed. In the sublime eighth chapter of Romans, Paul asserts that we, and the whole creation, groan in labor pains as we await "the redemption of our bodies" (Rom 8:22-25). We are speechless in the presence of a promise that we can barely grasp; it leaves us with an enigma. On the one hand, there is our mortality and finitude: what God intends will not reach its fulfillment in this life. On the other hand, Jesus' resurrection is the sign of signs that God can and will redeem what he has created in the future he intends for this world.

NOSTALGIA FOR THE ABSOLUTE

Today we inhabit a cosmos in which we experience God as elusive. The sacramental universe of the Bible and premodern cultures has been shattered. It has not always been so. To overcome the disenchantment of life in Western countries today, some historians of religion and culture romanticize the High Middle Ages as the exalted fusion of revelation and reason, spirit and sacrament.[16] While this fusion was never seamless, the world of the twelfth and thirteenth centuries was filled with God. Wherever you turned, there were images of God—in churches, in wayside shrines, in processions bearing images and statues, in a recurring cycle with its days of fasting and feasting.

The goal of philosophy was to manifest the wholeness of the creation in God so that there would be no ontological barrier between the sacred and the mundane: holy realities manifested themselves through ordinary ones, through water, bread, and wine. God was confessed as the cause of all things. The symbolic words and gestures of worship made the Creator present in the midst of the creation. Medieval and, to some extent, even Reformation-era Christians were at home in this enchanted universe. Everything in their world, from philosophy to farming, witnessed to the fathomless mystery of God, the One who was behind everything we are and have and who could be counted on to order it for good. The mystery of God (Col 1:15-20) was the dazzling, impenetrable cosmic reality beyond human grasp that nevertheless disclosed itself, most fully in the life, death, and resurrection of Jesus Christ. Long after the scientific revolution, traditional movements, like the Amish, have remained in this enchanted universe. To the extent that they are no longer primarily farmers or have accepted the digital revolution, they are being catapulted into the disenchanted universe of mainstream society.

---

[16]For a critical but not dismissive summary of theology at that time, see Bernard J. Cooke, *The Distancing of God: The Ambiguity of Symbol in History and Theology* (Minneapolis: Fortress, 1990), 157-84.

Today we in the West are estranged from the mystery of Christ, in whom all things hold together. We live in a disillusioned, demythologized cosmos in which evidence of God is, at best, found in the shards of a shattered world-view. This is a breathtakingly vast subject at which we can only hint. The point at issue is whether symbols can have a meaningful reference point if there is not a personal God, the Maker of heaven and earth, who is present to his creation. Through science we have discovered a boundless universe of cause and effect, yet also of seeming randomness. The popular scientific worldview asserts that no claims can be made for the divine, not just for the premodern picture of a God of intervention, of miracle, but of a force beyond that of matter.[17] The God of the universe has become a stranger to Western society. Believers might still have a place for God in their hearts, but there is no room for God in the world.

The Enlightenment sought the emancipation of humanity from its enforced submission to religion. By means of science and philosophy its thinkers concluded that we inhabit a universe whose source cannot be known. Humanity must seize the freedom to make a home for itself in this world within the bounds of reason and rational inquiry. Much good came from the freedom of the human mind to explore the natural world: modern science has given us spectacular discoveries of medicine and inventions of technology. The problem arises when claims of autonomy and finality are made for human creativity.

Many people in our society grew up with an awareness of religion—and perhaps even an experience of God. But the public place of Christianity in our culture has receded to the point that seekers after God need to go to the margins of our culture in search of him. They often bring two responses with them. George Steiner, the philosophically minded American literary critic, concludes that "the ancient and magnificent decline of the architecture of religious certitude" leaves us with "nostalgia for the absolute."[18] Many of us still long for God, perhaps even for the God of the Bible. We welcome

---

[17]Critical theologians have engaged this complex debate from many vantage points. Gordon Kaufman has done so profoundly, but has he done so at the cost of a trinitarian God who is both transcendent and immanent? See Gordon D. Kaufman, *In Face of Mystery: A Constructive Theology* (Cambridge, MA: Harvard University Press, 1993).

[18]George Steiner, "Nostalgia for the Absolute," CBC Massey Lecture 1974 (Toronto: Canadian Broadcasting Corporation, 1974), 5; audio available at www.cbc.ca/radio/ideas/the-1974-cbc-massey-lectures-nostalgia-for-the-absolute-1.2946821.

experiences of intimacy and transcendence, moments of an enchanted universe, but can no longer take the leap of faith. The massive popular literature on spirituality, deliberately distinguished from religion, testifies to this widespread nostalgia.

A second attitude often accompanies—or displaces—the first one. Many believers once swam in Matthew Arnold's "sea of faith" when it was full. But now the poet hears only "its melancholy, long, withdrawing roar."[19] What remains in the wake of the "withdrawing roar" in liberal religious and academic culture is a polite cynicism. Jackson Lears, the American social historian, speaks of this phenomenon as one of "elegiac regret."[20] In the twentieth century the wake of the "withdrawing roar" has been all the more intensified by the horrors of that century's endless violence, from Verdun, Auschwitz, and Nagasaki to Cambodia, Rwanda, Iraq, and Yemen. This rape of the human body and spirit has almost stripped us of the capacity to imagine a good God who rules the cosmos. Are we left with merely a reluctant agnosticism, at once nostalgic and cynical?

When the innocence of childhood, our first naiveté, has been wrested from us, can we enter into a second naiveté, a fresh receptiveness to the possibility of love and truth? That is one of the profound questions modernity asks of itself. Addressing a boundless question like this is beyond the scope of this book except at two related points. First, orthodox Christian thought has responded that only a trinitarian theology is ultimately sturdy enough to keep symbolic language and ritual from being self-referential, that is, having as its ultimate reference point not human experience but divine reality. Second, we can most fruitfully begin our postdisillusionment pursuit of God in worship. By worship I mean specifically the church's Sunday assembly around Word and Table as well as the more general realm of the luminous and liminal, the threshold between the empirical and the ineffable. In church history good theology has arisen out of worship, not the other way around. This is especially so in an age in which all rational, propositional claims of truth are suspect.

---

[19]Matthew Arnold, "Dover Beach," in *The Norton Anthology of English,* ed. M. H. Abrams (New York: Norton, 1962), 2:905.

[20]T. J. Jackson Lears, *No Place of Grace: Antimodernism and the Transformation of American Culture 1880–1920* (New York: Pantheon, 1981), 145. He is speaking specifically of nineteenth-century Romanticism as mourning for what is dead.

Our first naiveté ends when we realize this and embark on the intellectual and moral quest for meaning. Our second naiveté begins when we realize that pure rationality addresses only part of what matters in life: love itself is beyond the reach of reason.

THE AMBIGUOUS INTERIM

We shall need no sacraments in eternity because faith will have become sight. Sacraments are the densest signs given to us for the ambiguous interim we inhabit on earth between the breaking in of God's reign and its consummation. In the sway of the Holy Spirit, the animator and medium of life, God's reign becomes tangible. In the Gospels Jesus casts out demons. At one point his critics accuse Jesus of casting out these evil spirits by the power of the ruler of demons. He takes their argument on forcefully, concluding, "But if it is by the Spirit of God that I cast out demons, then the kingdom of God has come to you" (Mt 12:28).

Jesus is put on the spot another time. Immediately before he ascends, his followers ask him if he will now restore God's reign. Jesus replies that it is not for them to know the times the Father has set but that they will receive the power of the Holy Spirit (Acts 1:6-8). Paul describes the Holy Spirit as God's "first installment," a promissory note to the church and the world that there is more of God to come (2 Cor 1:22; 5:5). The church itself is the primal sacrament of the divine down payment: the body of Christ is the prolongation of the incarnation. The church is the Spirit's servant in offering tangible evidence that God's reign enters time and space. Bread that is shared locates Christ among us around the Lord's Table and the tables of the world. These tangible signs take us beyond the ambiguities of our mortal life long enough to let us taste—and even see—the promised new age of healing and justice for all.

This nearness of God's reign is not an ethereal reality that lifts us above the world; it is an earthly reality, hard evidence that love cannot be banished from the plane on which we "live and move and have our being" (Acts 17:28). I think of the refugee mother with three children of her own, barely surviving. The woman in the next tent of the refugee camp dies and leaves an orphaned daughter. Something greater than her woes—by faith we would say the indwelling presence of the Spirit—comes to the mother so that she can take the orphan into her arms and life.

I think of such an unequivocal sign in my own life. It concerns a double death. Within the space of four days, my cousin's husband and daughter died. We were blackened with grief. The day before the first funeral was Good Friday. Grasping for solace I went to church with a friend. The solemnity of the occasion took us to the heart of the sacred narrative, recounting the naked experience of Christ's death on our behalf in word and sacrament. I returned to the grieving family, persuaded that the wonder of God's love embraced our sorrow as well.

Most of the time in most of our lives we struggle to become aware of spirit taking on flesh. We long to recognize God's embodiments. In the Christian narrative there are two root signs of the realm of love, from which all others grow. They are baptism and the Lord's Supper. Their simplicity helps to make their meaning transparent. They hallow water, bread, and wine—elements that were primal to natural existence in the Mediterranean world in which the gospel arose. Water is the womb of life; without it we perish. Bread and wine are the staff of life; they slake our hunger and quench our thirst. In the gospel these elements become the bearers of salvation's narrative. As water is poured, new life arises; as bread and wine are shared, we ingest Christ. These primal rituals will be explored in later chapters.

THE LANGUAGE OF TRANSCENDENCE

Although we seldom stop to think of it this way, language also has a sacramental nature. Intelligence speaks. Ideas become tangible as they are mediated by the human voice. In the Christian understanding of revelation there is an interdependence between material and linguistic signs. Augustine is famous for saying that when you add the element to the word you have a sacrament.[21] The word tells the story behind the element; the act demonstrates the reality referred to in words. To put it another way, both the language of *en-act-ment* and the language of *en-voice-ment* (forgive the term) convey God's involvement with the creation. Both of them are mediations of spirit. The church is fatally impoverished when it prefers one over the other.

George Steiner argues that "any coherent account of the capacity of human speech to communicate meaning and feeling is, in the final analysis,

---

[21] *Tractates in the Gospel of John, Nicene and Post-Nicene Fathers,* ed., Philip Schaff, Vol VII (Grand Rapids: Eerdmans, 1980), 344.

underwritten by the assumption of God's presence."[22] Another way of saying this is that in Western cultures meaning making has presupposed transcendence; that is, there is an uncaused absolute beyond the relative reality of created existence. Nathan Mitchell, a theologian, expands on Steiner's train of thought in two complementary ways that are relevant to our pursuit. One way is that linguistic and other symbols disclose what they symbolize. Meaningful communication depends on the assumption that there is a transcendent reference point for our symbol making. At the same time, there comes a point beyond which they cannot take us. Then, "we experience the certitude of divine meaning surpassing and enfolding ours."[23] Because our ritual words and acts have limits in what they can grasp and express, we realize there is a reality beyond our reach that we call God. Sacraments designate both what is revealed of God and what remains hidden.

It is this foundational assumption of transcendence that secular society does not share with Christianity. It has shed the garment of tightly woven religious fabric that Christian culture had sewn together over many centuries. Eighteenth-century Enlightenment philosophers, like Immanuel Kant (1724–1804), argued that religion could claim only subjective certainty. The unintended consequence of that claim in the nineteenth century was the relativizing of religious claims and the exalting of reason. In the end, materialism displaced metaphysics.[24] An a-theistic worldview goes on to discredit signs of the divine that earlier times had found necessary to arrive at the meaning of life. In short, a world without God, a world that is self-referential, one in which there is no beyond, has become plausible.

To apply this way of thinking to the Lord's Supper, all that this worldview can claim as true is that a community gathers around a performance that calls a past event to mind. Bread and wine still have a symbolic role, but their reference point is immanent. Only the humanity of Jesus is left; only hope that is generated by human aspiration is credible. Kant allowed for people to make faith claims, but he insisted that faith claims could not be truth claims in a verifiable way. This worldview has profoundly shaped yesterday's intellectual

[22]George Steiner, *Real Presences* (Chicago: University of Chicago Press, 1989), 3.
[23]Nathan Mitchell, *Real Presence: The Work of the Eucharist* (Chicago: Liturgy Training, 2001), 85.
[24]Richard Tarnas, *The Passion of the Western Mind: Understanding the Ideas That Have Shaped Our World View* (New York: Ballantine, 1993), 346-54.

culture and today's popular culture. The church in Western Europe and North America is still in the midst of a centuries-long struggle to take seriously this account of reality and to shape the church's languages to address it.[25] Charles Taylor reflects on this as well:

> Now it is true that a great deal of our political and moral life is focused on human ends: human welfare, human rights, human flourishing, equality between human beings. Indeed, our public life in societies, which are secular in a familiar modern sense, is exclusively concerned with human goods. And our age is certainly unique in human history in this respect.[26]

What is at stake here? We long to know whether the signs, symbols, and sacraments of the gospel disclose something of God or whether they are our own projections onto an empty universe. Unless we take this possibility seriously, neither our worship nor our mission will be believable. To keep this vast aspect of our topic within bounds, let us look at only one reason that accounts for this seismic shift in worldview from belief to unbelief. It is the reality of radical evil. To begin with, evil is an unfathomable enigma in every religion that believes in an all-loving and all-powerful God.

Job and the psalmists of old pled for signs that God is indeed what is said of him. The psalmist cries out, "Why, O LORD, do you stand far off?" (Ps 10:1). He then laments the ways in which the wicked prosper. In the midst of his dirge a moment of divine disclosure opens itself to him. "But you do see!" the poet finally realizes. "Indeed you note trouble and grief, / that you may take it into your hands" (Ps 10:14). Israel both protested the inscrutability of God and, by faith, bowed to the ruler of the universe. The authors of *Divine Providence & Human Suffering*, a study of patristic teaching on this theme, conclude "that none of the ancient Christian writers ever experienced more than a passing difficulty in accepting the two concepts as perfectly compatible with one another."[27] This does not mean that in their losses both individuals and communities experienced no anguish; rather, in the end their anguish did not destroy their belief in a good God.

---

[25]For a breathtakingly vast and insightful charting of this territory, see Charles Taylor, *A Secular Age* (Cambridge, MA: Harvard University Press, 2007).

[26]Taylor, *Secular Age*, 569.

[27]James Walsh and P. G. Walsh, *Divine Providence & Human Suffering*, Messages of the Fathers of the Church 17 (Wilmington, DE: Glazier, 1985), 11.

In a time when agony over evil and suffering can make belief incredible, the church and its worship lack integrity if they do not take the reasons for this skepticism to heart. Only when we do so do our wordsmithing and symbol making become persuasive. Our models for integrity of speech and act before an unbelieving world come from people and movements that have risked moral dissent without counting the cost. Martin Niemöller, like his fellow minister Dietrich Bonhoeffer, was among the minority who could not keep silent in the face of the evil that was Nazism. In punishment for his protest, Niemöller was imprisoned in the Dachau concentration camp. Even there he refused to be silent. He preached for his fellow inmates in language shorn of presumption, conventionality, and surface. His purified language arose out of his own purgation. In a Communion service on Maundy Thursday 1945, Niemöller made an audacious claim to the ragged circle of prisoners gathered around the Lord's Table. This claim, in the simplest words, was that beyond the wrenching loss of everything that had to do with home, which all of them had endured, that "despite all this, we are at home."[28] He had earned the right to speak of God from within a seemingly godless experience of the world.

Many people experience the signs, symbols, and sacraments with which the gospel is proclaimed as broken from their roots, like cut flowers that have wilted. For them the cultic acts of Christian tradition are no longer doors into the sacred. The church has been engaged in a half century of self-scrutinizing reform of all the dimensions of worship—setting, music, symbols, and the verbal and ceremonial aspects of its ritual life—to make them believable. This is the case in both the liturgical and charismatic movements, albeit in different ways. Inseparable from society's scrutiny of the holy sounds and gestures of ritual expression has been its scrutiny of moral expression, of how Christians live what they profess. In most church circles there is the awareness that in a skeptical—even cynical—age like ours, deeds must come before words. Unless we do justice and love kindness and walk humbly with our God (Mic 6:8), even our most precious language will be unpersuasive. This purgation, even humiliation, gives integrity to Christian worship and witness. At the center of this new reality is the Holy Spirit. Our task is not to get in the way

---

[28]Martin Niemöller, *Dachau Sermons*, trans. Robert H. Pfeiffer (New York: Harper & Brothers, 1946), 78.

of the Spirit, who draws people to Christ both through us and in spite of us. "For we do not proclaim ourselves; we proclaim Jesus Christ as Lord and ourselves as your slaves for Jesus' sake" (2 Cor 4:5).

Those of us who stay in the church are not immune to the crisis of faith. In trembling faith we continue to recite and reenact the ancient narrative. We let it ring in our ears and record it with our eyes. We touch it. In doing so we are not alone, as individuals or as a generation, but members of a cloud of witnesses, the whole company of Israel and the church (Heb 11:1–12:2). When we as individuals cannot believe, the people of God across the ages believe for us. They continue to recite and reenact so that we might again come to the point of encounter seen in the Gospel story of the father with his stricken son pleading with Jesus. The man cries out, "I believe; help my unbelief" (Mk 9:24).

By reenacting the long narrative, Israel sought to show that the Lord of heaven and earth keeps his promises. God rescues the Hebrews from their Egyptian bondage. When the Israelites in the wilderness are famished, God promises to "rain bread from heaven" for them (Ex 16:1-8); God overturns the power of oppression through the suffering of his people on behalf of others (Is 40–55); in the midst of the utter destruction of Jerusalem, the city of God, Jeremiah, the traumatized prophet, discovers that even there God's "steadfast love . . . never ceases" (Lam 3:22-24); and, finally, we are awestruck that in the early church the Father himself, in the Son, suffers on the cross in solidarity with creation and breaks the power of evil over it (Mk 10:45; Mt 26:26-29; Col 2:9-15; Eph 2:13-16).

> Eternal God,
> you gave your people of old a cloud by day
> and a pillar of fire by night.
> Guide us as you guided them
> with your counsel,
> and afterward receive us with honor,
> so that although our flesh and heart may fail,
> you may be our strength
> and our portion forever.[29]

---

[29]Arthur Boers, Barbara Nelson Gingerich, Eleanor Kreider, John Rempel, and Mary Schertz, *Take Our Moments and Our Days: An Anabaptist Prayer Book Advent Through Pentecost* (Scottdale, PA: Herald Press, 2010), 2:212. Used by permission. All rights reserved.

It is this two-sidedness that characterizes Christian faith and worship in our time in the secular West. On the one hand, there is the awfulness of evil and suffering, magnified by the technology of war. On the other hand, there is affirmation of the Bible and the church that pierces the darkness with light: God is at work mending the world. The definitive sign that God's love for the creation cannot be thwarted is the bodily resurrection of Jesus. Here again we encounter the limits of language. Paul's most spectacular claim is that we too will rise from death to eternal life. Our physical body will become a "spiritual body"; our perishable body will become "imperishable" (1 Cor 15:42-58). Our mortal self, the body that gives us our identity, will inherit immortality. Thus, it is the body—Christ's and ours—that is the final evidence the New Testament offers that love cannot be thwarted.

On their own, Christians in the Global North will not find the way from a precritical to a postcritical faith in the transcendent. In the Global South (and its presence in the North Atlantic world as immigrant cultures), in the midst of poverty and powerlessness, a purified church has found a way to hold together its lament (think of the four million civilians who died in the Congo's civil war) and hope. It is not only because the ecstatic is more at home in African cultures, for example, than in European ones that much of the worship in the Global South is charismatic—God's immediate presence in the face of overwhelming loss is such an unmistakable reality that it overflows into the gifts of tongues and healing. God's love is tangibly at work. Whether or not people there use the term, there is a sacramental dimension to their deeply spiritual reality. Theirs is not the religion of the otherworldly: people's minds are set free from fear in this world; people's bodies are set free from disease in this world.

Bold and unashamed claims of the goodness of God come to us from the body of Christ in cultures from the Global South. But, of course, these claims must become incarnate in our culture in order to ring true. Our starting point is our inherited words and gestures—in worship and the arts—which are bruised reeds of revelation, always in danger of being uprooted by the wind of doubt. Even those whose heart is set on Christ can sometimes barely believe them. Therefore, the holy calling of symbol making in and for our time, proclaimed and enacted, calls for a combination of modesty and passion—

empathy for our culture's barren experience of the realm of spirit, yet openness to words and deeds and silences that point beyond themselves. Sometimes we have to build a symbolic rhythm backwards: at the beginning all we have is silence, removed from the sounds and sights that no longer reveal. After those ancient signs—joining in a ceremony of footwashing or a few bars of once beloved music like "Comfort Ye" from Handel's *Messiah*—are experienced anew, they become life-giving to us. The hidden reality behind these rediscoveries is the Holy Spirit. If we let her in, the Spirit convinces us to trust ourselves to speak words that carry an echo of God's Word and make signs that embody God's deeds. In that moment the agonizingly ambivalent experience of life is pierced, and we encounter love, forgiveness, and belonging. This is the "mystery of Christ" (Eph 3:4). In the words of T. S. Eliot, "The hint half guessed, the gift half understood is Incarnation."[30]

---

[30]T. S. Eliot, "Four Quartets," in *Collected Poems 1909–1962* (London: Faber & Faber, 1977), 212-13.

3

RITUAL, SACRAMENT, AND SPIRIT

INCARNATING THE TRANSCENDENT

A SACRAMENTAL UNIVERSE is one in which all of creation mediates its Creator. Everything God made has the potential to mediate the love and harmony with which it was created. The creation is an organic whole in which all things are related to one another and God. When creation along with humanity fell, the capacity of matter to reveal spirit was marred. In the incarnation and resurrection of Christ, matter's capacity to mediate spirit was restored. Paul describes the outcome of Christ's death as "a new creation" that we enter through faith in him (2 Cor 5:14-19).

The raw material of a sacrament is an element of nature, like oil, that locates God's healing presence in a sick person's body or mind. Through the Holy Spirit the raw material becomes a promise of divine nearness. A sacrament embodies God's initiative as well as our human response.

Such particular instances of nearness are expressions of a cosmic reality: the sacramental is the eruption of God's kingdom in a specific time and place. Jesus' healings were sacramental in that the presence of Jesus—his voice, hands, and touch—brought God's power to bear on a specific person. Yet another way to talk about the mystery of matter mediating spirit is to think of it as a door to the realm of the sacred. Our ultimate interest is not the door but that to which it gives us access.

The sacramental is the indwelling of the ordinary by the divine. Let us take the example of language. From early childhood onward we have two ways of speaking. One of them is discursive, the language of information and fact: "I took my car to the garage this morning." The other way of speaking is symbolic, words and gestures sewn together to take us outside the limits of information and fact into an alternate reality beyond the one to which we are normally confined. Think of Martin Luther King Jr. and the civil rights movement. The intensified words ("I have a dream") and deeds (the march to Selma) of the organizers and participants opened to people a new reality that they had not been able to imagine. When these evocative words were performed, they became life-giving. Thus the indwelling of the ordinary by the divine has the capacity both to evoke the past and to open up the future.

Ritual is the collective term for signifiers, symbols, and sacraments, for all that takes us across a threshold from fact to meaning. Philippe Buc stresses that definitions of ritual like this one were brought into being in the twentieth century by sociologists and anthropologists. He further cautions us against concluding that we understand what people hundreds of years ago meant when they carried out rituals as we understand them.[1] At the same time he asserts that ritual is common to all societies. It is as if humans intuitively reach for something that eludes them in ordinary life. They participate in lean, stylized, repeated gestures and words that carry them across a boundary that has confined them. Tom Driver has shared his understanding of this role of ritual in our communal life:

> Ritual controls emotion while releasing it, and guides it while letting it run. Even in a time of grief, ritual lets joy be present through the permission to cry, let tears become laughter, if they will, by making place for the fullness of tears' intensity—all this in the presence of communal assertiveness.[2]

When ordinary acts have taken on extraordinary meaning, they are stylized for easy and memorable repetition and given communal expression. That is to say, ordinary meals Jesus shared with people took on deeper significance, focused intensity through his death and resurrection. As they were repeated in the apostolic communities, the gestures, words, and food of a shared meal were simplified so as to be easily and recognizably performed.

Ritual structures usually emerge to commemorate a revelatory event and then evolve in form over long periods of time. Their transformative quality

---

[1]Philippe Buc, *The Dangers of Ritual: Between Early Medieval Texts and Social Scientific Theory* (Princeton, NJ: Princeton University Press, 2001), esp. 9-11, 223-31, 248-55.

[2]Tom F. Driver, *The Magic of Ritual: Our Need for Liberating Rites That Transform Our Lives and Our Communities* (San Francisco: Harper, 1991), 156.

rises like yeast the more worshipers memorize the words and gestures. Ritual behavior is often criticized for being innately conservative; that is, it reinforces old habits that are impervious to change. Religion has become, more than anything, a force of oppression through its symbolic practices. It is said that the closer the revolution of 1789 came in France the more meticulous court etiquette and religious observance became a bulwark against change.

But this stereotype is not necessarily true. We have already seen the radical interpretation given to symbolic words and gesture in the US civil rights movement. We will see in chapter nine how the faithful performance of the Catholic Eucharist in 1980s Chile had revolutionary consequences. Ritual has the capacity to overthrow as well as reinforce assumptions and behaviors. Whether for reactionary or revolutionary purposes, ritual gives reinforcement and structure to community. The power of ritual is released by the unselfconscious participation of those gathered, to the point of losing themselves in the ritual reality. Being unselfconscious is not the same as being mindless. An unselfconscious participant is aware but responding at a deeper level than the self-conscious persons who must read and follow instructions all the way through the event, all the while pondering whether they are sincere in what they are doing. At the same time, the meaning of the event is different for each participant.

To illustrate, I once visited a fellow student's home village in a German-speaking enclave in Hungary. Timothy let me know that morning prayer was held every weekday at eight o'clock in his local Reformed church. Did I want to attend? Of course. The congregation of eight old women in black shawls and dresses, plus my friend from seminary, the minister, and I, entered a long silence. Then we sang a hymn followed by the same psalm recited every Monday and so on. There was a short sermon. This was followed by a long set of invariable responsive prayers. All of the worshipers, Timothy included, were lost in their chantlike responses. Only I was reading from a book. The eight sisters in black had never ventured far from the village of their birth; Timothy had lived in Berlin, the great metropolis of Central Europe. The morning prayer service was spacious enough to allow for shared words and gestures as well as highly different life experiences.

In contrast to this unselfconscious participation, meaning making in mainstream twenty-first-century Western culture is highly rational, technological, and individualistic. Our constructed rituals lack the aura that surrounds inherited practices, like morning prayer in rural Hungary. In order to give our gestures such an aura, we turn to what is novel. This then leads to a compulsion in some churches to offer something original every Sunday to hold people's attention. At some point in the pursuit of authentic worship we conclude that only novelty and informality are genuine. This is a modern and especially American fallacy.

Consequently, we no longer communicate unselfconsciously by means of commonly held gestures. We can no longer be gathered together into a community by a single set of symbolic words and acts as an objective reality that will carry us through times of festivity or mourning. Because Christianity is no longer the dominant public religion, fewer and fewer people find a home in the inherited meaning of its ritual events. I remember reading an analysis of the success of a megachurch in Southern California. To its credit, this congregation had tapped into popular culture and its symbolic structure, such as popular music performed in a glamorous style. The meeting place deliberately did not look like a church—no cross, not pulpit, no Lord's Table; the centerpiece was a band. This congregation of fifteen hundred had relegated Holy Communion to a side chapel holding forty people once a month. The reason for this, it was explained, was that the Lord's Supper had no meaning for people who were suspicious of anything traditionally Christian.

It is much easier for faithful rituals to be lost than for them to be created. A friend of mine grew up in a village in East Germany. It was the custom there when young people in the church were to be confirmed that the mother of the oldest confirmation candidate would festoon the street leading to the church with boughs and ornaments. By the late 1960s fewer and fewer people were attached to the church. The year my friend was confirmed she was the oldest member of the class. My friend's mother, whom tradition designated as the decorator, concluded that this outward display was an imposition on their nonchurch neighbors and had outlived its appropriateness.

There was integrity to this way of thinking in a pluralistic society. On the other hand, it was disorienting to the families of believers who relied on the decorating of the street as the sign that the village was ready for the festivities leading to the confirmation service. Once the aura of a particular ritual has been shattered, it is almost impossible to recreate it. Street decorations for confirmation never happened again in that village.

RITUAL AS INHERENT TO COMMUNITY AND COMMUNICATION

Even though inherited ritual patterns have been broken and are often irretrievable, it is crucial to remember that symbolic communication is inherent to being human. Even with the loss of shared, bequeathed practices, we still retain the capacity to borrow and innovate with words and signals that disclose meaning. Here are three examples that illustrate how this happens.

First, there are natural gestures that take on expanded meaning. I remember the story of an old woman during the 1990s war in Yugoslavia. She described how Serbs and Croats had always coexisted. It was natural to greet neighbors as you met them at the market or sporting events. When propaganda succeeded in making enemies of the two cultures, hostility became so intense that most Croats and Serbs refused to acknowledge one another on the street. The old woman was part of a minority of those who refused to go along with this antagonism. These few folks made a practice of greeting all their neighbors with words and a handshake. Often the offer was spurned. Suddenly saying hello had been invested with amplified significance. Now this ancient gesture had unmistakable and newfound depth. It affirmed, "I acknowledge you as my fellow human being; I refuse to let hatemongers determine that my neighbor is my enemy."

Then there are acts that bring memories to life and accumulate them. When I was a child, one of the high moments of our family life was lighting the candles of the Advent wreath. I was so eager that my mother had to stop me from lighting all four candles on the first Sunday of the season. She explained that by lighting one candle a week we heighten our anticipation of Christmas. We were not alone in what we did, she went on to say, but united with countless believers across the centuries who marked the time leading up to Christmas the same way. But that was not all. Our mother told us about the comfort she felt as an immigrant teenager in Winnipeg carrying on this sturdy gesture from the lost world of Russia, of which few traces remained. For us children, both of these layers of memory amplified the act of Advent candle lighting.

Finally, there are occasions when improvisation is called for and words give way to actions. In the Gospels, one of Jesus' biggest challenges is to convince his followers that authority is a moral trait and not a hierarchical advantage. Jesus rebukes James and John when they appeal to him to sit on his left and right side in glory (Mk 10:35-40). Jesus' words do not sink in. At the Last Supper there is another argument about who will be first in the kingdom. Suddenly Jesus arises, reaches for a towel, pours water into a basin, and washes the disciples' feet (Jn 13:3-17). Slaves were used to washing masters' feet but servants did not expect to be served by their master. Jesus' words about servanthood couldn't pierce his friends' hearts. But a startling, upside-down gesture—possibly spontaneous—reached them. A deed did what words stammered to express.

The church has inherited from Jesus the role of being a sign maker. It is God the Spirit, of course, who makes our sounds and signs luminous. Our task is to "employ human gesture and ceremony in structuring the presence of that encounter."[3] In order to do that, we need to find a grammar, an agreed-upon arrangement of words and gestures, adequate to the truth we struggle to express. This is what we mean by the term *ritual* when it is used in a religious sense: piecing together sounds and signs that come to life through the Holy Spirit.

BECOMING PRACTICAL

Let us now take these principles of ritual and relate them to congregational worship and pastoral care. To begin with, there is the problem of technical terms. We should not be intimidated by the long list of definitions that comes with every approach to the world of liturgy. There is no single set of precise meanings to the terms used, either within the church or in academic disciplines like ritual studies. Terms and concepts help us to think clearly about what we are doing, of course, but their purpose is ultimately practical: to help us recognize and enter the sacramental universe waiting to be discovered.

Ritual is the most encompassing category we have for clothing God's transcendence in immanence. At its simplest it is stylized, patterned, repeatable, habit-forming behavior. It consists of ordinary gestures that are contracted in their form

---

[3]Xavier John Seubert, "Ritual Embodiment: Embellishment or Epiphany?," *Worship* 63, no. 6 (1989): 403.

and expanded in their meaning. Singing a hymn, for instance, gathers and stylizes the emotions of a congregation: my self is caught up with the selves of others. When we sing a hymn like "And Can It Be" at a baptism, the wonder "that thou, O God, shouldst die for me" is intensified and shared.[4] If we sing that hymn at every baptism, it accumulates further layers of association. And so the layering of ritual, and the experience of those layers, continues to expand.

Rituals that most profoundly carry us with them—visual, tactile, or oral— are marked by five characteristics: rite, use of natural elements, repetition, universality, and a sense of belonging. Each trait is individually significant, but all five of them together fulfill the event. First, in the world of ritual, the simpler and less embellished the rite, the more powerful it is. If the action has to be explained in more than one sentence, it is too complicated for its intended purpose. To illustrate, almost all of the accounts of meals in the Gospels, including the Last Supper, describe Jesus as taking, blessing, breaking, and giving the bread (Mt 26:26-28). If these primal gestures are obscured in the celebration of Communion by competing words and actions, their power diminishes.

Second, the use of an appropriate natural element creates an immediately recognizable similitude. The church's act of anointing with oil for healing, for example, arises from its ordinary medicinal use. But rather than being applied literally, to an afflicted part of the body, it is applied symbolically: oil traces the sign of the cross on the participant's forehead to enact God's nearness to the whole of the afflicted person's need.

Third, there needs to be ease of repetition for both the presider and the participants. Litanies call for the assent of the worshipers to the petition that has just been offered up. In the pastoral prayer, a cue after an intercession by the leader, like "in your mercy, Lord," is followed by "hear our prayer" as a congregational response. Anything longer runs the risk of drawing worshipers away from the act of praying to the mechanics of the prayer. Constant novelty in form undermines the natural flow and the unselfconsciousness of the occasion. For example, if you introduce a new order of service for Communion in your congregation, use it exactly as it is for at least a half dozen times before you experiment with changes.

---

[4]Charles Wesley, "And Can It Be," in *Sing and Rejoice: New Hymns for Congregations*, ed.. Orlando Schmidt (Scottdale, PA: Herald Press, 1979), #5.

Fourth is universality. It has two dimensions. First, stark and stylized gestures and their accompanying words, repeated from year to year, constitute the vocabulary that comes closest to being understood by all. Think of ballet and poetry. Simplicity in form and speech, well executed, has the capacity to include children as well as adults with all levels of ability. To illustrate, the story is told of a mute teenager in a rural nineteenth-century Pennsylvania Mennonite congregation. Because he could not speak, everyone assumed he could not understand. No one considered him a candidate for baptism. There came a Sunday when his peers were to be baptized. After they had answered the questions concerning their loyalty (Do you renounce . . . ? Do you turn . . . ? Do you believe . . . ?),[5] the candidates knelt one after another so the bishop could baptize them. The gestures were simple and repetitive. The cleansing nature of water was evident as it rolled down the forehead of each candidate. Suddenly the mute teenager darted out of his pew and ran to the front. The father tried to stop his son, but the bishop raised a hand to hold back the father. The boy knew exactly what he wanted: he took his place at the end of the line of candidates and waited to be baptized with them. By his posture, his determination, his yielding himself to the pouring of water, he had answered the questions for which he had no words.[6]

There is a second aspect of ritual that makes it universal: repetition. Take the example of a wedding. In our culture we prize uniqueness. A ceremonial occasion is memorable for our culture when it has music or vows completely different from anyone else's. This is the modern and particularly American fallacy I have already mentioned. To be sure, there is something unique about any two people pledging their lives to each other. But an equally exciting aspect of a wedding is the performance of traditional words and gestures by the couple and the presider, making this ceremony their own. In so doing, they enter a solidarity with their parents and grandparents who had entered marriage with this same rite.

Fifth, ritualized words and gestures create a sense of belonging. Joining in symbolic enactments over time gives a tangible sense of community and identity: we are the people who gather every Sunday to praise our Maker and

---

[5]John D. Rempel, ed., *Minister's Manual* (Newton, KS: Faith and Life Press, 1998), 48.
[6]Richard J. Lichty, *Meetinghouse on the Plain: Plains Mennonite Congregation Remembering 250 Years* (Harleysville, PA: Plains Mennonite Church, 2015), 218.

renew our resolve to live for the upside-down kingdom. But the power of good ritual can also create community on and for a single occasion. I remember a funeral where we stood, bereft of words and gestures, at the grave of a friend who had died before his time. Suddenly, the minister invited each of us to place a shovelful of earth into our friend's grave. Our hearts stopped when we heard the first thud of earth on the coffin. Instantly, we became aware that lifting a shovelful of earth was the unequivocal initiation rite that made our solidarity with our friend, his wife, and one another unmistakable.

When we think of *ritual*, what may come to mind first are its most elaborate manifestations, such as a Renaissance mass sung with pomp and circumstance in a Gothic cathedral. We ask ourselves, does anything less really meet the requirements of the term *ritual*? Of course, such music in such a place can glorify God, but it is not the model for ordinary congregational worship. Thinking too much about Gothic cathedrals (as I am prone to do) can lead us to conclude that the heart of ritual is ceremonial complexity and extravagance. We can miss the point that ritual has a primal simplicity. It is a rhythm of form and movement that carries worshipers through acts of praise, prayer, and proclamation. Good liturgy has a clear shape that the worshiping community internalizes. Because it knows where it is going, the freedom to improvise without getting lost increases. Good liturgy is sturdy enough to keep the concerns of the moment from taking over and elastic enough to allow for interruptions. Good liturgy speaks to more than one social class.

I have friends who are members of a charismatic Anglican church. As someone who is not used to that much freedom in worship, I have asked them if the intensity of immediate experience doesn't overwhelm the fixed form. They are quick to answer that this is not the case. They explain that even the most charismatic members see experience and form as complementary. They rely on the fact that ecstatic expression is part of a larger whole that can be counted on to carry the congregation through all the stages of the service.

Some churches seek to be led by the Spirit without structure. Charismatics of a certain bent will argue that the Spirit is always improvising and shouldn't be "formed." From another perspective, biblicists of a certain bent claim that since there is no fixed form of worship in the New Testament, there should be none in the church today. They conclude that faithful Christians need no form or pattern. Some would go so far as to deny that they have any rituals. Yet on closer examination this is not the case.[7] Sometimes rituals are so straightforward and have become so unselfconscious that we don't realize we are engaging in them. For instance, Quakers place great weight on the inner life and make little of outer gestures. But they do have rituals. At one point in my life I attended a Quaker meeting from time to time. I noticed that when the clerk entered the meetinghouse and sat down, conversation ceased and worshipers entered a shared silence. Similarly, at the end of the meeting when the clerk arose and departed, conversation resumed.

I once experienced such unselfconscious participation in an internalized pattern in the worship of an Old Colony Mennonite congregation. The service that Sunday included a wedding. The minister delivered his admonition to the couple and then spoke the vows in a clearly formulaic, but by no means lifeless, fashion. Afterwards, I went up to him and asked for a copy of the wedding service. He was genuinely puzzled at my request and assured me that he had used no written form and that his words had been inspired by the occasion.

EXPRESSING THE INEXPRESSIBLE

Once we are aware that symbolic words and gestures characterize all expressions of community, we can learn what makes them life-giving. The primal forms of ritual performance are music and poetry. They are our models for shaping worship because of the stylized and compact way they express the imaginings of the mind and desires of the heart. They are the media that come closest to expressing the inexpressible—wonder, passion, trust, grief. There is an ancient saying, attributed to more than one of the fathers, that summarizes the symbiosis of prayer and music: "The one who sings, prays twice." Music and poetry both create harmony as well as dissonance. They marry each other in hymnody. Music carries words in a way that makes what is being portrayed accessible to people for whom the prosaic language of belief no longer speaks. It gives the soul a voice.

---

[7]Arthur Paris's in-depth study of black Pentecostalism's communal praise demonstrates that there is a clear pattern of worship that worship leaders, musicians, and preachers embrace. Theirs is simply a more elastic way of following a rhythm than a Eurocentric one. Arthur E. Paris, *Black Pentecostalism: Southern Religion in an Urban World* (Amherst: University of Massachusetts Press, 1982).

Elie Wiesel, the Holocaust survivor, recounts a haunting incident from the concentration camp in which he encountered Juliek, a fellow prisoner:

> I heard the sound of a violin. The sound of a violin in this dark shed where the dead were heaped on the living. What madman could be playing the violin here at the brink of his own grave? . . . I could hear only the violin and it was as though Juliek's soul were the bow. He was playing his life. The whole of his life was gliding on the strings—his lost hope, his charred past, his extinguished future.[8]

This articulation of realities that are universal is the holy calling of music. The church does well not to tame it because it can speak of the infinite in ways that other languages cannot. At the same time, music and musicians have been willing over the centuries to humble themselves to be the handmaidens of faith. They are willing to compose vehicles for words. This is true of most religions, certainly of Judaism and Christianity. We know that the psalms were chanted in temple and synagogue and that early Christian music was shaped by this tradition.

One of the earliest forms of Christian liturgical music is that of the Chaldean church. Its origin is in ancient Syria, today southern Iraq. I once attended a Chaldean service in Basra, Iraq. I was told beforehand that their chant dates in its present form to the sixth century in a style of Aramaic similar to what Jesus spoke. Its distinctive meter and sound evoked an otherwise lost world, echoing sounds Jesus might have chanted.

In Western church hymnody, songs that are not a fixed part of the liturgy evolved slowly into a separate genre. Singing, in the style we perceive to be traditional, began in Germany in the late Middle Ages. At the Reformation, hymn singing became the favorite vehicle for expressing the exuberance of renewed and owned faith. By contrast, in England the Baptists were the first hymn writers, beginning late in the seventeenth century. In the massive revivals led by John and Charles Wesley, hymn singing came into its own. Methodist hymnody has left an enduring mark on most forms of Protestantism and has a place in Catholic hymnals today. One need only call to mind a hymn like "O for a Thousand Tongues" to experience the spirituality it first embodied. Similar in its scope and creativity is the contemporary church music scene,

---

[8]Elie Wiesel, *Night* (New York: Avon, 1969), 107.

using music and language styles in the idiom of popular culture as well as improvisations on chant, like that of the Taizé monastic community.

Poetic form is another primal manifestation of ritual expression—density of language, leanness of expression, and multivalence of meaning. In the presence of the poetic, readers or hearers find themselves agreeing with the author because the poet has named exactly what is normally elusive and out of reach in our experience. An ancient opening prayer begins with these words: "Almighty God, to you all hearts are open, all desires known, and from you no secrets are hidden."[9] When one has entered into the vulnerable space such words provide, one is naked before God. Nothing more needs to be said. In fact, any elaboration would obscure and detract.

Like other poetic forms, liturgical expression is condensed in form and expansive in meaning beyond the capacity of prose and conversational speech. Think of a Communion service in a diverse congregation whose members hold to different understandings of the atonement. Words purged of cliché and acts purged of decorativeness open worshipers to the universally recognizable act of breaking bread and pouring wine. Worshipers are taken to a primal, sometimes even precognitive, level beneath and before rational articulation. What remain are the words and gestures enacting Jesus' self-giving and the worshipers' reception of the gift. Here literal language concerned with explanation and instruction is out of its depth.

I experienced the multivalence of meaning and its importance when I was a member of a collective of authors who wrote a prayer book. One of our members became concerned that the intercessions for morning and evening prayer were heavily weighted toward social justice and said little about personal witness to Christ. Another member defended the existing content of the prayers. Neither person was willing to give ground. At the next meeting yet another member brought the following proposal for the petition that was under scrutiny. "Your gospel is peace for all people. We pray for the church in all places, that we may speak boldly for Christ." The two contenders both liked it. Proclaiming a gospel of peace has an application both to the hearts of believers and to conflicts in the political realm. "Speak[ing] boldly for

---

[9]*Book of Alternative Services of the Anglican Church of Canada* (Toronto: Anglican Book Centre, 1985), 185.

Christ" can be both an unashamed witness to Christ's power to change the human heart and a courageous appeal to enemy factions in a civil war to stop shooting and start negotiating. Both affirmations are true and can be prayed for sincerely in the same capacious words.

A NOTE ON TERMINOLOGY

A word needs to be said about the terminology commonly associated with ritual. One of the terms is *rite*, derived from the same root. It has more than one application. A rite is a specific liturgical form, often attached to a historical practice. Thus, Catholics follow either the Latin rite (derived from Roman practice) or the Eastern rite (derived from Eastern and Oriental Orthodox practice). But one may also talk about the rite of footwashing, a specific form for the enactment of an action.

Another term with more than one meaning is *ceremony*. Historically, the word was commonly used by Anabaptists in place of *sacrament*. As it is mostly used today, *ceremony* is the particular set of gestures that accompany an act of worship. In liturgical churches, for example, the reading of the Gospel is accompanied by distinct ceremonial. The reader moves to the place of reading in the middle of the congregation, often accompanied by cross and candle bearers, and does so with greater deliberateness than for the other readings. This act is often accompanied by instrumental or vocal music and framed by an antiphon between the reader and congregation.

Ritual activity occurs with varying density. The least layered type is the *sign*. More layered is the *symbol*. And densest of all is the *sacrament* or *ordinance*. An object that simply points beyond itself is a sign. A sign can literally be that: a triangular, yellow road marker that means "yield." Usually the meaning of a sign makes sense to anyone who is part of its culture and language. A sign is an arbitrary designation we agree on, external to the reality it's pointing to.[10] In some churches people make the sign of the cross or talk about the passing of the peace as a sign of Christ's welcome.

A *symbol*, as it is widely understood, has a less obvious but more profound meaning than a sign. A symbol is multivalent, holding together meanings

---

[10] An exception to this is the use of *sign* in *Confession of Faith in a Mennonite Perspective* (Scottdale, PA: Herald Press, 1995), where *sign* has a meaning close to *sacrament*.

that stand apart in everyday life. It comes to our aid when thoughts fail us. For instance, on one level the cross is a sign. It has come to designate a place or person as Christian. But at a deeper level the cross is a symbol, a repository of two thousand years of religious experience. It evokes realities that cannot be reduced to a single reference point. One of them is literal, Jesus' crucifixion in Jerusalem. Another one is metaphorical, the self-giving asked of Jesus and of those who follow him.

The concept of symbol is historically contentious in its meaning. This contention has much to do with the setting in which the church of the patristic era practiced its symbols. A dramatic shift of context came about during and after the reign (306–337) of Constantine the Great (274–337). Increasingly, especially after he moved the capital city from Rome to Byzantium (renamed Constantinople after himself), Constantine fostered an alliance with the church. With the consent of most of its leaders he made the church into a public institution with elaborate buildings and ceremonies that paralleled those of the state and that ruled with the state. It is in this sense that Roman and Greek society was Christianized. This process was completed in Asia Minor and in Europe south of Scandinavia by the time of Charlemagne in the eighth century. As the fusion of church and state evolved, people increasingly belonged to the church as a mark of belonging to the empire. The reference point of the church's symbolic acts changed with it. The Sunday worship of the church became a public event presided over by clergy with a passive congregation. Infant baptism became the normal act of initiation. Salvation was communicated by sacraments that were effective in and of themselves. This evolved partly because it could not be expected that most citizens were church members because they had come to faith in an existential sense, that is, by putting their trust in Christ.

Hilary Mantel describes this kind of religiosity:

> To keep at bay the misfortunes of the world [the ordinary man] followed the prayers framed for him in Latin, a language he did not understand, attributing a mechanical efficiency to their enunciation, heaping them up as if he could build a staircase to a capricious God.[11]

---

[11]Hilary Mantel, "The Magic of Keith Thomas," *New York Review of Books*, June 7, 2012, 38-39.

At the same time, renewal movements over the centuries, led by nuns and monks as well as diocesan clergy and laity, sought to bring people to existential faith and discipleship. Ultimately this unfulfilled impulse led to the Protestant Reformation. It was a protest against externalized religion. In order to make clear that one becomes a Christian through faith in Christ alone, some Reformers went so far as to reduce symbols to external signs that had no mediating power. We shall look at this crucial development in the chapters concerning the Lord's Supper.

SACRAMENTS

Finally, we come to the most important form Christian ritual takes. The term *sacrament* is the Latin translation of the Greek word for "mystery." In the New Testament, *musterion* is the word chosen by Paul to describe Christ's hiddenness before his incarnation. Now this mystery has been disclosed by the Spirit. The divine disclosure is that "the Gentiles have become fellow heirs, members of the same body, and sharers in the promise" (Eph 3:2-11). The core idea here is that Christ's hiddenness is being revealed. Soon this understanding of mystery was applied to the Lord's Supper as the densest medium of Christ's revelation. Other forms of disclosure, like baptism, were also named as mysteries.

Sacramental worship, in its original sense of a mystery being revealed, is like the ladder in Jacob's dream on which "the angels of God were ascending and descending" (Gen 28:11-17). The angels mediate between heaven and earth; they are messengers between the realms of spirit and matter. Jesus uses this metaphor of the ladder to describe himself: "You will see heaven opened and the angels of God ascending and descending upon the Son of Man" (Jn 1:51). He is the One in whom God takes on flesh, takes on our nature. His humanity is the paradigm for God's self-disclosure. His human nature becomes the ladder by which we ascend to God. Because Christ is the meeting point between God and humanity, some streams of contemporary theology describe him as the "primordial sacrament." Paul says something similar when he speaks of "the glory of God in the face of Jesus Christ" (2 Cor 4:6). Matthew, Mark, and Luke take this notion of incarnation in another direction. In them, the meeting point between God and humanity is described in political language, as a kingdom. The Gospel writers trace the incursions God's reign makes in the person, teaching, and healing of Jesus (Mt 12:28), and then in his death and resurrection. The church is made up of those who have heeded God's invitation and cast their lot in with this ever-coming kingdom. The church prolongs Jesus' presence in time and space. Sacraments are concrete extensions of that presence. David Brown sums it up for us: "As symbol is to action, metaphor to language, and image to art, so sacrament is to religion. Each is trying to move us analogically, to take us to a different place."[12]

All these representations open us to a reality beyond our present awareness. Sacraments "take us to a different place" by means of an object accompanied by ritualized words and actions. They carry us across the threshold from the literal to the numinous. They come with the promise of God's presence in this place and time.[13] "Sacraments are the occasions, rather than the cause, of grace, which God alone causes."[14] This summary of a thirteenth century debate preserves a notion dear to lean liturgical traditions: that things have no inherent power to cause grace. Rather, they have the capacity to bear grace.

A crucial distinction needs to be noted at this point between the sacramental and mystical path.[15] Participation in sacraments, especially the Eucharist, can be the occasion for "feeding on Christ" in a mystical encounter. This possibility is part of much Catholic teaching. It is also part (surprisingly) of the eucharistic theology of some Reformation thinkers, among them Ulrich Zwingli and Dirk Phillips. One could go so far as to say for both of them that the real presence of Christ in the Holy Supper is *not* sacramental but mystical. The strength of Zwingli's and Phillips's thinking is that the Lord's Supper puts its participants on the mystical path, a subjective experience of Christ. Its weakness, in my judgment, is that there is no promise of an objective presence always being attached to the Breaking of Bread and the sharing of the cup (1 Cor 10:16-17). For Zwingli and Phillips, an encounter with Christ depends on whether one receives the gift of mystical experience.

---

[12]David Brown, "A Sacramental World: Why It Matters," in *The Oxford Handbook of Sacramental Theology*, ed. Hans Boersma and Matthew Levering (Oxford: Oxford University Press, 2015), 609.

[13]There are two other modes of presence parallel to the sacramental in a complementary way. One is the mystical, the unbidden, unmediated encounter with Christ. The other is the ethical, the mediated encounter of Christ in the other that happens through self-giving.

[14]Joseph Warrykow, "The Sacraments in Thirteenth Century Theology," 222 [218-234] in Boersma, Levering, *Sacramental Theology*.

[15]James Finley, *Christian Meditation: Experiencing the Presence of God* (New York: HarperCollins, 2004), esp. 101-89, gives a luminous description of the mystical path.

The mystical path to God is the counterpoint to the sacramental one. The mystical path is the naked experience of God—purifying but often also overwhelming and disorienting. It is a state of ecstasy, of self-transcendence, religious as well as sexual. This happens religiously when we receive the Spirit's gift of oneness with Christ. It happens sexually when we receive the gift of oneness with a spouse. This sacred state is not something we can bring about. All we can do is prepare ourselves for it.

By contrast, sacraments signify a presence that is not seen but is imparted; sacraments are the clothes God wears to come to us: he dresses in our flesh to meet us on our terms. Christ's sacramental nearness is God's promise that in the Breaking of Bread the Spirit will make Christ present to the celebrating congregation and to each believer; Christ needs only to be received by faith, however weak and battered that faith might be. When we take the bread, we receive the body of Christ.

SHIFTS IN THINKING

There are two defining shifts in late-twentieth-century thinking about sacraments that reclaim neglected aspects of teaching. They are creating convergences of thought and practice across denominational lines. One of them is the resurgence of trinitarian theology. The second is the emphasis on action rather than objects as the heart of sacramental reality. Both of these shifts are in evidence in the literature cited below. They open the way to a convergence and complementarity of views.

Trying to speak about the "threeness" of God takes us to the edge of mystery. By his very nature God is beyond human grasp. Gathered together in the Bible are revelatory images of the divine as Source, Word, and Presence that confess both God's transcendence and immanence. These images become more tangible in the New Testament because of the incarnation and the steadfast presence of the Spirit in and beyond the church. Taken together, they show us enough of God to live by. It is often said that writers of the New Testament arrived at an implicit trinitarianism because they had to: only then was the church able to confess everything of God that had been revealed to it.[16]

---

[16]This teaching was made explicit in the Councils of Nicaea (325) and Constantinople (381). From them the Nicene Creed emerged.

The Trinity is the lynchpin of Christian belief, worship, and theology. It is the fastener that prevents the wheel from sliding off the axle: without it everything would fly apart. Our interest in this immeasurable topic is how the threeness of God accounts for his transcendence and immanence. God as God in himself is boundless and unfathomable. God's revealed names are Father, Son, and Spirit. We complement these titles with descriptions of the roles and characteristics of God, such as Source, Word, and Presence. Before there was time or place, God as Spirit moved over the face of the deep. Through the Son, the Word, God created all that is. Through Moses and the prophets, this God spoke. "In these last days [God] has spoken to us by a Son, whom he appointed heir of all things, through whom he also created the worlds" (Heb 1:2). Since Jesus' departure from the plane of this world, the Spirit has prolonged Jesus' presence and power in the church and in creation. The Spirit is the animator of the sacramental.

In the New Testament, Christ's incarnation is the densest point of divine disclosure. John asserts that "no one has ever seen God. It is God the only Son, who is close to the Father's heart, who has made him known" (Jn 1:18). Speaking of Christ's cosmic significance, Paul makes the audacious claims that "in him all things hold together" and "in him all the fullness of God was pleased to dwell" (Col 1:17, 19). Paradoxically, we know the divinity of Christ through his humanity. As I have said before, in that sense Christ himself is the primordial sacrament. The incarnation extends from the birth and ministry of Jesus to his death and resurrection. When he leaves this realm, his human nature goes with him and becomes part of God. This is what the letter to the Hebrews means when it speaks of the Son interceding for us with the Father (Heb 4:14-16). These are the most profound descriptions we have; all other reflections of God present in the world are grounded and measured by them. From these descriptions we take the confidence that what is created has had its capacity to express the Creator restored. In the church's self-giving, its sacramental actions—whether liturgical or missionary—are little analogues of the incarnation; they prolong Christ's humanity in time and space. The whole of incarnational reality constitutes the sacramental universe.

Although we seldom consider it, almost always happening upon God is a mediated experience. Earlier in the book I mentioned the intense spiritual encounters of my coming-of-age years in natural settings. I was awestruck that I could be alone with God. But, in fact, I was being borne up in God's presence by the tangible testimony of the sun's warmth and the lake's breeze. When Christ "became a natural man for natural men,"[17] he revealed a holy oneness between spirit and matter that is within our everyday reach. At its simplest, we inherit these little analogues of the incarnation, prescribed words and gestures through which we are given a place of belonging. Then we improvise on them, like the woman I mentioned from war-torn Yugoslavia, who reinvented the handshake as a protest against rulers who tried to make neighbors into enemies. Stanley Grenz describes the dynamic of such occasions well. "These acts are an indispensable means whereby the group is placed ritually within a narrative that constitutes them as a community."[18] It is common to think that the path to spiritual vitality transcends outward things. However, the highest intention of religious gestures is the opposite: to provide tangible forms for the Spirit to inhabit.

Inseparable from God's self-giving in the incarnation is God's self-giving in the Holy Spirit. The Spirit is that of God, which indwells the church, each believer, and the whole creation. According to John, the Spirit is the person of God who continues the ministry of Jesus in time and space (Jn 16:5-15). The petition for the Spirit in the Communion prayer in appendix one richly illustrates this reality: "Send now your Spirit upon us so that the bread we break and the cup we share might be a communion of the body and blood of Christ. Send now your Spirit upon us so that we, and all who bear his name, might live lives conformed to Christ." We remember not only the historical Jesus but also the living Christ who feeds us with himself and sends us into the world as little incarnations.

AN EXERCISE IN SACRAMENTAL REALITY: BECOME WHAT YOU HAVE EATEN

In the apostolic church there was an intensity of faith in the presence of the risen Christ, an encounter that expressed itself sacramentally, mystically, and

---

[17]Pilgram Marpeck, in *The Writings of Pilgram Marpeck*, ed. and trans. William Klassen and Walter Klaassen, Classics of the Radical Reformation 2 (Harrisonburg, VA: Herald Press, 1978), 85.

[18]Stanley Grenz, "Baptism and the Lord's Supper as Community Acts," Anthony R. Cross and Philip E. Thompson, eds. *Baptist Sacramentalism*, Studies in Baptist History and Thought 5 (Waynesboro GA: Paternoster, 2003), 91.

ethically. In fact, these three dimensions were often inseparable parts of the church's and the believer's identities. Paul calls the bread of the Lord's Supper a communion/sharing/participation in the body of Christ (1 Cor 10:16-17). This is a double entendre, referring both to Christ's tangible presence in the shared elements and the community that eats and drinks them. In 1 Corinthians 12 "body of Christ" clearly refers to the congregation. Both expressions of *body* are essential to the meaning of the Breaking of Bread. In Corinth and elsewhere there is a sense of Christ's nearness beyond the believers' ordinary awareness of him, but, as Joseph Martos recognizes, "that presence seems to have been a pervasive presence in the group's praying and eating rather than a localized presence in the food."[19] There is also Paul's confession: "It is no longer I who live, but it is Christ who lives in me" (Gal 2:20), suggesting a mystical oneness. And finally there is an ethical expression of the presence of Christ in the bodies of believers, who become "a living sacrifice" (Rom 12:1). In another example of ethical embodiment, described by Matthew (25:31-46), Jesus is so fully identified with the hungry, the stranger, the prisoner, that to provide for them is to provide for Jesus.[20]

In the patristic era, the church moved from a primarily Jewish context to a primarily Greek one. Theologians turned to thinking about the "mysteries" of the church in Greek categories. This is an exceedingly complex and varied

---

[19]Joseph Martos, *Doors to the Sacred: A Historical Introduction to Sacraments in the Catholic Church* (Garden City, NJ: Doubleday, 1982), 240.

[20]I have found the following texts clarifying and insightful on the subject of Christ's presences. F. J. Leenhardt, "This Is My Body," in *Essays on the Lord's Supper,* by Oscar Cullmann and F. J. Leenhardt (Cambridge, UK: Lutterworth, 1958), 24-85, an attempt to overcome Protestant reductionism; Edward Schillebeeckx, *The Eucharist* (London: Sheed & Ward, 1968), in part a response to Leenhardt using the concept "transignification"; John D. Rempel, "Critically Appropriating Tradition: Pilgram Marpeck's Experiments in Corrective Theologizing," *Mennonite Quarterly Review* 85, no. 1 (2011): 59-76, my attempt to apply the above shift to Free Churches; Scott W. Bullard, *Re-membering the Body: The Lord's Supper and Ecclesial Unity in the Free Church Traditions* (Eugene, OR: Cascade, 2013), historical and current examples of radical thinking on real presence; Tad W. Guzie, *Jesus and the Eucharist* (New York: Penguin, 1974), a radical Catholic restatement of real presence; Paul Bernier, *Bread Broken and Shared: Broadening Our Vision of Eucharist* (Notre Dame, IN: Ave Maria Press, 1981), the outworking of Christ's presence in doing justice; and William Crockett, *Eucharist: Symbol of Transformation* (Collegeville, MN: Liturgical Press, 2990), esp. 78-121, fresh language for old debates on the subject. Anthony Cross and Dale Stoffer both apply the rethinking of the past half century to their traditions: Anthony R. Cross, "Baptismal Regeneration: Rehabilitating a Lost Dimension of New Testament Baptism," in *Baptist Sacramentalism 2,* ed. Anthony R Cross and Philip E. Thompson (Eugene, OR: Wipf & Stock, 2008), 150-59; and Dale Stoffer, ed., *The Lord's Supper: Believers Church Perspectives* (Scottdale, PA: Herald Press, 1997), a collection of papers on the theology and practice of Holy Communion from different denominational perspectives.

development that evolved differently in the East than it did in the West. In these novel cultural settings, after the intensity and intuitiveness of first-generation faith, believers were inevitably moved to ask, "In the legacy Jesus left us, what is the relationship between the sign and the thing signified?"

We have noted that an early and implicit understanding of a mystery or sacrament was that what is signified is also present in the sign. This is what makes a sign a sacrament. Christians believed that the crucified and risen Christ was among them in a surpassing density of presence in the Eucharist. This was signified by the words *body* and *blood* as a way of describing the whole person. This language spoke to Jewish Christians because the shedding of blood was part of their sacrifices. There was a simple realism at work here.

Because they lived in a Mediterranean diaspora, Jews were surrounded by Greek culture and shaped by it. The Gospel of John is an example of this fusion. Via Rabbinic Judaism and through its own mission, like Paul's address to the Athenians (Acts 17:16-34), Christianity entered the world of Greek philosophy. Its language had to evolve to keep pace with the issues being raised.[21] The inevitable question with which patristic theologians grappled was what happens to grant believers sacramental participation in Christ.

In the fourth century, thinkers like Gregory of Nyssa and Ambrose of Milan believed that the elements of bread and wine were indeed transformed into the body and blood of Christ but not in a sensual, quantifiable way. The way in which they conceived of the relationship between the ritual act and that which it signifies is often called "metabolic realism" because the elements themselves are changed.[22] Gregory's language moves between the metaphorical and literal. He argues that just as the divine "mingled" with the human in Christ's incarnation, so "now also the bread that is sanctified by the word of God is changed into the body of God the Word."[23] Ambrose also moves between the metaphorical and the literal, but his use of the word *flesh* in describing the outcome of the prayer of consecration moves toward the literal: "When consecration has been added, from being bread it becomes the flesh of Christ."[24]

---

[21]Daniel J. Sheerin lays out this evolution in the thought of the defining figures of the early patristic era by sampling their sermons and lectures in *The Eucharist* (Wilmington, DE: Glazier, 1986).

[22]William Crockett, *Eucharist: Symbol of Transformation* (Collegeville, MN: Liturgical Press, 1990), 78-105.

[23]Sheerin, "The Great Catechetical Oration," in *Eucharist*, 63.

[24]Sheerin, "On the Sacraments, Book 4" in *Eucharist*, 77.

Thinkers like Augustine of Hippo brought another mindset to this burning question. They were drawn to what is often called "symbolic realism," the notion that ritual actions participate in the reality they represent but are not identical with it.[25] In other words, when we take Communion, the Holy Spirit makes the elements the means by which we participate in an encounter with Christ. Yet the elements are not transformed so as to be identical with the body and blood of Christ. In his most famous sermon on the Breaking of Bread, Augustine tries to account for the double affirmation that after the ascension Christ is at the right hand of the Father in heaven but also in the Eucharist. He contends that in a sacrament one thing is seen and another is understood.[26] What is to be understood is that *we* are the body of Christ. In the consecration, Augustine reminds his hearers, bread becomes body and wine becomes blood, yet the weight of the celebration falls not on the elements but on the congregation. The congregation as the body of Christ is Augustine's central eucharistic motif.[27]

It is remarkable that we have almost no evidence that these different under-standings of what happens in the Breaking of Bread caused conflict in the church from the fourth to the ninth centuries. Apparently the shared convic-tion that believers truly receive the very person of Christ in the Holy Supper was sufficient commonality to allow for different cultural and philosophic expressions of how this presence comes about. However, the ground had shifted by the ninth century. The official position of the church became metabolic realism of an increasingly materialist sort.

At the time of the Reformation many Catholics shared the concern of Protestants for a spiritual reception of the sacraments. However, Protestants concluded that the teaching of transubstantiation—whose goal it was to prevent a materialistic interpretation—had proved incapable of correcting Catholic practice. As a consequence, there was an outburst of Protestant attempts to develop eucharistic theology and worship directly from the practice of the New Testament and postapostolic church. It is one of the great tragedies of Western Christianity that the meal of unity became one of discord. That story will come later.

---

[25]Crockett, *Eucharist*, 78-105.
[26]Crockett, "Sermon 272," in *Eucharist*, 94.
[27]Crockett, "A Discourse on the Lord's Day Concerning Holy Pascha," in *Eucharist*, 99-102.

A postscript to this turn of events is that most historic Western churches have found themselves in a "disenchanted" world. By contrast, the historic churches of the East as well as indigenous, Catholic, and Protestant churches in the Global South are at home in an "enchanted" world. All their cultures have an immediacy to the created order that the Western church also had before the Renaissance and Reformation. Theirs is a world that is at home in the Bible, with its miracles and demonic forces.

What might such unselfconscious participation in an enchanted universe look like within modern Western culture? Is it even possible? Here is a preliminary response. Teasing out the assumptions of any worldview is a high-wire act in which it is easy to lose one's footing. To oversimplify, there are many religious and secular critics of those extreme currents of rationalism and materialism whose origin lies in the Enlightenment.[28] Today there are schools not only of spirituality but also of philosophy that challenge the absolute priority reason has been given in the West in how we arrive at meaning. They see a role for intuition and for liminality, and boundary experiences that take us beyond language and rationality. This rethinking helps to bridge the philosopher Gottfried Lessing's "broad ditch" between the general claims of religion and the particular facts of history.[29] By that, Lessing meant that the human quest begins with historical facts that are contingent. Between rationally arrived at claims and the universal truths of religion there is an unbridgeable chasm because reason rejects any claim of the supernatural. Thus, we can know only the verifiable world of matter; the world of spirit—if it exists—is beyond reach.

This has been a premise of modern thought since the Enlightenment. Extreme rationalism, which has a religious as well as a secular expression, is unreceptive to paradoxical thinking, that is, an approach to reality in which two claims can both be true, for instance, that humanity is both blessed and fallen. This way of interpreting the world is fundamental because paradoxes give structure to religion's deepest insights. The kind of rationalism I have

---

[28]For instance, Carl Jung, *Psychology and Religion* (New Haven, CT: Yale University Press, 1960), 14; Michael Polanyi, *Personal Knowledge: Towards a Post-Critical Philosophy*, corrected ed. (Chicago: University of Chicago Press, 1962); and John Polkinghorne, *The Faith of a Physicist* (Minneapolis: Fortress, 1996).

[29]*Werke, vol 23*, ed., Pederson, von Olshausen. 23, 47-49 as quoted in Taylor, 363.

mentioned claims the opposite: that the law of contradiction is absolute. Similarly, some kinds of scientific thought make a sharp distinction between intellect and emotion, reason and imagination, aligning themselves with rationality as an objective human faculty and the exclusive medium of verifiable knowledge. Such rationality claims the objective truth of the scientific method and its mastery of the factual realm; it assigns emotion and intuition to the subjective realm, in which truth claims are not possible.

The realm of the incarnational and sacramental can be grasped only where there is openness to the human capacity for imaginative as well as rational perception. The metaphorical imagination is at home in the realm of spirit; it apprehends truth that would otherwise be inaccessible to us. Yet this world of spiritual potency is brought home to us only by the gaze of faith. Belief in a sacramental universe means that the distance between a sign and what it signifies has been shortened and brought within reach.[30]

Sacraments are at once a condensation and an intensification of a whole world. Gerard Manley Hopkins's uses two evocative images for this reality. Our earth is, "charged with the grandeur of God." Why is this? Because God's Spirit "broods" over it.[31] Sacramental words and gestures concentrate and stylize the story of salvation. They engage all our senses. Together they unleash our imagination and our memory and bring within reach the human and divine promises that ground us and offer us a place of belonging in the vastness of the cosmos. Rituals with a sacramental intensity are capable of constituting communities because they have a density of encounter, a power of evocation, that make shared meaning tangible in the midst a life that is agonizingly ambivalent. Love lives side by side with estrangement; hope is haunted by death. Sacraments are a form of the gospel that persuades us of the elusive but life-giving truth that love is stronger than death. They are promissory notes that "touch and handle things unseen."[32]

There is a core of such notes that enact the gospel. They are outward and visible signs of inward and spiritual grace. Infant baptism and dedication

---

[30]I thank Scott Holland for this notion in his "Signifying Presence: The Ecumenical Sacramental Theology of George Worgul," *Louvain Studies* 18 (1993): 38-55.

[31]Gerard Manley Hopkins, "God's Grandeur," in *The Poems of Gerard Manley Hopkins*, ed. W. H. Gardner and N. H. MacKenzie, 4th ed. (Oxford: Oxford University Press, 1970), 66.

[32]"Here, O My Lord, I See Thee," *Hymnal: A Worship Book*, #465.

designate God's claim on a newborn life and God's promise to keep the child in his care. Confirmation and believer's baptism mark someone's coming of age and coming to an owned faith. Marriage and other rites of family and community enact pledges of fidelity on their anniversaries. Ordination and other ministries, including consecration to a life of celibacy, empower people to live the vocation to which they are called. Anointing with oil invokes God's healing nearness on those crushed by afflictions of body and soul. A Christian funeral accompanies those who loved the deceased person with the claim that even death cannot interrupt God's care for us.

In these holy moments we are borne up by gestures and words not of our own making. Of course, each of these transitions can be—and is intended to be—profoundly personal for all of those involved. But, ultimately, what attracts us to life-giving rituals is their universal role: they act and speak equally to and for all Christians at precarious—and in the same breath—transcendent moments.

4

THE SACRAMENTALITY
OF TIME

"I'M LATE, I'M LATE, I'm late for a very important date," cries the Mad Hatter in *Alice in Wonderland* as he pushes his way through a crowd. "No time to say 'hello,' 'good-bye,' I'm late, I'm late, I'm late."[1] We're amused by the Hatter's behavior because we know it describes ours as well.

Time is elusive. We want to master time, but it masters us. We want to set it aside, but we get caught up in it. In the Bible, time belongs to the created order of things (Gen 1:14-19; 2:2-3). Time, like all of creation, has limits, but time itself is not a result of the fall. In an age when endless war and human-made environmental destruction leave us with a sense of futility, it is of utmost importance to affirm that the movement of time has meaning. It places decisions before us, like that faced by Abram and Sarai when God said to them, "Go from your country and your kindred" (Gen 12:1-3). Time is our friend because it opens the possibility of change to us. Because we know we are going to die, we savor every second allotted to us to live. Even though we are bound for eternity, we rightly love this life because it is the only one we know. The problem lies not with loving life but with trying to possess it. Like our life, time is a gift from God. It cannot be hoarded—it can only be lived, either selfishly or unselfishly.

In Israel's exodus from captivity in Egypt to Canaan, the Promised Land, liberation came to them in the movement of time. In Hebrew belief, time was not static or cyclical but linear: God acted in time to rescue people and set them free. The devotional as well as the prophetic literature of the Old Testament gives pride of place to waiting on God. When the time is right, God will

---

[1] *Alice in Wonderland*, directed by Tim Burton (Burbank, CA: Disney, 2010).

act. Thus, time has a sacramental character; it is the medium of God's engagement with humanity, an intensification of time in which novelty is possible.
Fate is the power that overrules freedom and compels creation to repeat an
endless, meaningless cycle. In Greek lore Sisyphus is punished for his mis-
deeds by having to roll a large stone to the top of a hill only to have it roll back
down again. He is fated to roll the stone up the hill again and again forever.
Grace is the opposite; it is the gift to act freely in the unfolding of time. Israel
was rescued from the Babylonian captivity it had seemed fated to endure.
Then came the cosmic act of liberation that restored the potential of time,
Jesus' death and resurrection. For Jews (Passover) and Christians (Good
Friday and Easter), by contrast, the liturgical year was a memorial of God's
freeing acts. The feasts and fasts marked God's great incursions into time and
space. Ordinary time anticipated extraordinary time each week and year.

In modern secular societies, by contrast, time has been flattened out. The
daily, weekly, and yearly complementary rhythm of work and rest has been
overtaken by stores that are open twenty-four hours a day and restaurants
that advertise all-day breakfasts. Industry and financial institutions are the
biggest culprits in this profanation of time ("time is money"). They demand
that people work whatever shifts are most efficient in making money seven
days a week because for them time is merely a commodity to be consumed,
not a rhythm that allots room for community and festivity as well as work.
The Sabbath was created for the safeguarding of all aspects of society's rhythm.
It was a collective agreement that shared experiences of time as liberating and
restoring are essential to human well-being. Until recently, Sunday played
this role in Western countries: it set limits for work and consumption on
behalf of believers and unbelievers alike. On the Sabbath, not only the density
of time but its pace changed. It set a boundary to the delusion that more, bigger, faster, better, mine is the path to fulfillment.

Technological societies, like ours, confuse quality of time with quantity of
time. All things, from dishwashers to scanners, "save" quantities of time for
us to "spend." We crave more time, but when we get it, we keep doing what
we were already doing—working, shopping, using digital devices, traveling.
A friend of mine is a minister in a fashionable urban congregation. He tells
me that, increasingly, people are coming to funerals late and leaving early. In

response, the congregation has asked that the funeral service be shortened and that it be held over the noon hour with the offer of a fifteen-minute stand-up lunch right after the service.

In traditional societies people have an instinct for different kinds of time. When someone dies, a different flow of time sets in, spacious and slow enough to allow one to sit with mourners, to cook for the bereaved, to ponder one's own mortality. There is a way out of relentless, undifferentiated time. As we have seen, it has its origin in the Hebrew and later Christian understanding of time. Through their rescue from the Egyptians, the early Hebrews experienced linear time: God had rescued them from the eternal return of time in which nothing ever changed. History came to matter a great deal to them: movement was possible; meaning was created not through endless repetition but through progression. Forgiveness freed people to live differently; protest made justice possible. Therefore, time mattered. But time was not unending; it was transcended by eternity.

A novelty entered Christian thought concerning time through the influence of Greek philosophy as it shaped Second Temple Judaism and early Christianity. In antiquity the Greeks had two ways of speaking about time. One of them was *chronos*. We get the word *chronology* from it. This describes events in the order of their occurrence. Here we are talking about linear progression.[2]

The other, and more intriguing, Greek word for time was *kairos*. This word talks about the quality, not the quantity of time. It concerns a moment that stands out from other moments, one that is pregnant with meaning and possibility. A modern instance of *kairos* time comes to mind. During World War II, Germany conquered Poland. After the war and into the 1970s, West Germany resisted repenting for the German devastation of Poland. In 1973 Willy Brandt, West Germany's chancellor, asked to lay a wreath at the memorial to the Warsaw ghetto, where numberless Poles—the majority of them Jews—had been murdered. The event was arranged. Brandt stepped forward and lay down the wreath. He stood erect for a moment and then fell to his knees in front of the memorial. All the tentative gestures of repentance by West Germans of good will, all the aspirations of Brandt's government, came to expression in

---

[2]The precise meaning of these concepts in their original setting has been debated. In Jewish and Christian thought they have taken on the meanings summarized above.

the planned laying of the wreath and, even more profoundly, in the unplanned kneeling down. It was a *kairos* moment, unmistakable in its sorrow for past sins and its plea for a new beginning. From that moment onward, the relationship between Poland and West Germany was changed.

Such times have a sacramental character, one in which time is the bearer of grace, in which time's power to redeem, rather than destroy, is restored. There are times that become pregnant with possibility, with novelty. Something new was birthed in the breakthrough brought about by Brandt's gesture of remorse and its reception by his Polish hosts. It is hard to overstate the significance of time as purposeful, forward movement for the nature of Western civilization. Hannah Arendt, the German and American political philosopher, speaks to the meaning of time in the Western world with her assertion that a just society can come into being only when forgiveness and promise making are possible:

> The possible redemption from the predicament of irreversibility—to be unable to undo what one has done, though one did not, and could not, know what he was doing—is the faculty of forgiving. The remedy for unpredictability, for the chaotic uncertainty of the future, is contained in the faculty to make and keep promises.[3]

The possibility of prying open a movement of time that has closed, that has locked in both friend and foe, both perpetrator and victim, arises in *kairos* moments within linear time. By contrast, there is no place for open moments in cyclical time, which can only repeat what has already happened. Similarly, the possibility of living justly in the future, whatever it brings, is vouchsafed by pledges we make to one another and that God has made to humanity. The American Jewish theologian Abraham Heschel describes this freedom from the seeming inevitability of fate in history as the "sanctification of time."[4]

There is a second level of significance for liberating moments in history. Through repetition, liberating moments evoke the original power of the event. The Spirit of God inhabits them again and again. This is the case when Moses convenes Israel to hear God's giving of the Law. He has just rehearsed Israel's

---

[3]Hannah Arendt, *The Human Condition* (Garden City, NY: Doubleday, 1959), 212.
[4]Abraham Joshua Heschel, *The Sabbath: Its Meaning for Modern Man* (New York: Farrar, Straus, & Giroux, 1978), 8.

rescue from Egypt. Then he says, "Not with our ancestors did the LORD make this covenant, but with *us*, who are all of us here alive today" (Deut 5:3, emphasis added). God's liberating encounter with his people is re-presented again and again and releases them from bondage again and again.

SABBATH

Any span of time can become one of forgiveness and promise making. But it takes its life from a paradigm that is repeated every seven days, every year, and every seven years. Every week there was a Sabbath (Ex 20:8-11), every year a Passover (Ex 12:1-27),[5] every seven years a Sabbath for the land (Lev 25:1-7), every forty-nine years a Jubilee in which lost land was restored (Lev 25:8-17). Each of these events was a *kairotic* transcendence of *chronos* time.

The origin of a day that puts ordinary time aside lies in God's day of rest in celebration of the goodness and completeness of creation. God had been busy creating a harmonious whole out of sunshine, flowers, fish, and people. All of them were interdependent, all of them belonged together, and all of them were kept from destruction by the steadfast, almighty love of God. After six days of fashioning the world out of chaos, God rested and commanded all creatures to pause with him and rest in his sovereignty over all of life (Gen 1:29–2:3). It is likely that this account of creation was written long after the giving of the Ten Commandments and is, in part, a meditation on the reason for the fourth commandment (Ex 20:8-11). Resting on the seventh day is the climax, the completeness of divine and human creating. It is a "palace in time," "adjacent to eternity."[6]

The keeping of the Sabbath is the first step in reversing the fall, in placing the world back into God's hands. In the fall, we tried to take the world into our own hands, insisting that we knew better than God what makes life good. This flight from God leaves us with the devastating realization that now the only meaning in life is one that we create. We worry that without our accomplishments we are nothing. Then the basis of human existence is no longer who I *am*—a child of God—but what I *make*. This shift is the defining premise of modern economic theories. In its unfettered forms, capitalism sees

---

[5]The account of the giving of the law in Deuteronomy (5:1-21) links Sabbath and Passover under the theme of freedom.

[6]Heschel, *Sabbath*, 15.

people only as doers: on weekdays they are producers; on weekends they are consumers. This way of seeing the world reduces time to undifferentiated quantities whose only purpose is to be filled with production and consumption. By contrast, Heschel says, "The seventh day is the armistice in man's cruel struggle for existence, a truce of all conflicts personal and social . . . a day on which handling money is considered a desecration."[7]

It is worth noting that the Hebrew commandment for a day of rest includes not only people of power and privilege, those who are rich enough to stop working at any time because they can make others work for them. The offer of the Sabbath is universal. Rest is extended not only to parents but to daughters and sons—who were in charge of household duties in that society. Further, it includes female and male slaves, as well as the cattle that draw carts and pull plows. Finally, sojourners—people from other tribes who have no rights in their host's culture—have a place in this day of liberation. Every Sabbath is a breakthrough of God's reign—all of God's creatures ceasing their striving and being equally at rest in God's steadfast love. The specificity of the seventh day—its twenty-four hours, its shared interruption of toil, its shared memory of liberation (Deut 5:12-15), its acts of unique festivity—is what gives it a sacramental density.

The most remarkable fact, then, is that the Sabbath was the first universal human right, the great equalizer. At least on one day of the week there were to be no masters and no slaves, no separate status for women or foreigners! The Sabbath was a dangerous day: think of the utopian visions it gave oppressed people about the possibilities of creating a just society.

RESURRECTION

Christianity inherited its understanding of time and history from Judaism. This was due in significant measure to the notion of God's kingdom. God ruled over creation, over history and the nations, and specifically over Israel. Time had a forward movement toward the fullness of God's reign at the end of time and through eternity. Theologically speaking, every moment in time has the potential to be a *kairos* one. This is so because time, like matter and space, is inhabited by God. A *kairos* or sacramental moment is one in which God's kingdom becomes tangible.

---

[7]Heschel, *Sabbath*, 29.

The final agent of this movement toward eternity was Jesus. "But when the fullness of time had come," writes Paul to the churches in Galatia, "God sent his Son, born of a woman, born under the law" (Gal 4:4). Liberating occasions in history, like the coming of Christ, have two levels of meaning. The first one is their power to break into and alter history. Just as the exodus from Egypt is the birth of freedom in the Old Testament, in the New Testament it is the resurrection of Jesus, whose power is mediated by the Holy Spirit from generation to generation (2 Cor 3:17-18).

It is the resurrection of Jesus on which the gospel pivots and on the basis of which a Christian understanding of time came into being. Early on the day of resurrection, the first day of the week, the two Marys, Joanna, and their friends were dumbfounded to discover the empty tomb (Lk 24:1-10). Later that same day Jesus accompanied two of his dejected disciples as they walked from one town to another. When they stopped for a meal, Jesus took bread, blessed and broke it, and gave it to them. In that moment they recognized him as the One with whom they had often sat at table (Lk 24:13-32). Later that evening he appeared to a brooding and grieving room full of his male companions. They "thought that they were seeing a ghost" (Lk 24:33-42). A week later a similarly startling encounter took place (Jn 20:24-29).

It became irresistible for Jesus' followers to meet on the first day of the week even after his ascension. They gathered in anticipation of an encounter like those of Easter Sunday. The association between Sunday and resurrection was quickly established. It became the day on which Jesus' friends broke bread in expectation of his presence. They called it the "Lord's day" (Rev 1:10). Soon every Sunday was thought of as a little Easter, a repetition of the day of Jesus' return from the dead. It was the weekly Breaking of Bread, above all else, that kept the delay in Christ's return and the end of time from becoming a catastrophe for the church: every Lord's Day Christ *did* return.

Later another term was added to describe the meaning of Sunday, "the eighth day of creation." Jews were already familiar with the term. It was favored because it suggested a new beginning for creation in which death would not have the final word.[8] For Christians, Sunday was the rehearsal of this hope,

---

[8]Marl Searle, "The Heart of the Liturgical Year" in Lawrence Johnson and Mark Searle, eds., *The Church Gives Thanks and Remembers: Essays on the Liturgical Year* (Collegeville, MN: Liturgical Press, 1984), 22.

setting those who joined in on it free from the fear of death and, thus, free to risk their lives for Christ.

In some settings, like Jerusalem, Christians continued to worship with Jews on Saturday and to keep that day as the Sabbath. Gradually, traits of the Jewish Sabbath were carried over to the Lord's Day. By the second century the weekly Day of Resurrection was also becoming the Christian day of rest. This shift was enshrined in law by Constantine at the beginning of the fourth century. It set a limit to work, consumption, and worry. Ordinary time was set aside for extraordinary time, drudgery for festivity. In Christian thinking, the setting apart of time became parallel to the setting aside of objects and places. Mark Searle describes it this way:

> Sunday, with its assembly, its preaching, its Breaking of Bread is essentially a post-resurrection appearance of the Risen Christ in which he breathes his Spirit upon his disciples for the forgiveness of sins and for the life of the world. As such, it is the point at which all the central images of the Christian year converge, and because the liturgical year is but a spinning of these images from week to week, the Christian Sunday may properly be claimed as the heart, not only of the liturgical year but of the Christian life itself.[9]

THE CHRISTIAN CALENDAR

The church year was an expansion of this paradigm. The annual re-presenting of salvation history from Advent to Pentecost shared the same notion of sacramental time. Its days and seasons were not merely adornments of cyclical time or *chronos* time. They were a rhythmic sequence that, like objects and spaces, had a density to them that made long-ago events, like Good Friday and Easter Sunday, tangibly present and effective again. This second level of significance of liberating events is the ongoing power they gain through repetition.

In the Middle Ages, Sunday as Sabbath was of lifesaving significance for peasants and their beasts of burden. All week they were beholden to their overlords—always at their beck and call. Only Sundays and feast days set a limit to the work that could be demanded of them. This arrangement provided

[9]Mark Searle, "Sunday: The Heart of the Liturgical Year," in *Alternative Futures for Worship*, ed. Lawrence Johnson (Collegeville, MN: Liturgical Press, 1984), 35.

the only time at their disposal for church, rest, and family. At the time of the Reformation the sanctity of Sunday was retained and even expanded. It was considered to be the ideal time for meditating on the Bible, suddenly widely available because of the printing press.

In people's zeal to keep Sundays set apart, they made lists of what was permissible and what was not. Frequenting public houses and entertainments like cock fighting, for example, were discouraged and in many places forbidden. These rules brought the danger of legalism with them. There is, for example, this story of an eighteenth-century Baptist woman in England leaving church on the Lord's Day. She came upon friends cheerfully sitting in a pub and joined them. Musicians struck up a tune and the woman, caught up in the spirit of the occasion, climbed onto a table and began to dance. On hearing about her extravagant behavior, the leaders of the Baptist congregation reprimanded her. The reprimand was not that she had gone to the pub or even that she had danced on a table but that she had done so on a Sunday.[10]

A collective day of rest had ripples that set limits in unexpected ways. For example, I once taught in a small city that was plagued with gang violence. One of my students reflected on her experience of that dangerous world as a child. She always looked forward to Sundays because there was a tacit agreement between residents and gang members (often their own children) that Sundays would be free of vendettas, robberies, and the like—if for no other reason than that grandmothers had to be able to get to church in safety. So, for children and parents, Sunday was the safest day for visiting and other forms of recreation.

THE SECULARIZATION OF TIME

With the coming of the Industrial Revolution in the nineteenth century, and its massive dislocation of people from country to city, the power of tradition was undermined. This included a disregard for Sundays and feast days that had set limits to the demands of employers on their employees.[11] This elimination of a day of rest was true also for beasts of burden. Thus, the solidarity

---

[10]Margaret Spufford, "The Importance of the Lord's Supper to Dissenters," in *The World of Rural Dissenters, 1520–1725*, ed. Margaret Spufford (Cambridge: Cambridge University Press, 1995), 91.

[11]Hans Meyer, "Anthropological Notes on Liturgical Time," *Studia Liturgica* 14 (1982): 8-13.

of creation—humans, animals, and nature[12]—that was to be restored each Sabbath was violated. "Time is money" was the employer's newly minted motto. Factory laborers worked under appalling conditions, including twelve-hour days, sometimes seven days a week. This was truly an era when time was flattened out; it no longer had peak times set apart from the work week, rejected by the powerful as too high a price to pay for social harmony. Trade unions arose to take up the cause of the powerless. One of their core demands was a work-free Sunday. Thus there arose an alliance of church and organized labor for fair working conditions—including Sunday as a day of rest—that persists today in countries like Germany and Italy. Almost no one seems to be conscious of this link among faith, consumerism, and shared rhythms of time.[13] Remarkably, this is truest in the United States, the most religious and at the same time most consumerist country in the Western world.

Even though most people today work fewer hours than they did in the nineteenth century, there are also fewer shared pauses. In the United States, and increasingly in Canada, there is not a common day of rest that allows families, as well as friendship and affinity groups, to meet. This individualistic arrangement of time goes against the grain of human community. Some European countries have taken the Christian calendar as a given, a historic pattern of time use, that can make life more just for people of any or no religion. Because Western society has Christian origins, Sunday has been its weekly day of rest. But it can also be a convenient day of rest for all, which does not impose Christian practices on multicultural societies. A common day of rest gives all of us the permission to linger over the newspaper as long as we want and to savor an extra cup of coffee without feeling guilty. On the Sabbath, the density of time changes but also its pace. It sets a boundary to rushing and consuming. It dismantles the delusion behind these impulses, that is, that more and faster and bigger and better shape the path to fulfillment.[14]

---

[12]This notion of practicing a sabbath for the whole creation was applied not only to the seventh day but to the seventh year, when fields were laid fallow for a year.

[13]I realize that I'm writing for people who have the security and leisure to read books like this one. There are many unemployed and underemployed people working for a minimum wage that forces them to hold down two jobs. They have little freedom to set the times of their work. My argument is intended not as a judgment on them but as an example of the unjustness of their situation and the need for a differentiated sense of time and its uses.

[14]See Michel Quoist's meditation "Lord, I Have Time," in *Prayers* (New York: Sheed & Ward, 1963), 96-99.

The larger issue at stake during and after industrialization, as we have seen, was the disenchantment of the world. The profaning of holy time is an integral, and often overlooked, dimension of secularization. In breaking the bond between humanity and nature, it legitimated the exploitation of nature. In a world in which spirit and matter were completely separated, the efficient production of material goods was the highest value. Like labor, time was merely a quantity at the disposal of those with power to use it to their advantage. Production and profit became ends rather than means. The new creed was that human accomplishment, rather than the providence of God, is the basis of creation's well-being. This premise became one of the fundamental shifts that constitute the modern age. Sunday, both literally and as a symbol, holds forth an alternative view of abundant living, in which human productivity and consumption and worry have limits imposed on their place in our lives. Every seven days we are called to enact this liberating truth.

5

BAPTISM

THE ART OF RISING FROM THE DEAD

DO YOU RENOUNCE THE EVIL POWERS of this world and turn to Jesus Christ as your savior? Do you put your trust in his grace and love and promise to obey him as your lord?"[1]

These words accost us, as if they are coming at us from another universe. What right does anyone, on this earth or anywhere else, have to ask such intimate, such intrusive questions? These are the first questions traditionally asked of candidates for baptism. The words are an unsparing request, uttered in a public setting, demanding that those being addressed declare themselves. At stake are the candidates' loyalties. Do they promise their allegiance to Christ or to another person or power?

Before coming to an owned faith, we believe what our parents believe. We are part of their identity. We belong to their family, culture, nation, worldview. God's provision for us often takes the form of belonging to them. But when these attachments are made absolute, they compete with God for our loyalty. To set our hope on the reign of God is to relativize the solidarities of birth and vocation and to embrace another solidarity, that of the body of Christ (Mt 10:32-39). In belonging to Christ we belong to all those who have come to him. Paul presents 1 Corinthians 12 as his treatise on the superseding of all secondary parts of our identity—culture, status, gender—by belonging to Christ through the Spirit. "For just as the body is one and has many members, and all the members of the body, though many, are one body, so it is with Christ.

---

[1]John D. Rempel, ed., *Minister's Manual* (Newton, KS: Faith and Life Press, 1998), "Baptism and Church Membership," 48. Original use in *Apostolic Constitutions, Book 7, Chapter 41,* 57 in Thomas Finn, *Early Christian Baptism and the Catechuminate: West and East Syria* (Collegeville: Liturgical, 1992).

For in the one Spirit we were all baptized into one body—Jews or Greeks, slaves or free—and we were all made to drink of one Spirit" (1 Cor 12:12-13).

Resolving who or what is sovereign in our lives is the most consequential choice we ever make. Most people make and remake that decision during different times and seasons of life. But it begins with yes to God's call, whether on a single occasion when "our heart is strangely warmed"[2] or in a long gestation. What happens to us is not of our own making. We are not left to our own devices. It is the Father who draws us to the Son through the Spirit, according to the Fourth Gospel (Jn 6:25-40; 14:8-17; 16:12-15). Our seeking of Christ is evidence of the Father working through the Spirit drawing us to him.

> I sought the Lord, and afterward I knew
>> he moved my soul to seek him, seeking me.
> It was not I that found, O Savior true,
>> no, I was found, was found of thee.[3]

We call this divine initiative and our human response conversion, however compact or drawn out it is. The process has inner and outer elements that are woven together in different ways in each person. At the heart of coming to faith is the experience of being loved. Often the love of parents is the first inkling we have that their love is the embodiment of an even greater love. They and others who are good to us love us because they have been loved, ultimately, by God. At some point our experience of love leads to the question Paul asked. "Do you not realize that God's kindness is meant to lead you to repentance?" (Rom 2:4). Conversion is a paradoxical reality. No one can come to the Son unless the Father draws them (Jn 6:44). This drawing enables us to turn from one direction to another (Mk 1:15). Within the embrace of God's love, we turn from what once mattered most to what now matters most.

This awesome change, which will take a lifetime to unfold, is enacted and sealed in baptism. In Matthew's description of Jesus' baptism we see the Spirit "alighting" on him, and a voice declares that Jesus is the Father's beloved Son (Mt 3:16-17). In John's record, Jesus says to a seeker, "No one can enter the

---

[2] This was John Wesley's description of his conversion. See *A Burning and a Shining Light: English Spirituality in the Age of Wesley* (Grand Rapids: Eerdmans, 1987), 203.
[3] Anonymous, "I Sought the Lord," *Holy Songs, Carols, and Sacred Ballads* (1880).

kingdom of God without being born of water and Spirit" (Jn 3:5). Geoffrey
Wainwright, a Methodist theologian, favors the term _enabler_ for the Spirit.
Enabling is different from coercing; it implies that we have the freedom to
cooperate with God or resist God.[4] In Paul's language we become "dead to
sin and alive to God" (Rom 6:11). In each of these images, divine and human,
inward and outward, Spirit and water are held together; the Spirit is always
sovereign, but the indispensable witness to the Spirit's work is water.[5] In the
dynamic of conversion, God as Spirit works inwardly and God as Son works
outwardly.[6] In the act of water baptism, all that has gone on in us is actualized
and sealed. Like all good rituals, baptism condenses and stylizes everything
that has led to our coming to faith as individuals, and at the same time gives
us a shared marker. None of us has a holier story than the other; baptism
makes all the stories equal.

In conversion and baptism everything is at stake: we have been taken from
one solidarity to another, from one core belonging (family, nation, profession,
political affiliation, or gang) to another (Christ and his body). This change of
solidarities is not only a personal move: it involves shifting our loyalty from
one community to another. Everyone belongs somewhere; Christians belong
to the body of Christ.

Extravagant language like this is found almost everywhere in the New
Testament. From the Gospels we learn that when people say yes to Christ,
their lives are no longer their own. When the woman who anointed Jesus' feet
with oil was set free from what had brought shame into her life, she never
turned back (Lk 7:36-50). When Paul was struck by blinding light so that he
might see that the One whose followers he was persecuting was the Messiah
he himself was waiting for, he was baptized and appointed to declare this
revelation to the outsiders of his day, the Gentiles (Acts 9:1-22).

In all these texts the initiator of the drama is God and not humans. This is as
true of the inward change of heart they underwent as it is of God's outward work
in them. In the world of the New Testament, inward stirrings to faith and outward

---

[4]Geoffrey Wainwright, _Doxology: The Praise of God in Worship, Doctrine, and Life_ (New York: Oxford, 1980), 92, 100.
[5]Pilgram Marpeck, in _The Writings of Pilgram Marpeck_, ed. and trans. William Klassen and Walter Klaassen, Classics of the Radical Reformation 2 (Harrisonburg, VA: Herald Press, 1978), 137-39, 142-43.
[6]Marpeck, _Writings_, 133-34, 193-95.

enactment of them are part of the same reality. In the minds of the biblical writers, the inner-to-outer time sequence does not lessen the unity of the event.

Paul's unforgettable image of baptism as death and new birth, as conversion from one life to another, dominates our understanding of coming to faith in Western Christianity. It is cut from the same cloth as the equally dramatic and formative images in Jesus' conversation with Nicodemus in John 3. Jesus answers his question about the way to life. He says we must be "born from above" (Jn 3:3), "born of water and Spirit" (Jn 3:5), and again, simply, "born of the Spirit" (Jn 3:8).

These descriptions form a bridge to the image that holds sway in the historic Eastern churches, that of Jesus' own baptism by John (Mt 3:13-17 and parallels). John's baptism is one of repentance, preparing people for baptism with the Spirit. But when Jesus is baptized, a novelty occurs. When he comes up out of the water, the Spirit descends on him like a dove. "And a voice from heaven said, 'This is my Son, the Beloved, with whom I am well pleased'" (Mt 3:17).

In one sense the baptism of Christ is unique. He is the Son of God, who needs no repentance, but is baptized out of solidarity with us. Yet, very early the church saw Jesus' baptism as the model for ours: in our baptism God declares us to be daughters and sons. It is in the density of the baptismal act, as its culmination, that the Spirit descends and a voice is heard calling the person being baptized "beloved."

THE ORIGIN OF BAPTISM

At the time of Jesus, Judaism practiced several ritual washings.[7] One of them was a baptism by which Gentiles confessed their faith in the God of Israel. Another water rite that we know through the ministry of John the Baptist was a baptism of repentance (Lk 3:15-22).

---

[7]The following are texts that have most shaped my thinking: G. R. Beasley-Murray, *Baptism in the New Testament* (Grand Rapids: Eerdmans, 1973), exegesis of New Testament texts concluding baptism is sacramental; Colin Buchanan, *A Case for Infant Baptism* (Bramcote, UK: Grove Books, 1973), against indiscriminate baptism of infants; S. Mark Heim, "Baptismal Recognition and the Baptist Churches," in *Baptism and the Unity of the Church*, ed. Michael Root (Geneva: World Council of Churches, 1998), 150-63, averring that the difference between churches is more ecclesial than baptismal; Marlin Jeschke, *Believers Baptism for Children of the Church* (Scottdale, PA: Herald Press, 1938), pastoral insights; Kevin Roy, *Baptism, Reconciliation, and Unity* (Carlisle, UK: Paternoster, 1998), pastoral and spiritual dimensions; and Mark Searle, "Infant Baptism Reconsidered," in *Living Water, Sealing Spirit: Readings on Christian Initiation*, ed. Maxwell Johnson (Collegeville, MN: Liturgical Press, 1995), 365-409, a novel defense of infant baptism that takes critics into account.

After Jesus' ascension, on the Jewish feast of Pentecost, Jesus' disciples were given an experience of ecstasy—such an intense indwelling by the Spirit that they could speak in languages not their own (Acts 2:1-36). This gave rise to the conviction that the resurrection of Jesus demonstrated he was the Messiah the Jews had hoped for. The disciples' early preaching consisted of interpreting Old Testament texts as finding their fulfillment in Jesus. The same Spirit who had given Jesus' followers the gift of tongues was also promised to all of Abraham and Sarah's offspring. The disciples urged their hearers to repent and be baptized (Acts 2:38). If they did so, the disciples promised, their sins would be forgiven. Three thousand of them did so that day. The apostles added two elements to John's baptism. One, it should be carried out in Jesus' name. And, two, they associated baptism with the gifts of the Spirit. These aspects were the building blocks of the developing doctrine of Christian baptism.

We do not know how it happened that the practices of baptismal washings in the Rabbinic Judaism of the first century so rapidly took on a novel meaning with reference to Jesus as the Messiah. Most Scripture scholars agree, however, that baptism was part of the origin of the church. In the charismatic character of early Christian mission there is experimentation and variety, but in all the settings into which the gospel is taken, a relationship is assumed between word and sacrament, between inner and outer. The same apostles who proclaim the narrative of Jesus and his Spirit urge their hearers to open their lives to the Messiah. The sign they receive when they do so is baptism.

The simplest way to explain this phenomenon is that both Jewish and Roman culture had an intuitive and unselfconscious sense that spiritual realities are actualized in physical gestures. This mindset was carried over into early Christian communities. They were "bilingual" in the sense that there was no separation between inwardness ("it is no longer I who live, but it is Christ who lives in me," Gal 2:20) and outwardness ("repent, and be baptized," Acts 2:38). To separate the two undoes the oneness of religious reality in early Christianity. We shall see that in some patristic and medieval thought the outward enactment in and of itself predominated and that some streams of the Reformation so emphasized the inward event that baptism's outward role as recapitulation and seal was endangered.

The apostolic and much of the patristic church claimed a distinctive intimacy in conversion to Christ. In his historical ministry, people were transformed by their encounter with Jesus. After he and Jesus met, Zacchaeus, the wealthy tax collector, gave half of his possessions to the poor (Lk 19:1-10). On the cross, Jesus' self-sacrificing love embraced the whole human race. In his death and resurrection, he overcame the power of evil to compel us, and he set us free to live the life he taught (1 Cor 15:20-22; 2 Cor 5:14-15). Paul describes Jesus' self-giving as if it were intended personally for each of us: while we were weak, while we were sinners, while we were enemies, Christ died for us (Rom 5:6-11). After rising from the dead Jesus continued these transformative encounters, like meeting his followers at the seashore (Jn 21:4-19).

After Jesus' ascension, the Holy Spirit becomes the presence of God that indwells the world. That Spirit is the bridge between us and Christ. Through the Holy Spirit, Christ is present in his body the church and in each believer. In prayer we meet him in a mystical way in contemplation and imitation (Phil 3:7-11). In Matthew Jesus makes a striking statement about where else he is to be found: in the stranger, the naked, and the imprisoned (Mt 25:31-40). And finally Christ meets us in a surpassing way in the Breaking of Bread (1 Cor 10:16-17).

The New Testament preserves a record of one crucial aspect in the development of the church's mission and its expression in baptism. The early church was soon confronted with an inescapable question: Who is baptism for? Is it only for the Jews to whom God's covenant had been given? Or can outsiders be invited into the covenant? In stylized form, Acts 8–17 narrates a Spirit-guided movement in which the apostles are led into encounters with Samaritans (Acts 8:25), an Ethiopian Godfearer (Acts 8:26-39), leading women among the Greeks (Acts 17:1-7), as well as Cornelius, a Gentile seeker, and his household (Acts 10:1–48). As Peter is reciting the acts of God in Jesus to Cornelius's household, the Spirit falls on all who hear the word. The Jewish Christians in the room are dumbfounded that pagans have received the same gift they had been given. Finally, a disoriented Peter composes himself and says, "Can anyone withhold the water for baptizing these people who have received the Holy Spirit just as we have?" (Acts 10:47). Later on, Paul gives vivid theological backing to the claim that through Christ the Gentiles have been called into the covenant God has made with Israel (Eph 2:11–3:10).

The accounts of conversion and baptism in the book of Acts do not always follow the same sequence. For example, the people at Cornelius's house begin speaking in tongues before they are baptized (Acts 10:44-48; cf. Acts 2:37-42). If we remember that the Holy Spirit is sovereign over all aspects of coming to faith, such differences are understandable. Like the incarnation, sacraments are acts of God's condescension, his coming to us on our terms. The church has given a theological sequence for baptism (grace, faith, repentance, confession of Christ, baptism, gift of the Spirit) but defers to the Spirit working through a different order.

The matter of the Spirit's freedom leads to the larger question of whether baptism is necessary for salvation. This has two aspects, one in relation to Christians and the other in relation to non-Christians. The former was first addressed in the early church when baptismal candidates, people desiring baptism, were martyred before that could take place. It was concluded that they were indeed baptized by the "baptism of desire."[8]

This question takes on another form in relation to people who have accepted Christ but see no need for baptism. This is sometimes the case when a believer grew up in a setting where church life as a whole, and baptism in particular, were not life-giving. Of course God welcomes everyone who seeks him; for some people, sorting out what is good and bad in their religious past takes a long time. A problem arises when we make an understandable personal struggle into a norm and conclude that baptism is optional. When we do that, in our often rationalistic mindset, we are dissecting what the New Testament holds together. To marginalize baptism is to be left without the seal of salvation, the recapitulation of the Spirit's work in us and our insertion into the body of Christ.

The most difficult form of this question concerns the salvation of people who believe differently from Christians or don't believe at all. Many of them live lives of self-sacrificing love. I would say that how they live is evidence of the hidden work of Christ in them, of the Spirit's enabling. They would not put it this way, but I would say that people who love their neighbors as

---

[8]Balthasar Hubmaier, "A Brief Apologia" in *Balthasar Hubmaier: Theologian of Anabaptism*, trans. and ed. H. Wayne Pipkin and John H. Yoder (Scottdale, PA: Herald Press, 1989), 301.

themselves have received a kind of baptism of desire. Having said that, I would add that God's ultimate intention for them is to come to know the Source of their love and be assured of this love in baptism.[9]

POST-NEW TESTAMENT DEVELOPMENTS: THE EARLY PATRISTIC AGE

As the church grew, baptismal images and practices inherited from Judaism were joined to images and practices that arose when the church entered the Gentile world. There seem to not have been many conflicts concerning the form of baptism. Immersion was the preferred one, probably influenced both by Jewish practice and Pauline theology. But there are early records of pouring and sprinkling where that was more practical.[10] The association of the Spirit with Jesus' baptism could be dramatized in the act of sprinkling or pouring. From third-century written records, we know that the formula stated in Jesus' commissioning of his followers (Mt 28:19, baptizing in the name of the Father, the Son, and the Holy Spirit) displaces baptism simply in the name of Jesus, as found in the book of Acts. Both of these practices are already present in the Didache, the earliest post–New Testament manual for ceremonies, probably composed in the first century:

> Regarding baptism. Baptize as follows: after first explaining all these points [above], "Baptize in the name of the Father, the Son, and the Holy Spirit, [Matt 28:19] in running water. But if you have no running water, baptize in other water; and if you can not in cold then in warm. But if you have neither, pour water on the head three times, "in the name of the Father and Son and Holy Spirit." Before baptism, let the baptizer and the candidate for baptism fast.[11]

Baptism by immersion (often threefold) remained the norm.[12] By the beginning of the sixth century Gregory of Tours records that King Clovis and

---

[9]The principles of a recent Vatican document can be applied beyond infant baptism: International Theological Commission, "The Hope of Salvation for Infants Who Die Without Being Baptized," January 19, 2007, Vatican document, www.vatican.va/roman_curia/congregations/cfaith/cti_documents/rc_con_cfaith_doc_20070419_un-baptised-infants_en.html.

[10]Paul F. Bradshaw, *The Search for the Origins of Christian Worship: Sources and Methods for the Study of Early Liturgy*, 1st ed. (New York: Oxford University Press, 1992); and Hans Boersma and Matthew Levering, eds., *The Oxford Handbook of Sacramental Theology* (Oxford: Oxford University Press, 2015), esp. chaps. 6–10, 20.

[11]"The Didache," in Finn, *Early Christian Baptism . . . in West and East Syria*, 36.

[12]Theodore of Mopsuestia, "Baptismal Homily 3," in Finn, 91-93.

his legions were baptized by immersion or pouring.[13] Both practices were carried over into the Reformation.[14]

Liturgical forms were carried from the ancient churches in Jerusalem, Rome, Alexandria, and Antioch into missionary settings in and beyond the Roman Empire, where they were adapted to the local society. There they were shaped by the prevailing cultural forms. But some ancient worship forms remained closer to Jewish practice, like those of the East and West Syrian Churches, outside the Roman Empire. Their worship forms bear a family resemblance to the rites of the four ancient bishoprics of Jerusalem, Rome, Alexandria, and Antioch but have unique traits. The most enduring of these are Chaldean (Iraq, Iran), Syrian (a much larger territory than today), Armenian, and Coptic (Egypt, Ethiopia).

The baptismal fragment in the presbyter Justin's *First Apology* articulates a foundational development. He describes the baptismal dynamic:

> Those who are convinced and believe what we say and teach is the truth and pledge themselves to be able to live accordingly, are taught in prayer and fasting to ask God to forgive their past sins, while we pray and fast with them. Then we lead them to a place where there is water, and they are regenerated in the same manner in which we ourselves were regenerated.[15]

Here we encounter, less than a century after Paul's letters to the Romans and the Colossians, elements of coming to faith that resemble those of Paul: believing the proclamation of the gospel, pledging to live accordingly, asking for forgiveness of sins. Then something that is not explicit in Paul is described. When the candidates have believed and committed and prayed and fasted, they are "regenerated" in baptism.

This description is baffling for people from lean sacramental traditions. If candidates have pledged themselves to live the gospel and asked God for forgiveness, aren't they already regenerated, or made holy, by God? What

---

[13]Michael Driscoll, "The Conversion of the Nations," in Geoffrey Wainwright and Karen Westerfield Tucker, eds., *The Oxford Dictionary of Christian Worship* (Oxford: Oxford University Press, 2006), 180-81.

[14]Nathan Mitchell, "Reforms, Protestant and Catholic," in Wainwright and Westerfield Tucker, 326-327; Klassen and Klaassen, *The Writings of Pilgram Marpeck*, "The Admonition of 1542," 185, 188, 193.

[15]As quoted in Maxwell E. Johnson, *The Rites of Christian Initiation: Their Evolution and Interpretation* (Collegeville, MN: Liturgical Press, 2007), 50.

more needs to happen? The common attempt to explain this ancient mindset is to refer to apostolic practice. There the Spirit leads seekers to Christ: they ask for forgiveness and pledge themselves to Christ's way. The church then offers them water baptism as an enactment of God's grace and their faith.[16]

Is this what is implied in Paul's images of baptism? His favorite one concerns dying and coming to life (Rom 6:1-11; Col 2:11-13; see also Acts 19:1-7). Is baptism merely a vivid simile for conversion, a tangible metaphor for an elusive mystical experience, an outward image for an inward reality? Or is it something more than that? Might it also be a condensing of what has happened inwardly over time into a pregnant outward moment? The goal of the remainder of this chapter is to pursue these questions.

On the basis of Justin Martyr's mid-second-century account of baptism, Killian McDonnell, a Catholic theologian, places together the "relationship between Christ receiving the Holy Spirit at baptism and Christians receiving the Spirit at theirs."[17] In Justin's understanding, the initiator of both the inward and outward stages of conversion is the Spirit. It is not the water that regenerates; rather, in the water the Spirit is locally present. It is in the water that the Spirit regenerates, bringing about the dying and rising of the believer in Christ.

Justin's claim that the medium of the Spirit is in the water is a tingling novelty to the sacramentally lean Protestant ear. The Synoptic Gospels, Peter, and Paul do not stipulate how we die with Christ and receive the Spirit in baptism. It could be argued from a lean Protestant perspective that ever-expanding patristic ritual errs in locating God's saving work in the water of baptism and in the oil of anointing, parallel to locating the body and blood of Christ in the bread and wine. Both points of view need to bear in mind that in the early patristic era there is not yet a fixed correlation between the sacrament, its ceremony, and its spiritual reality.[18] Here we are not talking about the extreme sacramental and antisacramental positions of later centuries.

---

[16]Alan Kreider lays out the formation of catechumens in the third and fourth centuries in several settings, noting their commonalities and contrasts. Alan Kreider, *The Patient Ferment of the Early Church: The Improbable Rise of Christianity in the Roman Empire* (Grand Rapids: Baker Academic, 2016), 133-75.

[17]As quoted in M. Johnson, *Rites*, 52.

[18]The editor of the fourth-century *Apostolic Constitutions* makes it clear that if the oil and chrism are not available, the water is enough, Finn, *Early Christian Baptism . . . West and East Syria,* 57.

McDonnell emphasizes that Justin intends and assumes that his description of how baptism happens is in keeping with Scripture. His claim about water as the Spirit's medium does not lessen the existential aspect of the act, that is, that it involves an encounter between the believer and Christ.

Neither exegesis nor liturgy had yet been put into a completely fixed form.[19] Both the theologies and the liturgies of baptism allowed for improvisation from the middle of the second to the end of the fourth centuries. This fluidity of form and freedom in worship has led many scholars and believers to consider the early centuries to be the golden age of the Spirit. Of special importance to our concerns are Brian Spinks's quotations and commentary from texts before and after the fourth century to show the contrasts between earlier and later formulations.[20]

The realm of baptismal belief and practice expands organically. Even from the time before Rome's toleration of Christianity, there are artistic depictions of Christian themes, including baptism, in the Roman catacombs. For instance, in the Callistus Catacomb the candidate is baptized in the nude.[21] This became common practice as an enactment of "strip[ping] off" the old life and being "clothed" with the new one (Col 3:5-11). Soon this symbolic act was expanded to include an even more astonishing claim, the laying aside of our mortality and the return to Eve and Adam's innocence. When Christianity became a public religion with public buildings, beginning in Constantine's reign, baptisteries with a pool and a high tower immediately adjacent to the church became common. The original reason for this innovation was to safeguard the modesty of candidates entering the water naked. These artistic and architectural expansions of baptismal symbolism are theology in visible form.

Baptismal liturgies become more elaborate as the church becomes inculturated in its host societies in the fourth and fifth centuries. In the Armenian

---

[19]It should be remembered that, before the age of printing, the scribe copying the manuscript made intended and unintended changes, and the presider at a service expanded and conflated prayer and ceremony according to the needs of the situation.

[20]Bryan Spinks introduces the development of regional liturgical traditions; he helpfully draws attention to their language and gestures: Bryan D. Spinks, *Early and Medieval Rituals and Theologies of Baptism: From the New Testament to the Council of Trent* (Burlington, VT: Ashgate, 2009). Relevant to our quest is his attention to the relationship between faith and baptism (pp. 48, 141), the symbolism of language and gesture (pp. 74, 87), the movement from adult to infant baptism (pp. 110-14, 126, 152), and early definitions of *sacrament* (pp. 135, 143).

[21]Everett Ferguson, *Early Christians Speak* (Austin, TX: Sweet, 1971), plate 2.

rite, about seventh century, the weight seems—on the one hand—to fall more and more on the outward enactment of conversion in the several anointings that take place before baptism. At the same time, the candidate has been prepared beforehand. The image of "a second birth" of the Spirit is prominent.[22] Baptismal theology is largely an exegesis of baptismal liturgy; as time passes, biblical references are sometimes interpreted more in light of the liturgy than the other way around.

THE LATER PATRISTIC AGE

Something happens to sacramental life in the course of the patristic era, in which the relationship between Spirit and form changes. A great deal of care is called for in analyzing this stage of the evolution of baptism so as not to import assumptions alien to the original setting. The shift involves both the density of the ritual action and the actors in it. The baptismal service becomes more and more elaborate. For instance, already in the third-century Syrian worship manual, the *Didascalia*, the power of the baptizer reshapes the nature of the event. It is the bishop—implicitly "in the person of Christ"—who looses the candidates from their sins and fills them with the Spirit.[23] For instance, anointing with oil, an early aspect of baptismal rites, has assumed a disproportionate role. Minute attention is given to the precise procedure and its allegorical meaning, as if the power lies in the esoteric priestly gestures themselves. It is hard to resist the conclusion that the Spirit is being confined by the intricacies of human ceremony.

On the affirmative side, there is still a rigorous time of catechesis before baptism in some regions. In the church of Jerusalem its length was three years. This practice continued for more than a century after Constantine became emperor so one cannot simply equate the shifts in baptismal theology and practice with the beginning of his reign. In many places the preparation for baptism was aligned with the development of the church year. This happened in different ways, but overall, preparation for baptism becomes a catalyst in the emergence of Lent as a penitential season. For example, forty days are given over to the preparation period for candidates. Soon it is common for

---

[22]E. C. Whitaker, *Documents of the Baptismal Liturgy* (London: SPCK, 1970), 60, 62, 65.
[23]Spinks, *Early and Medieval Rituals*, 19.

baptism to occur on Easter eve or morning, to place it within the framework of the Lord's death and resurrection.[24]

What is it that has changed in the practice and understanding of baptism? The shift lies in the role given to the components of the ritual. For instance, the exorcisms and anointings begin a week before the baptism and continue as a part of the baptism itself. It is as if the increasing density of the outward ritual slowly crowds out attention to the inward change in the candidate (or compensates for the lack thereof?). Added to that, the questions to the candidate focus more and more on faith as assent, for example, to the Apostles' Creed, with less and less explicit reference to faith as trust.[25]

Two factors need to be kept in view in trying to make sense of ancient Christian practices. One, fairness in assessing these ritual shifts requires that modern, Western people not impose an antisacramental mindset (either secular or Christian) uncritically on another worldview. The assumption that material gestures and objects cannot express spiritual realities had its origin among more radical Reformers in sixteenth-century Europe and its flourishing after the eighteenth century by means of modern worldviews, like the Enlightenment and common-sense realism. To make a practical comparison, it is often remarked that in some Global South cultures ritual events in evangelical churches look and feel more like fourth-century Mediterranean worship than like similar events in northern European and North American Protestantism.[26]

The second factor is conditional on the first. The nonsacramental conclusion of some liberals and evangelicals is that in studying these texts one has the growing sense that sacraments and the gestures accompanying them take on an objective power to change persons. This power, inherent to a sacrament, then becomes the primary dynamic rather than a secondary one, that is, in

---

[24]Not surprisingly, there is great variation in the development of the liturgical year and the events associated with it. Some of the variation is standardized in the early Middle Ages and again in the liturgical movement of the past century.

[25]Egeria, *Egeria: Diary of a Pilgrimage*, trans. George G. Gingras, Ancient Christian Writers 38 (New York: Newman, 1970), 122-25.

[26]For example, the dissertation of the Mennonite theologian Aristarchus Sukarto, "Witnessing to Christ Through Eucharist: A Proposal for the Java Christian Churches to Contextualize and to Communicate the Gospel to Its Community," ThD diss., Lutheran School of Theology at Chicago, 1994, www.dropbox.com/s/3bu89kkecxqjjfq/Diss_Sukarto_Witnessing%20to%20Christ%20to%20 Eucharist.pdf?dl=0.

which it actualizes the inward working of the Spirit. To what extent is this interpretation based on a careful and correct exegesis of the biblical texts and their settings we have looked at, and to what extent is it an alien exegesis, imposing an eighteenth-century mindset.

This question is made more complicated by the increasing practice of infant baptism, which was known to have been practiced as early as the second century but became the dominant form of baptism in the course of the fifth century. It needs to be remembered that bishops in the third and fourth centuries, who assume that baptism on confession of faith is the norm, nevertheless make provision for the baptism of infants alongside adults. At the same time, the lengthy pre- and postbaptismal catechesis by Cyril of Jerusalem in the late fourth century shows how long baptism on confession of faith remained the dominant practice of the church.

It is clear that, for example, Gregory Nazianzus, Cyril of Jerusalem, and John Chrysostom taught and expected an interior transformation of the candidate in conversion and baptism. They expected the new Christian to share experientially in union with Christ and the gifts of the Spirit.[27] At the same time, there are hints in the writings of these very figures that there is a waning of this existential piety in the church of their day. It is instructive that the upsurge of monasticism at this time was, more than anything else, a protest against the waning of conversion and transformation in relation to baptism. Theodore of Mopsuestia and Cyril of Jerusalem both argue against the assumption of some of their flock that these rights are not "magical."[28]

Side by side with these theological and liturgical apologies for believer's baptism stands the already existing practice of infant baptism. It begins before the Constantinian era and has its own logic. Patristic theologians speak as if the act of professing faith is essential for those who are of age but imply that such a profession is not the heart of baptism. Before it is a human act, baptism is a divine one. This understanding explains why children of believers were baptized alongside believers without apparent dissonance. A

---

[27]M. Johnson, *Rites*, 121-24; and Kilian McDonnell and George Montague, *Christian Initiation and Baptism in the Holy Spirit: Evidence from the First Eight Centuries*, 2nd rev. ed. (Collegeville, MN: Liturgical Press, 1994), 226-88.

[28]Hugh M. Riley, *Christian Initiation* (Washington, DC: Catholic University of America Press, 1974), 185-97.

striking example is Hippolytus's *Apostolic Tradition* from as early as the third century.[29] Mature believers are examined with regard to their faith and manner of living and then exorcised before the day of baptism. On the day of baptism they assemble. The rubric says, "And they shall baptize the little children first. And if they can answer for themselves, let them answer. But if they cannot, let their parents answer or someone from their family."[30] The heart of the matter, so this reasoning goes, is God's sacramental offer of belonging to Christians and to their children. It is God's initiative in baptism that saves and not our response.

Infant baptism is an apt illustration of the gradual nature of the change in ecclesiology. It seems to have been practiced as a minority form of baptism since the second century. Initially, it seems to have been given to children along with their parents when pagan parents came to faith in Christ. This is a complex and disputed question. Something of a convergence in ecumenical scholarship is in evidence today. The gist of it is as follows. Infant baptism has an early but uncertain origin. There is liturgical evidence that it was practiced alongside believer's baptism in the third century. As we have just seen in *The Apostolic Tradition*, there are rigorous stages of preparation for adult candidates. Yet parents of Christian children are baptized without any sense of contradiction. At the same time, believer's baptism continues as a widespread practice among Christian families (that is, not only for pagan converts) through the sixth century. Current research suggests that for over four hundred years infant-versus-confessional baptism was not a church-dividing issue.

However, this understanding of baptism—that it is offered to believers and their children—gradually becomes anachronistic in medieval societies East and West. First of all, masses of people in the Roman Empire are increasingly joining the church with a wide range of motives. Second, in some settings whole populations are baptized under compulsion. It can no longer be assumed that they are Christian in the sense of putting their trust in Christ or that they will raise their children in a Christian way.

---

[29] At one time liturgical scholars claimed Hippolytus as author and an origin of about 215. This date was used to imply, among other things, the early routine practice of infant baptism. Current scholarship places it within Roman liturgical developments between the fourth and fifth centuries. See Bradshaw, *The Search for the Origins*, 89-93.
[30] Whitaker, *Documents*, 4-5.

In light of this development, is there validity to the charge that prebaptismal exorcisms and anointings as well as an elaborate water rite are slowly displacing the inward change expected in the candidate, especially when they are applied to infants? Has the subjective response been overwhelmed by the objective initiative? It is hard not to see in this development of sacramental theology a semiconscious pastoral rationale for the mass baptism of adults and infants who do not bring personal faith to their baptism.

The English Baptist patristics scholar A. W. Argyle begins his documentation of this trend with strident language. He calls it "materialistic decadence" (quoting G. Lampe, an Anglican) and "a failing to grasp the Biblical doctrine of grace" (quoting T. Torrance, a Presbyterian).[31] What does Argyle mean when he uses these terms? Concerning both grace and materialism, he argues that grace had become "a quasi-material force" that saves by means of the water.[32] He goes on to note that in the conquests of Christian rulers, baptism had become the required sign of those who submitted to defeat. In this case, baptism meant submission first to political, not spiritual, authority.[33]

The Hungarian-French Catholic sacramental theologian Alexandre Ganoczy addresses patristic baptismal theology from a different perspective. It raises other problems. He cautions against the dualism of certain fathers, like Ignatius, for whom baptism is enlistment in the fight against the world. He worries about Clement's insistence, based on Hebrews 6:4, that postbaptismal sin is unforgivable. He cautions against Justin Martyr's preoccupation with baptism as illumination that immediately sanctifies the convert. He praises Irenaeus's incarnationist baptism (being brought into the process of creation's restoration) but cautions that Irenaeus doesn't take sin seriously. Finally, he faults Tertullian's defense of believer's baptism as graceless.[34]

---

[31] Alec Gilmore, ed., *Christian Baptism: A Fresh Attempt to Understand the Rite in Terms of Scripture, History, and Theology* (London: Lutterworth, 1959), 188. See also pp. 187-222. My impression is that while Argyle correctly identifies a trend, he overstates his case by not doing justice to the oneness between the inward and outward dimensions of conversion in the fourth century.

[32] Gilmore, *Christian Baptism*, 188.

[33] Gilmore, *Christian Baptism*, 191. Argyle also notes that there were contrary impulses, like Canon 2 of the Council of Nicaea (325), that counsel against premature baptism, but that they were heeded only by a minority of church leaders.

[34] Alexandre Ganoczy, *Becoming Christian: A Theology of Baptism as the Sacrament of Human History* (New York: Paulist Press, 1976), 50-60.

These profiles are the backdrop for the definitive patristic theology of baptism in the West, that of Augustine of Hippo. To counter what he considered false views of the church and human nature, Augustine took existing catholic tradition and expanded it into a comprehensive defense of infant baptism. Augustine's first accusation arose from the controversy between Donatists and Catholics. The former were concerned for the purity of the church. As a consequence, they practiced rebaptism of people who had defected from their faith during persecution.

Augustine argued that everyone who has been baptized with water in the name of the Trinity is marked by that act for life: they cannot lose the grace they received. Similarly, and related, the baptisms conferred by a presbyter who is morally unworthy still confer the grace that the sacrament unfailingly conveys. Augustine concluded that baptism cannot be called into question by either the person baptized or the one baptizing. In order to do so, he developed the claim that a sacrament is always "valid" if it is properly performed, that is, with water in the name of the Trinity. Baptism makes an indelible mark on the person's soul so that he or she belongs to Christ. However, the sacrament is not "fruitful" for discipleship unless it is received in faith.[35]

This difference between *validity* and *fruitfulness* is hard to grasp for people outside baptismal traditions that stem from Augustine.[36] They fear that in church history, the term *valid* has been interpreted by clergy and laity alike to mean that if you are properly (validly) baptized, you are "safe" regardless of the life you choose to lead.

Augustine's second defining controversy concerning baptism arose from his debate with Pelagius, the British missionary who had come to Africa. We gather from fragments of his writings (largely destroyed by his detractors) that Pelagius believed humanity had never lost its identity as being in the image of God and that its sin consisted not of an underlying condition but of deliberate human acts of evil. Pelagius was not opposed to infant baptism, but he saw it as the gift of illumination; it was not necessary for salvation from sin.

Augustine's retort arose out of his sense of the tragedy of human nature. Because of Adam's sin, all are sinners and guilty, even for the sin we inherit. To

---

[35] Augustine, "On Baptism: Against the Donatists," in *An Augustine Reader*, ed. John J. O'Meara (Garden City, NY: Doubleday Image, 1973), 206-11.

[36] As we shall see in chap. 6, Augustine's theology of the Eucharist is cut from different sacramental cloth.

clinch his argument, Augustine presented an exegesis of Romans 5. Bible scholars today translate the pivotal verse, Romans 5:12, as "because all have sinned." Augustine relied on the Latin mistranslation "in whom [Adam] all have sinned."[37] Because all have sinned, only baptism could save newborns from condemnation, even though they could not receive it in any measurable way by a personal act of faith. Augustine's teaching gave the practice of infant baptism a theological coherence it had lacked until then. Quite practically, he argued that all children born within the Christian social order had to be baptized, even if it required coercion. This stance undermined Augustine's earlier stance that baptism was complete only with the baptized person's inner conversion. Baptism and conversion remain separate realities in many of his writings.

For outsiders to this way of thinking, it seems that the infant baptism of whole populations, as understood by Augustine and church teaching built on his views, underscores the "sacramental minimalism"[38] of his views. Although he speaks of "conversion of heart," when all is said and done, salvation from hell is achieved in baptism alone.[39] With Augustine's teaching, the logic of infant baptism, whether of a child of believing parents or not, gradually displaces the logic of baptism on confession of faith as the norm of the Western church.

MIDDLE AGES

Much of the development of baptismal thought and practice after the liturgical and cultic foundations sketched out above was organic in nature. There are, however, two developments that can be tracked. They both have long-term consequences. One concerns the shifts in the practice of confirmation. In the early patristic era, *confirmation* meant the bishop's prayer and anointing of the adult believer with the Holy Spirit. It took place as an inseparable aspect of baptism immediately before or after the water rite. Communion completed the service. This sequence (a prayer for the Spirit following baptism) and the timing are immediately recognizable to Free Church people and are widely followed today. The comparison becomes more complicated when these two practices, confirmation and immediate Communion, were

---

[37] Augustine, "The Grace of Christ and Original Sin," in O'Meara, *Augustine Reader*, 476.
[38] M. Johnson, *Rites*, 189, 200.
[39] O'Meara, *Augustine Reader*, 461-64.

continued when infant baptism became common. In some settings only a bishop could confirm. The service of confirmation was then adjusted to the bishop's schedule. Because dioceses were large and bishops traversed on foot or horseback, confirmation was sometimes administered years after the infant's baptism so that confirmation came to be seen as a separate sacrament. Ironically, this practical problem was turned into a pastoral opportunity to reassert the link between faith and sacrament. Gradually, preparation for confirmation became a time of intensified instruction for youth to prepare them for full participation in the church, most important of which was their first participation in the Eucharist.[40]

In my judgment, one cannot say that infant baptism and an established church are of a piece historically. The theology and practice of infant baptism had a logic of its own before Christianity became a state religion. At the same time, an instinct toward believer's baptism continued to shape the practice of initiation. The evidence from baptismal catechesis and church architecture makes it clear that baptism on confession of faith continued to be practiced through the sixth century in already missionized parts of Europe. For example, the baptistery of the Church of Saint John in Aix-en-Provence, France, was built in the sixth century. Four feet deep and broad enough for immersion, it was clearly designed for adults. A very similar architecture exists in the contemporaneous Justinian church on the Greek island of Paros.[41] But this lingering intuition is soon overtaken by the completion of the fusion of church and state in both East and West. By the end of Charlemagne's reign in the West (d. 814), for example, the church as an institution was coterminous with the empire; its sole rite of initiation was obligatory baptism of all citizens of the realm in infancy.

Partly related to the movement from credobaptism (believer's baptism) to pedobaptism (infant baptism) was the slow movement in the West from immersion as the normal (but not exclusive) form of baptism to sprinkling and pouring. By the seventh century there are small stone fonts only large

---

[40]The separation of initiation rites never occurred in the Eastern Orthodox and Oriental churches. This situation, however, creates different problems for dissenting churches that arose in the West. In the East, none of these rites—baptism, confirmation, or Eucharist—requires an existential act of faith *when administered to infants* for it to be received fruitfully.

[41]From a personal visit to both of those sites.

enough to immerse a baby. Immersion remained the only form of baptism in the East, but in the West it fell increasingly out of use between the twelfth and fourteenth centuries.

As has been mentioned, the fullness of the ancient catechumenate for adult baptismal candidates (catechesis, exorcisms, answers to questions) was no longer possible when the rite was applied to infants. What remained were anointings, the giving of salt, and the sign of the cross; these could be given equally to adults and infants. Gradually, the ceremonies once leading up to baptism over several weeks or months were telescoped into a single action applied to the infant candidate. The priest would meet the family at the church door to offer a highly condensed form of initiation in which the candidate's godparents answered the questions directed at the baptismal candidate, who by then was always an infant. Then the priest with the family went to the front of the church for the baptism.[42] This disjointed form was the last visible reminder of the fact that all these practices had once belonged to the baptism of believers.

When the Protestant Reformers began their drastic revision of worship practices, they removed the dense cluster of gestures carried over from adult baptism and applied to infants, on the grounds that they were made up of confusing practices that obscured the central act of baptism. Unknowingly, they were removing the last liturgical evidence of the adult catechumenate.

Finally, there is a largely unexplored matter concerning the shift in Western initiation practices. Did the sacramental changes, that is, the separation of baptism, confirmation, and Communion, come about only through practical concerns, such as the long waiting periods for the arrival of a bishop to confirm a child? Or were there implicit shifts in philosophy and theology in which confirmation became a rite that retrieved the role of the candidate's faith in the total process of initiation? Thomas Aquinas was typical of theologians from the High Middle Ages and late medieval era who made the case for confirmation as a time for the child to profess the church's faith and to receive the fullness of the Holy Spirit. It is the ultimate consummation of baptism, the fullness of the Spirit, the capacity to confess Christ publicly.[43]

---

[42]M. Johnson, *Rites*, 260.

[43]Robert Miner, "Aquinas and the Sacrament of Confirmation," in Matthew Levering, Michael Dauphinais, eds., *Rediscovering Aquinas and the Sacraments* (Chicago: Hillenbrand, 2009), 31-32, 34.

THE REFORMATION

Through the work of universal councils of the church and of individual clergy and laity, the spiritual, moral, and liturgical reform of the church was addressed again and again in the course of the centuries.[44] By the beginning of the sixteenth century many clergy and laity alike concluded that the church, its leaders, and its institutions were incapable of radical reform. Those who were most impatient broke with the papacy. The psychological freedom this rupture made possible opened the door to a new movement of the Holy Spirit, allowed for an unfettered criticism of the medieval church, and spawned an urgency to return to the sources, the apostolic and patristic eras, as the basis for their teaching authority. For simplicity's sake, the comparisons I shall make among the Magisterial Reformers (those who founded territorial churches, that is, allied with a regional state and its magistrates) will focus on first-generation leaders and regions of original influence in German-speaking territories, the Low Countries, and England. In chronological order they are Martin Luther (North Germany), Ulrich Zwingli (German-speaking Switzerland), Martin Bucer (South Germany and England), John Calvin (Geneva, northern France, and Low Countries), and Thomas Cranmer (England).

One of the many consequences of this revolution was the Protestant rejection of the Roman Catholic Church's seven sacraments. Reformers like Martin Luther and Pilgram Marpeck agreed with this judgment. It is an overlooked fact that part of their interest was to expand—not narrow—what was meant by the category of sacrament. For example, both Marpeck and Luther spoke of "love of neighbor" as a sacrament in the sense of being an act that incarnates grace. Marpeck also included rituals like footwashing in his list of ceremonies. But all the Protestant Reformers, except the spiritualists, made baptism and the Lord's Supper the defining sacraments or ordinances because they had been ordained by Christ.

All the Reformers of territorial churches (Luther, Zwingli, Bucer, Calvin, Cranmer, and their colleagues) kept the practice of infant baptism. All of them revised and simplified the baptismal liturgies they had inherited. Bucer and Cranmer kept and even expanded confirmation with a lengthy catechesis beforehand; the others favored a disciplined time of catechesis in its own

---

[44]The flowering of mysticism among laity as well as clergy is a striking example. See Bernard McGinn, *The Harvest of Mysticism in Medieval Germany* (New York: Herder & Herder, 2012).

right. All of them, de facto, made confirmation the basis for admission to the
Lord's Table.[45] They provided differing theologies of infant baptism because,
among other reasons, they had adopted different understandings of sacraments. Only Zwingli and Bucer briefly grappled with the possibility of baptism
on confession of faith as the norm. Their theologies of baptism were largely
coherent. A part of this coherence was their commitment to a rite of initiation
that provided entry in a Christian social order of which church and state
together were stewards.[46]

There was also a reformation within the Catholic Church through the work
of the intermittently meeting Council of Trent from 1545 to 1563. Rites were
simplified, superstitions suppressed. Theologically, the teachings regarding
sacraments and baptism in particular were reaffirmed and Protestant "devi-
ations" condemned.[47] On the matter of baptism, the Council agrees, in the
most basic sense, with the Magisterial Reformers in the necessity of infant
baptism for salvation from original sin.[48]

There is one exception to the focus on infant baptism in these churches.
Even before the Council of Trent, reform-minded Catholic scholars had
prepared the outline for an adult catechumenate and baptism. The reason
for this revival of a lost initiation rite was the victory of Christians over
Muslims in Spain. This state of affairs called for evangelization, as did the
conquest of lands beyond Europe by Spaniards and Portuguese.[49] By contrast,
the Dutch and the English, who entered the race for empire almost as soon
as the Iberians, give no evidence for the instruction and baptism of adults
in Protestant-controlled missionary settings during the sixteenth century.
In this matter the Catholics had overlapping concerns with the Anabaptists,
except for two essential differences. One was the Catholic association of

---

[45]The role of confirmation as a rite with analogous aspects to believer's baptism, especially that of a
personal profession of faith, was of great importance to the *Trilateral Dialogue on Baptism* (2012-
2017) of the Catholic, Lutheran, and Mennonite churches for this reason.

[46]To understand reformational theologies of infant baptism in the words of their proponents, readers should examine the proponents' texts or at least summaries of their positions in compendia
like Maxwell Johnson, *Rites*, 309-61. See Dagmar Heller, *Baptized into Christ: A Guide to the
Ecumenical Discussion on Baptism* (Geneva: World Council of Churches, 2012) for a judicious
assessment of different teachings on baptism.

[47]Peter Walter, "Sacraments in the Council of Trent and Sixteenth-Century Catholic Theology," in
Boersma and Levering, 314, 321, 325.

[48]Boersma and Levering, 314-15.

[49]Spinks, *Early and Medieval Rituals*, 152.

mission with colonialism. The other was that Anabaptists considered Europe as much a missionary setting as lands far away.

ANABAPTISM

Divine initiative and human response. The most revolutionary criticism the Anabaptists made of late medieval Christianity was its understanding of the church. At the heart of this critique was the role of sacraments in a church that included all members of society. For the radicals, the church was a called-out people rather than the whole of society. It was to be a charismatic community, a priesthood of all believers (a notion also affirmed by Martin Luther) who exercised gifts of the Spirit rather than acting according to a hierarchical order. Its expectation of members was similar to that of a monastic order; the community was to consist only of people whom the Spirit had drawn to Christ. Conversion led to a death to self and to discipleship modeled on the Sermon on the Mount. This stance is evident in the earliest Anabaptist confession of faith, the Schleitheim Articles:

> Baptism should be given to all who have learned repentance, amendment of life, and faith through the truth that their sin has been removed by Christ; to all who want to walk in the resurrection of Jesus Christ and be buried with him in death so that they can be resurrected with him; and to all who desire baptism in this sense from us and who themselves request it.[50]

Anabaptist baptism was an enactment of this understanding of the Christian life. Underlying this cluster of assertions concerning the church was the rejection of its sacerdotal structure, which stipulated that the sacrifice of the Mass for the remission of sin could only be offered by the hierarchical priesthood (pope, bishops, and pastors) standing in the "person of Christ."[51] It was only through participation in their mediations of grace that one could be saved. The experience of Anabaptists in the Catholic Church, the church of

---

[50]Michael Sattler, "The Schleitheim Articles [1527]," in *The Radical Reformation*, ed. Michael G. Baylor (Cambridge: Cambridge University Press, 1991), 174.

[51]Vatican II describes this role differently: *sacerdotalism* is the teaching that "through the ministry of priests, the spiritual sacrifice of the faithful is made perfect in union with the sacrifice of Christ, the sole Mediator. Through the hands of the priests and in the name of the whole Church, the Lord's sacrifice is offered in the Eucharist in an unbloody and sacramental manner until He Himself returns." Walter Abbott, ed., *Documents of Vatican II* (New York: American Press, 1966), 535.

their upbringing, was that people believed they were saved simply because their baptism had taken place. The initial protest of the radicals against the baptism in infancy of whole populations was not theological but moral. They charged that the "obedience of faith" (Rom 16:26) was not evident in the lives of many of the baptized.

Then came the Anabaptist theological arguments for baptism. Their foundation was the church as the visible, historical, "unglorified body of Christ on earth."[52] Its model of discipleship is the unglorified Christ himself during his earthly ministry. The Anabaptist dissent was not the rejection of the visible church as the ark of salvation but its re-creation.

The outwardness of the Christian life—bearing the cross of Christ in everyday life, visibly dissenting from social structures (governmental and religious) where faithfulness compelled it—was the heart of Anabaptist discipleship. Such a stringent lifestyle could be lived only in the company of fellow believers. According to the Great Commission of Christ (Mt 28:16-20), this community is entered through teaching, conversion, and baptism. The spiritualizing of the church by the Magisterial Reformers, following Augustine, as an invisible and inward number of devout souls among unbelievers with whom they share membership in the outward church, went against the grain of Anabaptism. In the movement at large, being church and reflecting on it were largely practical and pastoral matters, buttressed with scriptural allusions. Balthasar Hubmaier,[53] whose ministry took place in Zurich, south Germany, and Moravia, and Dirk Philips,[54] who was active in the Low Countries and northern Germany, were among the few who offered well-considered pastoral theologies of the church. This universal body becomes visible through many local embodiments into which believers are initiated.

But it was Pilgram Marpeck who made widely held but implicit assumptions explicit. Once he had arrived at a conceptual framework, he followed its logic beyond where most Anabaptist thinking had gone. For Marpeck, the church had a sacramental character. Perhaps one could say, using a twentieth-century

---

[52]Pilgram Marpeck et al., *Later Writings by Pilgram Marpeck and His Circle*, vol. 1, especially *Marpeck's Response to Caspar Schwenckfeld's Judgment*, trans. Walter Klaassen, Werner O. Packull, and John D. Rempel (Scottdale, PA: Herald Press, 1978), 75-155, esp. 84-87.

[53]Balthasar Hubmaier, "On the Christian Baptism of Believers," 95-149.

[54]Dirk Philips, "The Congregation of God," in *The Writings of Dirk Philips*, ed. Cornelius J. Dyck, William E. Keeney, and Alvin J. Beachy (Scottdale, PA: Herald Press, 1992), 350-82.

notion, that the church itself was the original sacrament. By this, Marpeck meant that the church was the extension of the body of Christ's humanity in history, the primal meeting point of inner and outer, spirit and matter.

It was Marpeck who made the most consequential application of the sacramental principle, not only theologically but also pastorally. To illustrate, for someone who has confessed faith before the congregation, "baptism is a door, and entrance into this church."[55] In his correspondence with Helene von Streicher, a spiritualist leader, Marpeck makes his case: "We must use the elemental voice, and other such material things as long as we dwell in the flesh. . . . But where the Holy Spirit moves and creates life there, too, the same physical reality becomes Spirit and life."[56] Through Gospel-mandated practices, like baptism, anointing, and love of neighbor, Christ's presence was prolonged in specific times and places.[57]

All the parties, Catholic and Protestant, agreed that the initiative for salvation is with God. We have seen that this was Augustine's passion in his understanding of salvation and baptism and became Luther's and Calvin's passion. For Luther, baptism, like salvation, was God's act alone. In its utter passivity the newborn infant is the ideal candidate for initiation into the body of Christ. This passivity in the reception of grace applies as much to adults being baptized as to infants. According to the French Lutheran theologian André Birmelé, the right liturgical ordering of baptism is for adult candidates to profess their faith only after the act of water baptism. This makes it clear that they had no role in the bringing about of their salvation.[58] In Birmilé's view, this order should also apply to the parents and sponsors in an infant baptism. Because of this stance, taken to its logical conclusion by Birmilé, the Lutheran position on baptism is the most radical in the Western church. It is an implied criticism not only of Anabaptism but of Roman Catholicism.

Luther's theology of baptism and the theologies of Anabaptist leaders were formed under different circumstances. Luther's experience as a monk was one of constant striving to earn God's favor. The Anabaptists shared Luther's

---

[55]Marpeck, "The Admonition of 1542," in Klassen and Klaassen, *Writings*, 227.
[56]Marpeck, "To Helene von Streicher," in Klassen and Klaassen, *Writings*, 379.
[57]Klaassen, Packull, and Rempel, *Later Writings 1*, "Pilgram Marpeck's Response," 76, 81-82.
[58]Conversation with André Birmelé at the Institute for Ecumenical Research, Strasbourg, September 8, 2016.

critique of works righteousness. However, their writings on baptism were composed a decade or so after Luther's break with Rome. Their protest was largely against the practice of the newly formed Protestant territorial churches of the Swiss and German states because they did not see many lives transformed by grace. This state of affairs (admitted by Luther himself) intensified the Anabaptist opposition to infant baptism: it seemed to them that it fostered passivity in the face of God's generosity.

Their concern was that the gift of grace needed to be received, that the person had to surrender to grace in order to be transformed.[59] There were different understandings among the radicals of how divine initiative and human response were expressed. For some, surrender and regeneration were given inwardly. This was the baptism of the Spirit. The outward baptism of water was offered when the candidate confessed Christ and the church confirmed the candidate's faith. Baptism reenacted all these aspects of the believer's salvation. For some of them, like Marpeck, the outward event was one with the inward event, so a term like *recapitulation* or even *actualization*, the making present of the inward event, would be a more accurate description of what happens in baptism. The implication of this latter view was that because water baptism was a recapitulation of the Spirit's inward work, water baptism itself was a Spirit baptism.

Baptism in the Spirit and in water as a divine act made clear that the gift of grace was unequivocal. But baptism as a human act was also unequivocal. It was a public "yes" to Christ that could not be undone, somewhat like the "I do" of a wedding vow. Giving every actor (Spirit, church, believer) their due is a challenge every denominational theology of baptism faces.[60]

For believer's baptism churches, baptism was a seamless initiation into Christ and the body of Christ. It located the believer's belonging to the

---

[59]Alvin J. Beachy, *The Concept of Grace in the Radical Reformation* (Nieuwkoop: De Graaf, 1976), 174-77, 214-17. Leonhard Schiemer, the German Anabaptist mystic, is clear that we are saved by grace but that it can be received only through our surrender and acceptance of the cross. See Leonhard Schiemer, "Concerning the Grace of God," in *Jörg Maler's Kunstbuch: Writings of the Pilgram Marpeck Circle*, ed. John D. Rempel (Kitchener, Ont.: Pandora Press, 2010), 215-17, 224-25. See also Menno Simons, "Christian Baptism," in *Complete Writings of Menno Simons*, ed. J. C. Wenger, trans. Leonard Verduin (Scottdale, PA: Herald Press, 1956), 229-47.

[60]Commission on Faith and Order, *Baptism, Eucharist, and Ministry* (Geneva: World Council of Churches, 1982), 10-17, is a seminal and widely affirmed attempt to rectify the imbalances in both infant and confessional baptism. See also Anthony G. Siegrist, *Participating Witness: An Anabaptist Theology of Baptism and the Sacramental Character of the Church* (Eugene, OR: Pickwick, 2013), 27-47.

body of Christ concretely in a congregation. The often taken-for-granted actor in this drama was the church as the agent of the Spirit. In its confirmation of candidates' faith with the offer of baptism and their initiation into the body of Christ, the church is not acting in its own power but as an instrument of the Spirit. In a similar way, believers are not acting in their own power but as instruments of the Spirit in witnessing to God's work of grace in their lives and pledging to live it out faithfully in the company of the congregation.[61]

Holding divine initiative and human response together was a delicate balancing act. If the imbalance in the pedobaptist position on baptism was to come down mostly on the side of divine initiative, the imbalance in the credobaptist position was to come down mostly on the side of human response. Sometimes the latter verged on making the candidate's sincerity the essence of baptism.

Finally, what about the fall and original sin in relation to baptism? Most Anabaptists rejected the Augustinian teaching of "total depravity," that is, that every aspect of our humanity and of the created order is fallen. In this view everyone born not only inherits sinfulness but bears the guilt of that depravity. As we have seen in Augustine, this anthropology provided the clinching argument for making infant baptism the normative baptism in the West.

Most Anabaptists accepted the teaching of original sin but rejected the biologic transmission of sin. Further, they believed that Christ's cosmic act of reconciliation included children. For them, neither sin nor guilt counted until the child had come of age.[62] A child came of age once he or she became capable of making simple moral judgments.

The claim that original sin (and to some minds original guilt) was not held against infants freed the Anabaptists and their descendants from the dread that unbaptized infants could not be saved. This shift in perspective prodded them to look at the New Testament baptismal references in a different light.[63]

Most Anabaptists and their descendants believed that in redemption God's image in us and in the whole creation is restored. Dirk Philips had the most

---

[61]Marpeck, in Klassen and Klaassen, *Writings*, "Pilgram Marpeck's Confession of 1532, 127, "The Admonition of 1542," 198, 214, 227.

[62]Marpeck, in Klassen and Klaassen, *Writings*, "Pilgram Marpeck's Confession of 1532," 127-33.

[63]Marpeck, in Klassen and Klaassen, *Writings*, "The Admonition of 1542," 203-22, 235-59.

suggestive thinking on restoration with his concept of "divinization," by which he means becoming participants of the divine nature.[64]

Incarnational logic. In chapter two we spoke about the Word becoming flesh as the ultimate embodiment of the relationship between Creator and creation: God has made the created world the medium of the uncreated one. The boundary between spirit and matter is permeable. As Gerard Manley Hopkins put the matter, "The world is charged with the grandeur of God."[65]

This incarnational reality has three characteristics. One, the world of matter has the latent capacity to reveal the world of spirit. Two, something of God's likeness is reflected in the universe because God created it good. Three, God's nearness is recognizable to the senses. Yet these characteristics are experienced in ambiguous and incomplete ways. This state of affairs will be overcome only when God's reign has fully come.

In the midst of this ambiguity and incompleteness there are times and places in which nature faithfully reveals God. There are two modes in which this disclosure comes to us. First of all, many people have had awe-filled experiences in nature. I once spent an extended time at Casa Cares, a hilltop Tuscan retreat house overlooking the Arno River Valley. Every morning I threw open the shutters and waited for the rising sun to pierce the mist, showing the shape of the steep hills and shining on the water until it sparkled. This extended, holy moment never failed to enchant me. On the simplest level, the scene was one of glistening beauty. But, beyond that, I was enchanted because all the parts of nature seemed to form a perfect whole. It was as if I were present at the creation! This harmonious moment was a symbol of the vast coherence of the created order. Further, it disclosed the Creator behind the creation. Terms like "sacramental universe" and "enchanted world" help to describe this reality.

Second of all, if the likeness of God is reflected in nature as a whole, could we not also say that it is reflected in particular elements of nature like the water of baptism and the bread and cup of the Lord's Supper? Free churches agree

---

[64]Philips in Dyck, Keeney, Beachy, *Writings of Dirk Philips,* "Our Confession Concerning the Creation, Redemption, and Salvation of Humanity," 69. See also "The Incarnation of Our Lord Jesus Christ," 145; "The New Birth and the New Creature," 294-296.

[65]Gerard Manley Hopkins, "God's Grandeur," in *The Poems of Gerard Manley Hopkins,* ed. W. H. Gardner and N. H. MacKenzie, 4th ed. (Oxford: Oxford University Press, 1970), 66.

with the premise that God is reflected in nature but have been hesitant to make deductions from it. Marpeck was exceptional on this point and ventured to follow this way of thinking to its conclusion. One of his favorite examples was the man whose blindness Jesus heals by putting mud on his eyes (Jn 9:6-11).[66] Marpeck's point is that Jesus' healing ministry demonstrates that what is spiritual and inward takes expression in what is material and outward. If God could save the world by taking on flesh, could he not come to us through the "flesh" of the church as the body of Christ, and as an extension of that, through the elements of everyday life, like mud, water, bread, and wine?

In order that we not answer that question too quickly, theologians point out that there is another side to creation, that is, its fallen, destructive power. In and of itself our experience of nature is ambiguous. For instance, not a hundred miles beyond the Arno Valley, an earthquake destroyed entire towns only months after I had left the retreat center.

If creation's meaning is ambiguous, can it be trusted to show us places of God's nearness? Most Christian traditions believe that Christ's taking on of flesh, his healing, his dying, and his rising began the restoration of creation. Paul addresses this already-and-not-yet nature of God's redemption. "The creation itself will be set free from its bondage to decay." Now the creation, and we ourselves, are "groaning in labor pains," awaiting redemption (Rom 8:19-23). The world of matter, and not only the world of spirit, is part of God's restoration.

Because this cosmic salvation is not yet complete, Spirit-inspired words and gestures need to accompany the church's use of physical symbols. That is why the eucharistic words of institution are essential to the Lord's Supper and why the trinitarian blessing is essential to baptism. In the power of the Spirit, material signs overcome their ambiguous nature and participate in the reality to which they point. For instance, when we baptize a believer, it is not the water itself but water in the service of the Holy Spirit that becomes a place where God's grace happens, where it becomes tangible.[67]

---

[66]Marpeck, in Klassen and Klaassen, *Writings*, "A Clear and Useful Instruction," 98-99.

[67]Heinrich Funck, the much-read eighteenth-century Mennonite minister, speaks in this vein of what happens *in* water baptism. Heinrich Funck, *A Mirror of Baptism* (Mountain Valley, VA: Joseph Funk, 1851; orig. German, 1744): the remission of sins in baptism by faith, p. 66; buried with Christ in baptism, p. 70; and baptized into the body of Christ, p. 98.

In Pilgram Marpeck's thinking, God's presence is not static and is not confined to objects. Objects, like water, are part of a dynamic. In baptism he describes the water as a "co-witness" to faith testifying to the presence of grace.[68] In this movement the Spirit embraces the believer who surrenders to the water and, in so doing, surrenders to the Spirit. The two are not identical, but in this moment they cannot be separated. We stumble over paradoxical assertions like this because the mind cannot fully grasp them. This is one of those realities we can know with our bodies but not our minds. In Marpeck's words, we use the elements of nature naturally because we still live in a natural state.[69]

Anthony Cross describes a similar current of thought, called "baptismal regeneration," present throughout Baptist history. He reviews and summarizes the literature. There is a similar emphasis on the Spirit as the animator of both inward and outward aspects of becoming a Christian and the inseparability of grace and faith. Faith and baptism are presented as one indissoluble event.[70]

This way of looking on it sheds light on the classic baptismal references: being "born of water and Spirit" (Jn 3:5) and being buried with Christ (Rom 6:4). The unselfconsciousness with which language like this is used in the New Testament suggests that divine initiative and human response, inward and outward, and their sequence are aspects of a single reality. Baptism in water and baptism in the Spirit are one.[71] How does such a baptism happen? God draws us to himself by the outward proclamation of the Word, as well as by the inward still, small voice. Those who hear it pray for faith to place their whole hope in Christ and God's reconciliation of the world through Christ. In the sway of the Spirit, the minister, on behalf of the congregation, asks the candidate to renounce the powers of this world and turn to Christ. If the answer is yes, the congregation, in the person of the minister, confirms

---

[68]Klaassen, Packull, and Rempel, *Later Writings*, 1: "Pilgram Marpeck's Response to Caspar Schwenckfeld," 75, 80f, 85f.

[69]Klaassen, Packull, and Rempel, "Pilgram Marpeck's Response," 82, 105.

[70]Anthony R. Cross, "Baptismal Regeneration: Rehabilitating a Lost Dimension of New Testament Baptism," in *Baptist Sacramentalism 2*, ed. Anthony R. Cross and Philip E. Thompson (Eugene, OR: Wipf & Stock, 2008), 150-59.

[71]*Baptist Sacramentalism 2*, Sean Winter, "Ambiguous Genitives, Pauline Baptism and Roman Insulae," 78-85, 88; Marpeck, in Klassen and Klaassen, *Writings*, "To Helene von Streicher," 383. This claim was part of the debate between Marpeck and Schwenckfeld, the spiritualist, who argued that only the inner baptism in the Spirit is part of salvation.

the work of the Spirit outwardly by baptizing the candidate with water. In baptism the whole movement of grace and faith is actualized and "sealed";[72] the believer is pried loose from the solidarity of sin and attached to the solidarity of grace, the body of Christ.

This incarnational understanding of believer's baptism offers a model of initiation that makes sense out of New Testament images of baptism in a way that a modern antisacramental or spiritualistic understanding of symbolic actions cannot do. Earlier in this chapter I made the case that the sixteenth-century radical reaction against popular Catholic sacramental practice veered toward an understanding that symbols are mere word signs with no participation in the realities they signify. Yet they continued to use New Testament language in a realistic sense; that is, in baptism we die and are buried with Christ. In the nineteenth century, forms of Protestantism with lean liturgical practice took a rationalistic bent in which they tried to argue why Paul's statement that we die with Christ could not mean what it plainly said. By contrast, the incarnational model applies the water of baptism sacramentally in a way that safeguards both the integrity of the Spirit's initiative and that of the believer's response.[73]

If one follows this incarnational logic, then *both* the rationalistic and spiritualistic interpretations of New Testament passages on baptism and the Lord's Supper lose their persuasiveness. What I mean by "spiritualistic interpretation" is the assertion that the very nature of God's communication with his creatures is in a spiritual and inward manner. But if this interpretation no longer determines the meaning of a text from the outset, there are other options than mere symbolism that are convincing as an interpretive key. For instance, it is then possible to interpret Romans 6:1-4 as a participatory reality and imagine that the mystery of dying and being buried with Christ truly can happen in a continuum of actions of the Spirit that culminate in water baptism.

If we turn to Paul's way of thinking, we see that the work of the Spirit in human beings is not restricted to inwardness. In Paul, faith comes through the hearing of "the word of Christ" (Rom 10:17). The hearer, the present preacher, and the original speaker are moved by what the physical ear brings

---

[72]Marpeck quotes Tertullian approvingly that "this bath is a sealing of faith," in the "Admonition of 1542," in Klassen and Klaassen, *Writings*, 197. See also Peter Riedemann, *Hutterite Confession of Faith* (Scottdale, PA: Herald Press, 1999), 185, 190.

[73]Beasley-Murray, *Baptism in the New Testament*, 130-32, 344-52.

them and what the physical voice speaks to them (Rom 10:14-17). Certainly the message is received by the human spirit, but the medium of the message is physical. That there is a temporal sequence to conversion (in other words, that it happens both inwardly and outwardly in order) does not seem to be problematic for Paul, or for the churches in Acts. There, as we have seen, even the order of the Spirit's acts, inwardly and outwardly, varies.

God's outer working is the other side of his inner working. The dynamic of water baptism is not a different, merely human, reality. If we look again at 1 Corinthians 12:13, we see that "in the one Spirit we were all baptized into one body." Conversion is inescapably personal, but it is not private. It is the movement from identifying with the powers of the world to identifying with God's reign. The Spirit is the seamless agent, the life-giving force, of the divine working in the church and in each believer.

God condescends to meet us fleshly and bloody creatures on our terms (Heb 2:12-19). The elements of nature reflect their Creator; they bless his creatures. For example, the church uses anointing with oil as a promise of God's healing presence. At the heart of salvation history are the elements of water, bread, and wine. God's intention in a sacrament is encounter. We join Christ in his dying and coming to life. The place where that happens is marked out by "water and Spirit" (Jn 3:1–8) in the presence of the congregation. In baptism, the church accompanies us to our death and awaits us as we rise from death.

Both understandings of God's engagement with his creatures, sacramentalism and spiritualism, run the danger of reducing God to our proportions. To be sure, sacramentalism run amok confines the Spirit to stipulated ritual gestures; it can be mistaken for the belief that sacred objects have intrinsic power. By the same token, spiritualism run amok confines the Spirit to what the mind can grasp; it can be mistaken for the belief that matter has no meaning in relation to God. Taken to their extreme, neither of them is hospitable to the mystery of God. Both approaches need to remember that inward and outward, spirit and body, are part of the wholeness God restored in the incarnation and the atonement. None of the Spirit's workings, mediated or unmediated, can be received other than by faith, which is also worked by the Spirit.[74]

---

[74]These thoughts coalesced as a meditation on Alf Härdelin's chap. 2, "The Sacramental Principle and the Nature of the Church," in *The Tractarian Understanding of the Eucharist* (Uppsala: Almqvist & Wiksell, 1965), 60-107.

Paul's image of conversion and baptism as death and new life is only one of the descriptions of coming to faith in the apostolic literature, but it is the most gripping and tangible one. It was cherished by the Anabaptists. Because of the very power of these images, most of them allowed that something happens in baptism. Theologians like Balthasar Hubmaier and the Moravian Hutterite Peter Riedemann did so very carefully. Yet Hubmaier held that when someone arises from the waters of baptism, that person belongs to the body of Christ and to the congregation who has just baptized that individual.[75] And Riedemann says, "Unless a person is born anew of water and the Spirit [referring to Jn 3:5] entrance into the kingdom of God is not possible." He adds that the water is bound by the Word: "the Word that is put into the water has this power."[76]

If you had pressed these theologians to describe exactly how that happens, they would have neatly separated image and reality to make clear that salvation happens when faith responds to grace. But the unselfconscious use of images that speak sacramentally over generations of time in treatises and confessions of faith suggests that this imagistic way of speaking helped them to say that something more than meets the eye was happening in the baptism of believers, something more than we have words for. This reality is born out in many parts of the New Testament. For example, the dynamic of the Spirit's work in coming to faith and being baptized happens in different ways (Acts 8:12, 14-17, 35-38; 10:44-48; 19: 1-6, etc.).

The dominant Mennonite and larger Free Church tradition heeded its instinct not to let conversion be separated from baptism. Part of the reason for that stance was Jesus' command to baptize. While baptism without conversion was a contradiction in their eyes, so was conversion without baptism. The coming to faith of an individual was incomplete without that person's *visible* incorporation into the body of Christ.

CONCLUSION

Two underlying thoughts deserve to be summarized. One of them is that Mennonite and other believers church ecclesiologies have been straightforwardly

---

[75]Balthasar Hubmaier, "On the Christian Baptism of Believers" and "Dialogue with Zwingli's Baptism Book," in Pipkin and Yoder, *Balthasar Hubmaier*, 146, 175.
[76]Riedemann, *Hutterite Confession of Faith*, 197.

sacramental in their doctrine of the church as the visible body of Christ. In other words, they describe the church as a tangible, historical community that is at the same time a spiritual fellowship. It is crucial at this point to add that the church is not the kingdom; it is the fallible forerunner of, the symbolic participant in, God's ever-coming reign.[77]

If my thesis is granted, that the churches that baptize only on confession of faith nevertheless express the sacramental principle in their understanding of the church, then the historic debate shifts. This means that the gulf between them has considerably lessened. Then the most difficult debate between liturgical folk churches and nonliturgical voluntary churches does not concern the meaning of the incarnation and its ongoing outworking. On that they agree, at the most basic level. The debate shifts to the character of the sacramental reality that flows from the incarnation. For instance, is the sacramental dynamic (in this case, in baptism) totally that of God's saving grace, or is it also made up of human faith? This more focused question has implications for the nature of the church: In what way is the church a visible historic reality? This more precise issue, rather than baptism in general, then becomes the defining unresolved issue between the two types of churches.

The second underlying thought has an ironic dimension to it. Believer's baptism churches have sought to safeguard God's initiative in salvation by locating it in the inward, unmediated realm of the Spirit. Infant baptism churches have acted out of the same concern. But they have safeguarded God's initiative by locating it in the outward, mediated realm of sacrament. If these two impulses could be seen to complement each other, then the old alternatives would appear in a new light.

---

[77]I am grateful for Anthony Siegrist's caution against "an ecclesial positivism."

6

THE MEAL JESUS GAVE US

NEW TESTAMENT AND PATRISTIC ERA

LONG AGO I MADE A VISIT to the Soviet Union. I was in Moscow on a Sunday and went to church at one of two legal Baptist congregations in the city. The church was already packed when I arrived, with only a few seats left in the balcony. The intensity of the singing and praying moved me deeply even though they were in a language I did not understand.

It was a Communion Sunday. From the balcony I could see everything that was happening. After the Communion prayer and the words of institution, the black-suited ministers and deacons took the bread into the rows. It was their custom for people to come to the end of the pew to receive the elements. As if against their better judgment, people arose before a server neared them, some with trembling hands. One old woman actually wedged herself between others and stuck her cupped hands forward to be sure she got a portion of the bread. In their hunger of body and soul, these persecuted believers knew this was no ordinary bread. In it, salvation had come within reach.

NEW TESTAMENT

Origins. The primal act of the Christian church is its gathering to eat bread and drink wine in memory of Jesus. In its gathered life, eating and drinking in memory of Jesus is the church's most profound enactment of the gospel. The Lord's Supper takes the narrative of Jesus' life, death, and resurrection and brings it to life in a deceptively simple gesture of breaking bread and sharing wine. At the Last Supper, Jesus, the faithful Jew, joined fellow believers across the centuries in the celebration of their rescue from oppression in ancient Egypt. Toward the closing of the celebration, Jesus took the last of four symbolic breads that were part of the Passover liturgy. It represented the lamb that bears the people's sin away. Jesus dared to claim that he was the one through whom redemption will come to the people. "This is my body, which is given for you" (Lk 22:19). The words he chose are unmistakable. Whatever precise meaning one might gave to this audacious assertion, the gist of it is clear: I give myself to you, for you, *now*. This is the message of Matthew, Mark, and Luke. To read Jesus' gesture as a mere sign of a separate reality is to impose a distinction that is not present in the text.

The Gospel of John goes even further. It is the most mystical and poetic of the four accounts of Jesus' life.[1] Perplexingly, it includes no record of the stages of the Passover food ritual, as do the Synoptics. Instead, the meaning of bread and wine as images of who Jesus is and what he offers is taken from the meals Jesus offered the multitudes in the course of his ministry. After his spectacular feeding of the five thousand in John 6, the crowds come back for more. Jesus sees that the people have not grasped the deeper intention of his miracle. "Do not work for the food that perishes, but for the food that endures for eternal life" (Jn 6:27). Skeptics among the crowd taunt Jesus. God gave our ancestors manna in the wilderness. Are you doing anything more than that?

Jesus is swift to reframe the discussion. "It was not Moses who gave you the bread from heaven, but it is my Father who gives you the true bread from heaven" (Jn 6:32). God is the hidden actor; it is God and not any human figure who feeds the hungry. Then Jesus blurts out, "I am the bread of life" (Jn 6:35) whom the Father has sent. For a few moments the crowd is spellbound. Then the skeptics resume their grumbling: we know this man's parents and where he came from. And it's not heaven! Jesus replies with cerebral language but quickly returns to the visceral language he began with; he becomes more extravagant with every utterance. "Whoever eats of this bread will live forever; and the bread that I will give for the life of the world is my flesh" (Jn 6:51). Five times in this passage Jesus offers his flesh to eat, and four times he offers his blood to drink.[2] This is a fiercely eucharistic text.

---

[1]It is generally agreed that the Fourth Gospel is not a straightforwardly historical account of events but more explicitly theological in its presentation of Jesus' ministry. John is also widely held to have had more than one author. Such investigations are valuable in grasping the intention of the text but are beyond the scope of this study. The canonical text is our focus.
[2]Raymond Brown, *The Gospel According to John I–XII*, Anchor Bible 29 (Toronto: Anchor Bible, 1966), 282. Brown notes that the Hebrew idiom "flesh and blood" means the "whole person." This

✓   In his exchange with the skeptics, we see that Jesus begins with less extravagant claims. First he is the "bread of life." After that he is living bread—whoever
eats of it will live forever. But then he raises the stakes, as if lesser language than
flesh and blood is inadequate to the intensity of the encounter and to what is
at stake.[3] The local skeptics take it that Jesus is speaking literally (Jn 6:52). Jesus
himself stays on that plane as if it is the only level of language that can make
unequivocally clear that eternal life comes through the flesh and blood of Mary
and Joseph's son. Jesus refuses to abandon his bloody language. The only con-
cession he makes in the stages of the conversation is to say that his claims are
believable only to those whom the Father has drawn to faith (Jn 6:44, 57, 65).

The sympathy of today's Western reader easily lies with the skeptics rather
than with Jesus. Even the disciples complain. Is it to mollify them that Jesus
explains, "It is the spirit that gives life; the flesh is useless" (Jn 6:63)? Is Jesus
dismissing what he just said as a provocative word game? Or could it be that
Jesus resorts to realist language to describe mystical experience? Whatever
path of interpretation one takes, the extravagance of the language itself resists
being reduced to the realm of metaphor; it refuses to be domesticated. Two
assertions frame the conversation that unfolds in John 6. First of all, God the
Father is the source of all that is given—not Moses, not even the Son himself.
The gift of salvation overflows from heaven above to earth below. Second, the
gift of God is nothing other than the Son, the Word become flesh (Jn 1:14).
Salvation is ultimately found not in ideas or codes or texts but in the flesh and
blood of the Messiah.

There is a partial parallel here with Paul's thought. The issue that both Paul
and John are grappling with is whether the Ascended One is still also the
Present One. Both writers make use of mystical as well as sacramental categories to assert the immediacy of Christ to the church. The mystical is anchored
in the sacramental: the sacrament locates Christ in the gathered congregation;
it opens the way to mystical oneness with him. John talks about Christ abiding in us and we in him (Jn 15:1-11). Paul confesses that Christ lives in him

interpretation moves the focus from body parts to the person but still retains the reality of personal
encounter, of real presence.
[3]Brown emphasizes a real encounter. He adds that while the discourse of John 6:35-50 makes allusions
to the Lord's Supper, it does so in images taken from contemporary Judaism (Brown, *Gospel According to John*, 286). But John 6:51-58 is so unmistakably eucharistic that this passage must be considered
a later theological riff on the preceding passage (Brown, *Gospel According to John*, 286-91).

(Gal 2:20). As profound as such *mystical* union with Christ is, it is a divine inbreaking that cannot be anticipated. By contrast, Christ's sacramental abiding carries the promise that the Spirit will make Christ present in a surpassing way in every time and place where believers gather to break bread in his name. This presence is a delicate analogy to the incarnation, to the coming into our world of the Word made flesh. I use the term *delicate* because the parallel is always incomplete. Both the incarnate and the eucharistic Christ are objective presences. But, in the former, certainty is given to the senses.[4] Can we say that in the sharing of the bread and cup of Communion the senses give us the certainty that Christ is present? Or must we say that certainty is given to the faith that receives these gifts? At issue is whether Christ is so fully identified with the elements that the senses "know" Christ. Would that mean that we receive Christ *in* the bread?

Or is the relationship between bread and body that of a parallel? Then we would say that we receive Christ *with* the bread or *when* we receive the bread. In either case, we receive the gift of Christ by faith. Through our experience of Christ in the Supper we recognize Christ's other presences—in a mystical meeting, in the face of sister, brother, neighbor, enemy (Mt 25:31-46). This divine human who once lived in Nazareth lives on in us. John 6 gives this confession eucharistic expression.

In John the incarnation is never far away. There is even a linguistic link between the theological case for Jesus' messiahship in John 1 and the sacramental argument for his messiahship in John 6: it is the word *flesh*. This striking and unexpected term is featured in another Johannine writing, the author's first letter: "By this you know the Spirit of God: every spirit that confesses that Jesus Christ has come in the flesh is from God" (1 Jn 4:2). One can argue from John 6 that the Eucharist is the perpetual reenactment of the incarnation. Yet how does one assent to such a breathtaking claim while also taking seriously the limits to this claim? For instance, we do not meet Jesus as he was before the resurrection. (Is this Paul's concern in comparing Christ's and our bodies?)[5] We meet Christ as he was after coming back from the dead: sensually

---

[4]Michael Welker, *What Happens in Holy Communion?*, trans. John F. Hoffmeyer (Grand Rapids: Eerdmans, 2000), 95.

[5]"Even though we once knew Christ from a human point of view, we know him no longer in that way" (2 Cor 5:16).

recognizable by his voice and gestures, by the mark of the spear and nails. Yet in his ability to be suddenly present or absent he was not bound by the limitations of mortal, physical bodies. Paul's meditation on the perishing body putting on imperishability attempts to find words for this reality (1 Cor 15:42-55).

Why did Jesus insist so passionately to those who sought him out that he is the bread of life (Jn 6:35, 41, 48, 51)? What is at stake for inquirers today? John's prologue, the most extravagant piece of theology in the New Testament ("the Word was God" [Jn 1:1]; "the Word became flesh" [Jn 1:14]), is the framework of the Fourth Gospel. Nothing loftier can be said of Jesus: there is no fuller disclosure of God. Most commentators agree that the theological refinement of John's writing suggests that it emerged as a single text only at the end of the first century. It attempts to address two generations of critics, both Jewish and Greek. Both of them disputed the finality of Jesus. The prologue is addressed to Greeks and Hellenized Jews; John 6 and other parts of John's Gospel are addressed to traditional Jews. John's most profound way of making his claim to these Jews is take the name of Yahweh (I am that I am) and extend it to Jesus by means of the "I am" claims, like "I am the bread of life" (Jn 6:35). To put it in other words, "I am one with him who made the world and called a people for himself out of Egypt." Later Jesus says it even more simply (and unequivocally): "The Father and I are one" (Jn 10:30).

It is striking that Jesus makes this loftiest of declarations by means of bread and wine, the humble elements of earth. In effect, the Lord's Supper as presented in John is the New Testament's clinching argument for the identity of Jesus and the nature of God's reign. There are certainly other ways of affirming this truth, but Jesus as bread is the most graphic and tangible. However, there is more than that to Jesus' words. The food of eternal life is the flesh and blood of Jesus; those who feed on it abide in him (Jn 6:53–56). "Whoever eats me will live because of me" (Jn 6:57). John 6:60-63 is a warning against a materialist interpretation of Jesus' words. But the urgent tone of the text makes a realist rendition much more compelling than a merely symbolic one. Only those who have devoured Jesus are on the path to eternal life. The Resurrected One, who bears the scars of his passion, abides within us—not a memory, not an experience, but a person. This oneness with Jesus who is one with God happens paradigmatically in the Breaking of Bread.

Encounter and absence. After Jesus' ascension, "body of Christ" language takes on two meanings beyond its literal sense. The historic body of Christ, that is, Jesus of Nazareth, is no longer near in sensually recognizable ways. But the mystical body of Christ comes to us in the Lord's Supper, that is, his real presence by means of signs. In addition, the church becomes the "body of Christ" as the prolongation of his resurrected body, and by extension its sacramental and missionary life become Christ's hands and feet by which he is recognized.

How does this language from the Synoptics and Paul connect to John's language of flesh and blood? In the Johannine mindset the claim for Jesus' messiahship is undermined if flesh and blood are only metaphorical realities (Jn 6:25-59). At the same time, it can be received only by those who have been "born of the Spirit" (Jn 3:1-8). This stance leaves us perplexed. Is the problem one of language? Are there conceptual and relational alternatives that go beyond either a literal or a metaphorical understanding?

It is common to say that Christ is spiritually present in the Eucharist. But *spiritual* has become such a broad term that it can hardly carry the concern of John 6, of an actual ingesting of Christ at the Breaking of Bread. Roman Catholics favor the term *substance,* that which makes an entity what it is, what gives it its true nature. The elements are "transubstantiated" so that their substance is the body and blood of Christ. But over the centuries it has been almost impossible to distinguish substance from locality and quantity.[6] In other words, how can Christ be present in his body and blood without being somewhere and having dimensions—the attributes of physicality?

In order to address this practical problem and to recast the issue into modern European thought categories, Edward Schillebeeckx, the Vatican II theologian, proposed the term *transignification*. He makes the case that it is the ultimate meaning of the elements that is transformed: to eat the bread

---

[6]To the Protestant mind this seems to happen even on the theological level. A favorite example is the Feast of Corpus Christi with the host on parade for adoration at a particular time and place. It builds on eleventh century Palm Sunday and Good Friday processions and the thirteenth century elevation of the host during mass. "In all of these trends the sacrament could be seen less as something to be eaten and drunk, more as a cult object to be venerated for its own sake outside the context of the mass.": Christopher Walsh, "Reservation" in Paul Bradshaw, ed., *The New Westminster Dictionary of Liturgy and Worship,* Louisville: Westminster John Knox, 2002), 404-6.

and drink the wine means to take to ourselves the whole person of Christ.[7] This assertion immediately throws up the question of how to speak about what happens in the eucharistic action, of taking to ourselves the whole person of Christ. One way of doing so is the language of the relational immediacy of Christ to the gathered community and each believer. Schillebeeckx favors the term *encounter* because it provides us with an analogy for how we meet fellow human beings: we let them in, they dwell in us, they change us. Their very person of spirit and flesh is received by our spirit and flesh.

Such relational language helps us to grasp the notion of the church as Christ's body: the head and the members are bound to each other as in 1 Corinthians 12. This understanding also flows into the church's missionary stance. Through his body, Christ faces into the world and gives himself to it. In him the reign of God has come near. Surpassingly through its participation in Christ in the Breaking of Bread, the church witnesses to and embodies the kingdom coming on earth as it is in heaven. In this way of describing mission, evangelism and justice are the seamless incarnation of the kingdom's nearness.

The earliest recorded reflection we have of how early Christians talked about the ongoing presence of Jesus in the church comes from Paul's rhetorical question, "The cup of blessing that we bless, is it not a sharing in the blood of Christ? The bread that we break, is it not a sharing in the body of Christ?" (1 Cor 10:16). The question's rhetorical nature suggests that Paul is quoting a familiar liturgical phrase and can count on the agreement of the people to whom he is writing. The key word here, however, is the inverse of John's focus on eating and drinking as the way of receiving Christ. It is variously translated as "sharing in," "participating in," "having communion with."[8] Participating in this meal unites us with Christ and one another. Paul's language is less extravagant than John's. Perhaps this was the case because belief in the incarnation was not under siege in the Pauline congregations as it was later on in the Johannine ones. In Paul's rendition of the words of institution, he uses the more restrained *body* and *cup* rather than *flesh* and *blood*. Paul's language is closer to Jewish covenant language. It is softer than the deliberately audacious language of John. Paul also

---

[7]Edward Schillebeeckx, *The Eucharist* (London: Sheed & Ward, 1968), 107-14.
[8]C. K. Barrett, *The First Epistle to the Corinthians* (London: Adam Black, 1973), 230-32.

contributes the profound double entendre of *body* as referring both to the person of Christ and to the church.

Jesus' command to remember him in the Breaking of Bread was shaped and recorded by the Gospel writers and Paul for the churches on whose behalf they were writing. The church in the age of the Fathers preserved these accounts (and rejected others) to show that we need all of those that were accepted into the canon to faithfully understand and participate in the Lord's Supper.

The claim the church made for the heavenly Christ's sacramental presence was, at the same time, an acknowledgment of his historic absence from our plane of reality. The ascension is understood in John (14:8–15:26) and Luke (Acts 1:1-11; 2:1-4) as the departure of Christ and the intensified presence of the Spirit indwelling our plane of reality to represent him. Paul develops the notion that Christ is made present by the power of the Spirit in the church and in each believer. Some commentators have coined the notion of "absent presence."[9] By that they mean that according to the usual measurements we make of someone's presence, the Jesus of history is now absent. Yet, as we have seen, the New Testament claims three forms of ongoing presence for Jesus. In a spiritual (mystical), sacramental (in the community that shares bread and wine), and ethical (in human acts of self-giving) manner, Christ is an actor in human affairs. Literal thinking inevitably becomes reductive, leaving us with only memories of the long-lost historical Jesus. Paradoxical thinking is necessary to account for the reality we experience.

There is an additional dimension to the paradoxical reality of the Lord's presence in the church and the world that is at the heart of the gospel. In Jesus, God and God's reign enter time and space. In the Synoptic Gospels the kingdom has come near in Jesus (Lk 11:14-20). In Luke 11, Jesus has just cast out demons. Onlookers are perplexed at the source of his power so they "kept demanding from him a sign from heaven" (Lk 11:16). Do you have evidence, they insist, that God's rule is present in you? After more debate about whose power is at work here, Jesus makes his case. "If it is by the finger of God that I cast out demons, then the kingdom of God has come to you" (Lk 11:20). To the skeptics Jesus audaciously replies that his finger is God's finger.

---

[9]Xavier Léon-Dufour, *Sharing the Eucharistic Bread: The Witness of the New Testament* (New York: Paulist Press, 1987), 75.

To put Jesus' deceptively simple identification of his finger with God's finger into theological categories, the incarnation is the entry point. That is to say, the kingdom comes from heaven to earth enfleshed in Christ. To be sure, God's reign existed in Israel prior to that and continues after Jesus' earthly life. After the ascension, his body, the church, becomes the sacrament of the kingdom.[10] The church is not only the embodiment of God's presence in time and space but a visible participation in a reality larger than itself. Christ's sacraments are an echo of both the incarnation and the kingdom. In the power of the Holy Spirit, they make Christ's nearness concrete and specific.

Sacraments, most profoundly the Lord's Supper, offer us this density of presence, this palpable nearness. The spoken narrative, its gestures, and the community gathered to enact them encounter the invisible presence of the host, the elements of the Lord's Supper. The communal partaking of bread and wine marks the place where Christ is met. By analogy with human encounters, our senses persuade us that Christ is present: as surely as we partake of the bread and cup, we are partakers of Christ. In turn, this Spirit-given encounter with Christ becomes the model by which we recognize other intimations that Christ is near—a liminal moment in nature, an act of altruism, a moment of mutual vulnerability.

In the New Testament there is another density of presence: Christ meets us not only outwardly but inwardly, not only sacramentally but mystically. John and Paul are at home in both realms and in the interplay between them. In John, we are "born from above" (Jn 3:3), yet we also ingest or feed on Christ (Jn 6:53). In Paul's way of speaking, the Spirit indwells our bodies (Rom 8:9-11); God's Spirit witnesses with our spirit that we are "children of God" (Rom 8:14). For John, feeding on the flesh and blood of Christ is the primal, paradigmatic embodiment of Christ. This emphasis is widely understood as a response to the threat of dualistic worldviews that claimed the material world was incapable of bearing spirit.[11] John's concern was to affirm God's hallowing of the material world as revelatory in the incarnation; God loved the world (Jn 3:16). His ultimate proof of the latent capacity of matter to disclose spirit

---

[10] Alexander Schmemann, *The Eucharist*, trans. Paul Kachur (Crestwood, NY: St. Vladimir's Seminary Press, 1988), 29-44.

[11] Brown, *Gospel According to John*, lii-lvi, is cautious about pre-Christian or proto-Gnostic influences but acknowledges dualism as a background threat in the writing of the Fourth Gospel.

was the Lord's Supper. We experience the world as embodied creatures. Receiving Christ in the Lord's Supper is more than a spiritual reality in the sense of being entirely inward, entirely beyond the limitations of the material world. Jesus, the One of flesh, indwells those who are of the flesh.

In Paul, the Lord's Supper does not have such a finely worked out, paradigmatic role. Meeting Christ mystically and meeting him sacramentally appear to be woven together in an interdependent way. Take the example of 1 Corinthians 12:13: "For in the one Spirit we were all baptized into one body." Here the weight falls on initiation into Christ's body by baptism. Yet the mystical seems to be a gift of the Spirit without an explicit eucharistic frame of reference. This is the case in Romans 8:15-16: "When we cry 'Abba! Father!' it is that very Spirit bearing witness with our spirit that we are children of God" and in Galatians 2:20: "It is no longer I who live, but it is Christ who lives in me."

All Christian traditions have tried to tame the wild and elusive language of Christ's nearness, which cannot be compelled or confined. At one extreme the church has undone the paradox of Christ's absent presence by reducing the mystery of God's reign to merely a sign of absence. At the other extreme the church has reduced the divine proximity to an object that can be adored.

The Last Supper and the Lord's Supper. Jesus' ministry embodies the kingdom. God's reign is present in the flesh: in Jesus' table fellowship with outsiders, in his teaching that loving God and the neighbor cannot be separated, in his healing of broken bodies and spirits. Jesus is the embodiment of the kingdom, and the church is the down payment, the sacrament of the kingdom—present but not yet fulfilled. Since Luke's Gospel is more focused on table fellowship than the other Gospels, we will follow its trajectories. There is a clue to this already-but-not-yet relationship in Luke's account of the Last Supper. After everything has been prepared, Jesus bares his heart to his friends. "I have eagerly desired to eat this Passover with you before I suffer; for I tell you I will not eat it until it is fulfilled in the kingdom of God" (Lk 22:15-16). The Passover celebration itself is eschatological: it has the hope that "next year in Jerusalem" the reign of God will come. Jesus repeats this vow after the third of four cups that make up the Passover ritual: "From now on I will not drink of the fruit of the vine until the kingdom of God comes" (Lk 22:18). This is a mystifying

statement. We do not know whether Jesus had a particular time sequence in
mind. But something of ultimate significance is about to happen: Luke's record
of Jesus' final hours is filled with anticipation.

The words of institution of the Last Supper are the crystallization point,
the gathered moment, of Jesus' ministry. They set in motion the coming of
God's sovereignty over all things through Jesus' atoning death and anticipate
a meal of reconciliation in the coming reign.[12] Second Isaiah is the source of
most of the images in Luke's portrayal; for example, the broken body and shed
blood of Jesus are the seal of the coming covenant (Isa 62:10-12, 65:17-25).
With his death, Jesus founds the saving community that will carry forth the
already inaugurated but not yet fulfilled kingdom.[13]

According to Luke, Jesus gives the loaf and cup to the disciples but
abstains himself. He insists, "I confer on you, just as my Father has conferred
on me, a kingdom, so that you may eat and drink at my table in my kingdom"
(Lk 22:29-30). There is an intimate affinity between the language of the
kingdom and the language of the incarnation: in both cases God enters time
and space under our conditions; redemption enters history. The atonement
is the fulfillment of the incarnation, the ultimate consequence of God's
solidarity with the creation. God's love in Jesus is relentless; it risks everything. On the cross, this nonresistant love confronts the cosmic powers—
and their local proxies, the Roman tribunal and the Jewish Sanhedrin—that
have come to destroy. Jesus enters the abyss on humanity and creation's
behalf. In him God overcomes these powers: they can no longer compel
our surrender to evil (Col 2:13-15). Our own complicity is forgiven, and we
are set free. The wall dividing us from one another falls (Eph 2:11-18).

The Lord's Supper manifests and prolongs this new creation. It gives us a
taste of life in the kingdom so that we can recognize and mark its incursions
into our everyday lives and the life of the world. Paul teaches that whenever
the church eats the eschatological bread and drinks the eschatological cup, it
proclaims "the Lord's death until he comes" (1 Cor 11:26). One of the few liturgical fragments we have from the first century is the congregation's shout when

[12]Rudolph Schnackenburg, *Gottes Herrschaft und Reich: Eine biblische-theologische Studie* (Freiburg: Herder, 1963), 173.

[13]Schnackenburg, *Gottes Herrschaft*, 174-76; and G. R. Beasley-Murray, *Jesus and the Kingdom of God* (Grand Rapids: Eerdmans, 1986), 265-69.

the coming of the Lord is proclaimed, "'Surely I am coming soon.' Amen. Come, Lord Jesus!" (Rev 22:20). These words partake of Jesus' own yearning to confer on his apostles a kingdom just as the Father has conferred one on him, "so that you may eat and drink at my table in my kingdom" (Lk 22:29-30).

Out of the ashes the phoenix arises. The One declared to be the victim is the victor! Jesus' resurrection is the cosmic confirmation that the reign of God has made an incursion into the world that cannot be undone. "There is another king named Jesus!" (Acts 17:7). Jesus' return from the dead is the reality that makes the table fellowship of Jesus' ministry and the Last Supper into the Lord's Supper. The kingdom has not yet come in its fullness, but with God's overcoming of death and fate in Jesus' victory, the conditions for its coming are in place.

Uniquely, Luke preserves the first communion with the Risen One in spellbinding language (Lk 24:28-35). Jesus meets two of his disciples travelling to the town of Emmaus on the evening of Easter. At first they fail to recognize him. But something prompts them to invite the stranger to lodge with them for the night. They sit down for supper, and immediately there is a reversal of roles: Jesus is suddenly the host and his companions the guests. Jesus takes the loaf provided for the meal, blesses it, and breaks it to share around the table (Lk 24:30). Instantly they recognize him, perhaps because they call to mind his gestures from shared meals during his ministry. It is not insignificant that even in this astonishing moment of improvisation, Jesus shapes this meal just as he had those of his ministry and of the Last Supper: in each case he "took," "blessed," "broke," and "gave" them the bread.

So persuaded are the two disciples that Jesus has come back from the dead that they run to Jerusalem to tell the other disciples: "They told what had happened on the road, and how he had been made known to them in the breaking of the bread" (Lk 24:35). Here the full weight of the narrative is on the encounter. The ritual gesture with the bread, surging with meaning, is the giveaway. It is Jesus, no one else, who gives *us* himself. The bread of affliction has become the bread of rejoicing. The giver of this bread is not a ghost—he can be touched. At the same time, the host at Emmaus has already entered a wider plane of reality. He disappears at will. Soon he will be lost to sight. The nature of Jesus' presence with his friends is changing even as its association with the Breaking of Bread is being reinforced.

This Lukan ritual of intimate encounter is a complementary image for Jesus' eucharistic presence to those of John (feeding on him) and Paul (being made one with him). It is baffling that the early church and the church of later centuries made so little of it. Almost nothing of the Emmaus encounter makes its way into eucharistic liturgies.[14] Is the marginalizing of its narrative already the origin of an impulse to take the Supper away from the expansiveness of an encounter to the confinement of an object?

The language John, Paul, and Luke use to describe Jesus' promised presence in the meal concerns a profoundly paradoxical reality. Someone who has left the plane of reality in which his followers first met him nevertheless meets them within time and space. It was the reality of this encounter and the physical signs accompanying it that allowed the church to survive the crisis brought about when God did not "restore the kingdom to Israel" in the generation of the apostles (Acts 1:6). The dynamic of these encounters that sustained the church during the long interim before the fulfillment of God's reign was the Holy Spirit (Acts 1:8), mediating Christ's heavenly presence on earth, in the church, in each believer, in the Holy Supper.

The sharing of bread and wine is the paradigm for that unmistakable yet elusive reality of a transforming encounter with Christ. The elusiveness of encounter and the vicissitude of human experience are transcended in the Lord's Supper.

PATRISTIC ERA

Early eucharistic liturgies. So profound was this reality of Christ's presence in the early church that a structuring of the sacrament's core arose early on to give secure ritual form to the ongoing participation of Christ in the world of time and space. Two facts stand out in this development. One of them is the indebtedness of the church to its Jewish origins for prayers that frame not only the Last Supper but other holy meals of the Christian community.[15]

---

[14]Matthew Levering explores this overlooked text as a potential source of eucharistic unity for the church today, using the striking example of Gertrude the Great's experience of eucharistic communion in the thirteenth century. Matthew Levering, "The Eucharist, the Risen Lord, and the Road to Emmaus: A Road to Deeper Unity?," in *Come, Let Us Eat Together: Sacraments and Christian Unity*, ed. George Kalantzis and Marc Cortez (Downers Grove, IL: InterVarsity Press, 2018), 150-69, esp. 164-68.

[15]R. C. D. Jasper and G. J. Cuming, *Prayers of the Eucharist: Early and Reformed*, 3rd ed. (Collegeville,

The other fact, the counterpoint of order, is that for two centuries the liturgical forms are not uniform, remain simple, and are marked by freedom for improvisation within the structure. The church's liturgical forms remain provisional and open to adaptation in new cultures because the church is not wedded to a single culture or political order. It is adaptable to new missionary settings.

"The Teaching of the Twelve Apostles," called the Didache (Teaching), is a worship manual from the New Testament era that reinforces the picture of simplicity and fluidity of form as long as it gives voice to the Gospel narrative.[16] There is disagreement as to whether the meal in this manual is a Lord's Supper or an *agape* (a full meal that frames the Breaking of Bread) or whether the distinction between the two was not yet firm. The Didache has an importance that goes beyond its historical moment. It was included in later collections of eucharistic prayers and translated into several Mediterranean languages. Its characteristics are instructive. For example, only the baptized may participate. Yet even the baptized who persist in unresolved quarrels may not come to the Table. The great prayer of thanksgiving speaks of spiritual food but—strikingly—without making explicit reference to Jesus' Last Supper, death, or resurrection. This lack might have been one of the reasons for the detailed inclusion of the New Testament accounts of the Last Supper in the canon. Paul's and Mark's records of the Last Supper are thought to have been written about the same time as the Didache.

Justin Martyr was a presbyter from Samaria whose later ministry was in Ephesus and Rome from 135 to 165. Two similar orders of service followed by Justin are preserved.[17] The service begins with readings from the apostles or prophets, a sermon on the readings follows, and then comes a prayer. The kiss of peace, the sign of reconciliation, begins the service of the Lord's Table. The presider offers a eucharistic prayer after which the deacons distribute the bread and wine. The themes of that prayer are clear, but the form is extemporaneous.[18]

MN: Liturgical Press, 1990), 7-12.

[16]"*Didache*," in Jasper and Cuming, *Prayers of the Eucharist*, 20-24.

[17]"Justin Martyr," in Jasper and Cuming, *Prayers of the Eucharist*, 25-30.

[18]Alan Kreider, *The Patient Ferment of the Early Church: The Improbable Rise of Christianity in the Roman Empire* (Grand Rapids: Baker Academic, 2016), 185-207, lays out the progression of worship in several third-century settings.

Thanks is given for the creation, for Christ's incarnation, for his destruction of "the principalities and powers" in his death, and for the food that is "the flesh and blood of the incarnate Jesus."[19] The words of institution follow.

A further development in liturgical structure comes from the early third century. It is called *The Apostolic Tradition* and was once credited to Hippolytus, an early third-century Roman presbyter. There are two orders of service, one following an ordination and one following a baptism.[20] The Communion in the ordination service is striking. Jesus' birth of the Virgin Mary is prominent in the remembrance narrative (*anamnesis*).[21] The lead-in to the words of institution emphasize Christ's voluntary suffering, destruction of death, and resurrection. Bread and wine that members have brought are blessed and shared. If members have also brought forward oil, olives, or cheese, these are also distributed to the participants. At the end of the order is the following rubric. "It is not at all necessary for [the presider] to utter the same words that we have said above. . . . Let him pray according to his ability. . . . But if anyone who prays, recites a prayer according to fixed form, do not prevent him."[22] In the baptismal Eucharist, the prayer for the Spirit (*epiclesis*)[23] is that it might come upon the people rather than upon the elements. The bread and cup are described as "antitypes" and "likenesses" of the body and blood.[24]

In the mid-fourth century much of the Didache and the *Apostolic Tradition* were included into a yet more elaborate eucharistic prayer called the *Apostolic Constitutions*. Unique to this prayer is its long and lavish praise to God for the creation before going on to praise God's redemption.[25] In contrast with Western ones, later Eastern prayers preserve brief references to creation.

Lex orandi, lex credendi: the law of prayer determines the law of belief. Gregory Dix, the Anglican liturgical scholar, makes the stunning claim that

---

[19]"Justin Martyr," in Jasper and Cuming, *Prayers of the Eucharist*, 29.

[20]"The So-Called *Apostolic Tradition of Hippolytus*," in Jasper and Cuming, *Prayers of the Eucharist*, 31-38.

[21]The Greek word *anamnesis* means "remembrance" and has the implication of calling the past into the present.

[22]"The So-Called Apostolic Tradition of Hippolytus," Jasper and Cuming, *Prayers of the Eucharist*, 36.

[23]The Greek word *epiklēsis* means "invocation" and refers to asking the Father to send the Spirit to come upon the eucharistic gathering.

[24]"The So-Called Apostolic Tradition of Hippolytus," in Jasper and Cuming, *Prayers of the Eucharist*, 37.

[25]"*Apostolic Constitutions*," in Jasper and Cuming, *Prayers of the Eucharist*, 104-7.

fixed liturgies came into being only when the church had become "reconciled to time" and moved from "an eschatological to a historical notion of the Eucharist."[26] He means that there is a correlation between the church's accommodation to the compromises of historical existence and the development of a fixed order of worship. The anticipation of the fullness of God's reign, with its flexibility and freedom to improvise, ebbs.

Dix's correlation becomes truer as time passes. In the liturgies of the fourth century, there is still some freedom for improvisation. In the ancient orders of worship that have been preserved, two complementary characteristics stand out. One of them is the development of ritual, the words and gestures that frame sacramental acts. In this the church is following Jesus' command. The other characteristic is the freedom to improvise on form, most especially in the eucharistic prayer. In this the church is heeding the ongoing presence of the Spirit. The more the church becomes linked to the empire, the more its rituals prize uniformity and suspect deviation and innovation.

In the course of the third century, congregations in some areas outgrew the private homes in which they were meeting. By the fourth century, well-to-do congregations were building public assembly halls. The shift in scale and location resulted in the structure of the service becoming correspondingly more formal. Even more significant in the shift from intimate community and the private sphere to a public event under state patronage was the greatly accelerated innovation in architecture and ceremonial brought about by the empire's favor. Churches began to be patterned on basilicas, the long auditoriums that housed public and imperial events. Roman (in the West) and Greek (in the East) court garments and ceremonial began to accompany the stages of the service. In contrast, the Syriac, Coptic, and Armenian liturgies, which arose outside the empire, retained more Jewish influence.

The patristic maxim "the law of prayer determines the law of belief" was first articulated by the presbyter Prosper of Aquitane in the mid-fifth century.[27] It was quickly taken up as a turn of phrase that made clear that worship is prior to belief in the sense of doctrine. What we believe about God arises from how we worship God. First, gradually the prayer for the Holy Spirit became more

---

[26]Gregory Dix, *The Shape of the Liturgy* (1945; repr., London: Dacre, 1975), 303-6.
[27]Gordon Lathrop, *Holy People: a Liturgical Ecclesiology* (Minneapolis: Fortress, 1999), 102-4.

and more explicitly focused on the "offering"; that is, what was brought to the Lord's Table was less and less the people themselves but rather the consecrated elements. The references to the elements as body and blood became less symbolic and more realist. Increasingly, liturgies spoke of offering the body and blood, not on the table but on the altar, as if it were a sacrifice in its own right and not the re-presentation of Christ's offering on the cross.

These developments resulted in a profound shift in the theology and ceremonial of the Eucharist in the West, which became a crisis in the ninth century. But the beginning of the shift is already in evidence by the middle of the second century. This is surprising in two ways. One of them is that the straightforward identification of bread and wine with body and blood increasingly departed from the more nuanced, personal, and paradoxical language of the New Testament. Second, this shift has to be taken seriously because it begins to happen so early. The modern reader observes these changes from a distance, but in the minds of third- and fourth-century liturgists and congregations, their changes in language remain in complete conformity with the New Testament.

Different philosophical backgrounds account for differences in the language and meaning of various schools of liturgy. In the early patristic era such differences did not seem to divide the church. Part of the reason for that was the fluid use of language to talk about the nature of the Holy Supper. It flowed among literal, analogical, and metaphorical forms of expression. For example, Justin Martyr wrote *Dialogue with Trypho* about 135. In it he describes "the bread which Christ handed down to us to do for us for remembrance of his incarnation . . . and the cup which he handed down to us to do, giving thanks for remembrance of his blood."[28]

In his *First Apology*, written about 150, Justin speaks about the same subject quite differently.

Just as our savior Jesus Christ, being incarnate through the word of God, took flesh and blood for our salvation, so too we have been taught that the food over which thanks has been given, by a word of prayer which is from him [Jesus], (the food) from which our flesh and blood are fed by transformation, *is both the flesh and blood of that incarnate Jesus.*[29]

---

[28]"Justin Martyr," in Jasper and Cuming, *Prayers of the Eucharist,* 27.
[29]"Justin Martyr," in Jasper and Cuming, *Prayers of the Eucharist,* 29. Emphasis added.

The realistic language is unmistakable! At the same time, it would be unfair historically to claim that Justin meant the same thing that Lanfranc (in the next chapter) did half a millennium later when he interpreted "the flesh and blood of that incarnate Jesus" in a physical manner. Using language without caring for its historical context has been the source of futile debate about sacraments over the centuries. In addition, it is well to recall the unselfconscious participation of third-century believers who lived in a sacramental universe, experiencing the physical and spiritual worlds as one. The theological inflections of eucharistic language were heard by ordinary people as part of the familiar flow of literal and metaphorical descriptions of the sacred.

Symbolic and metabolic realism. However, beginning in the late fourth century the influence on Christian ritual by different contexts and philosophies became noticeable. There were two broadly different ways developing to describe how we receive Christ in the Eucharist. One of the approaches to the mystery of Christ in the Supper, described today as metabolic realism, is associated with Ambrose, the late-fourth-century bishop of Milan. This phrase means that the elements were changed into the body and blood of Christ in a sacramental way. That is, the incarnate Christ was "truly" received in the transformed elements but not in a physical way. The outcome of this teaching was an increasing focus on the elements consecrated by a priest as the medium of the real presence rather than the whole Eucharist as the action of the congregation. This concentration on the elements as Christ's body and blood was, in turn, increasingly buttressed by the popular belief that communicants consumed the body and blood of Jesus as he had been in his earthly life. This notion is the background of stories in the High Middle Ages about bleeding hosts. The Catholic Church, and later the churches of the Reformation, strove to correct this materialist view.

The other fourth-century approach to the eucharistic presence of Christ, symbolic realism, is associated with Augustine.[30] Today it is popular to say that a symbol stands outside the reality it represents. For example, the bread at Communion is described as "merely" an external sign of Jesus' body but not a bearer of it. Against this view, there are two key characteristics of a

---

[30]William Crockett, *Eucharist: Symbol of Transformation* (Collegeville, MN: Liturgical Press, 1990), 88-98.

symbol in the ancient understanding, rather like two sides of the same coin. One is that it is in the nature of a symbol to participate in the reality it represents. The other, and corresponding, characteristic is that the symbol is not identical with that reality. For example, bread broken and wine shared offered believers participation in the body and blood of Christ, but they themselves were not that reality.

The fluidity of this symbolic language allowed for its extension in another direction. In a catechetical sermon Augustine says the following:

> If, then, you wish to understand the body of Christ, listen to the Apostle as he says to the faithful, "You are the body of Christ and His members" (1 Cor 12:27). If, therefore, you are the body of Christ and his members, your mystery has been placed on the Lord's Table, you receive your mystery.[31]

Augustine reinforces this in a later sermon. "The bread which you see on the altar, sanctified by God's word, is the body of Christ. . . . If you received worthily, you are what you received."[32] The change that happens to the bread is instrumental; it is not an end in itself. It is intended to bring about a change in those who eat it. The ultimate evidence of the presence of Christ in the Supper is that it makes those who commune in Christ's body into his body, again and again.

In hindsight one can see that the implications of the Ambrosian and Augustinian approaches led in contrary directions. Their profound commonality is that both positions were grounded in the incarnation, in the physical world as the bearer of the spiritual world. Both positions safeguarded the paradoxical relationship between spirit and matter. There is no record from the late fourth century that these positions were thought to be in opposition to each other.

We have already taken note of another commonality. In the patristic and early medieval eras, the church itself was commonly spoken of as the "sacramental body of Christ" and the Eucharist as his "mystical body." These terms fit with the belief that the prolongation of the incarnation occurred in the visible church and most densely there in the encounter with the incarnate One

---

[31]Daniel J. Sheerin, "Sermon 272," in *The Eucharist*, Message of the Fathers of the Church 7 (Wilmington, DE: Glazier, 1986), 95.

[32]Sheerin, "Sermon 272," in *Eucharist*, 95.

in the Lord's Supper. The seminal writing of Henri de Lubac documents a profound shift in the sacramental thought that peaks in the High Middle Ages. In this transposing of thought, an inversion takes place. The church is no longer primarily the sacramental but the mystical body of Christ; the Eucharist is no longer primarily the mystical but the sacramental body of Christ.[33]

A number of theological and liturgical changes accompanied and accelerated this inversion. As has been mentioned, when the communal nature of early Christian worship ebbed starting in the fifth century, the holy objects of bread and wine became more and more the focus of the celebration (the sacramental body of Christ), displacing the congregation (the ecclesial body of Christ). At the same time, the presbyters, the bishop's assistants in each congregation, gained an expanded sacramental status. That is, by means of their ordination they were given the unique power of "confecting" a sacrament, that is, being the instrument by which Christ is made present. This shift can be loosely correlated with a change in terminology from *presbyter* to *priest*.

Increasingly, what became essential to the Lord's Supper was not the presence of the people but the presence of the priest. The congregation lost its role in the eucharistic action in two ways. One loss was the role it had once shared with the priest, of offering the bread and wine in the eucharistic prayer. The other loss was its place as the ultimate object of transformation, that is, the congregation being remade into Christ's body. The decisive reality of the eucharistic liturgy was now the transformation of bread and wine into body and blood, whether or not it was shared among the congregation. As an extension of this cluster of changes there was a gradual movement away from thinking of the Holy Supper as a re-presenting of the one sacrifice of Christ (Heb 9:24-28) to the notion that Christ's sacrifice was repeated in a bloodless fashion through the power of the priest in every mass. Taken together, these developments favored the Ambrosian approach to sacraments with its focus on the elements.

The social location of the church is an essential dimension of these pivotal shifts. The change in the church's role in relation to government and society came about in the West in the centuries between Constantine (who granted

---

[33]Henri de Lubac, *Corpus Mysticum: The Eucharist and the Church in the Middle Ages*, trans. Gemma Simmonds (Notre Dame, IN: University of Notre Dame Press, 2007), 141-80, esp. 162-75.

toleration to Christianity at the beginning of the fourth century) and Charlemagne (who completed the mass conversion of populations in the empire, often under coercion, by the end of the eighth century). The significance of this shift for an understanding of the church and its ceremonies, especially baptism, is much debated, but directly relevant to a changing understanding of the church. As I discussed in the chapter on baptism, initially it seems to have been given to children along with their parents when pagan parents had come to faith in Christ.

The next stage in the development of baptismal practice came when it was offered to children in danger of dying. The defining subsequent step was the baptism of children of masses of nominal converts, especially under Charlemagne; by this point the personal faith of the parents as essential to the sacrament recedes. The stages we have all too briefly traced of development from a private, minority community to a public institution, to which one belonged by civil obligation, are inseparable from the evolution of infant baptism and the Eucharist.

Of relevance to the development of the Lord's Supper is the shift in ecclesiology, as described above by de Lubac.[34] Between the fifth and eighth centuries the established church moved from being a gathered church, where one chooses to belong, to a mass church in which membership of the whole society is obligatory. This shift meant that the communicant coming to the Lord's Table could not be assumed to come with an existential faith open to an encounter with Christ. This necessitated pastoral instructions that mandated a minimum disposition on the part of the communicant, which consisted of not placing a moral obstruction in the way of the sacrament. Out of this the understanding of the sacrament grew: the sacrament accomplishes what it signifies even without the condition of active faith. This principle was expressed in the term *ex opere operato*, literally, "from the work that is worked."

By the sixth century, the eucharistic liturgies of the various regions were fixed in their basic shape, although elaborations continued to be added for centuries. In the East, the Divine Liturgy of Saint Basil the Great[35] and the

---

[34]Scott Bullard helpfully locates de Lubac's great insight historically and theologically in Scott W. Bullard, *Re-membering the Body: the Lord's Supper and Ecclesial Unity in the Free Church Traditions* (Eugene, OR: Cascade, 2013), 66-84.

[35]"The Byzantine Liturgy of St. Basil," in Jasper and Cuming, *Prayers of the Eucharist*, 114-24.

Divine Liturgy of St. John Chrysostom[36] were expanded and gradually became the normative Eastern Orthodox services. A parallel path was followed by the Eastern Oriental churches on a nation-by-nation basis. In the West, there was interplay between the status of the Liturgy of Rome and those of other leading bishoprics, like Milan and Toledo, until the Roman rite became the sole norm at the time of the Reformation.

---

[36]"The Liturgy of St. John Chrysostom," in Jasper and Cuming, *Prayers of the Eucharist*, 129-34.

7

THE MEAL JESUS GAVE US

MIDDLE AGES AND REFORMATION

MIDDLE AGES

Discord at the Lord's table. By the end of the Carolingian era in the ninth century, liturgical practice in the West had been standardized.[1] The Roman rite was the first among equals. Other rites, like the Milanese, had a similar structure with some distinctive ceremonial and architecture. For example, in the Milanese rite, the baptism of adults was followed by footwashing. All the official eucharistic rites had become more complex, with the addition of private and silent prayers by the priest and acts of devotion in the vernacular by the congregation at various points in the service. It had also become less communal, with the parts originally given to the congregation taken over by the priest's assistants.[2] Rood screens were built between the nave and the sanctuary to keep lay people away from the altar and the holy objects arrayed around it. As the understanding of the Eucharist became more materialistic, the notion arose that the spilling of even a drop of the wine would be an act

---

[1] I have found the following texts especially helpful for understanding the sacramental theology of the medieval period: David Aers, *Sanctifying Signs: Making Christian Tradition in Late Medieval England* (Notre Dame, IN: University of Notre Dame Press, 2004), esp. chaps. 1 and 3, debate on the Eucharist prefiguring the Reformation; David Broughton Knox, *The Lord's Supper from Wycliffe to Cranmer* (Exeter, UK: Paternoster, 1983), the stages in reconceptualizing the Lord's Supper; Ian Christopher Levy, Gary Macy, and Kristen Van Ausdall, eds. *A Companion to the Eucharist in the Middle Ages* (Boston: Brill, 2011), comprehensive, based on the latest scholarship; Gary Macy, *The Banquet's Wisdom: A Short History of the Theologies of the Lord's Supper*, 2nd ed. (Ashland City, TN: OSL, 2005), esp. chaps. 4 and 5, a succinct overview; and Godefridus J. C. Snoek, "The Process of Independence of the Eucharist," in *Primary Readings on the Eucharist*, ed. Thomas J. Fisch (Collegeville, MN: Liturgical Press, 2004), 37-76, origins and consequences of the medieval shifts in the Eucharist.

[2] The exception to this development was monastic worship, in which the sisters and brothers had an active part in the Mass and the liturgy of the hours.

of sacrilege. Therefore, the cup was withheld from the laity. In addition, the dread of unworthy Communion inhibited people from taking even the bread of Communion more than once a year. To compensate for this development, the practice arose of displaying the bread and cup to the congregation for adoration. For centuries this adoration remained the normal form of the people's participation in the Mass.

If the central act of worship for lay people was veneration, the central assumption of worship was that the consecration of bread and wine by the priest made Christ miraculously present in the host and chalice. Ironically, worshipers received the host's sacramental grace not by eating it but by gazing on it, especially immediately after the words of institution were spoken. In keeping with this visual reception of Communion, architecture and art focused increasingly on eucharistic images as an expression of teaching as well as an inspiration for devotion.[3]

In the midst of these developments, about 840, King Charles the Bald requested a treatise on the Eucharist from the monks in the monastery of Corbie in France. Paschasius Radbertus was the first one called to this task.[4] Astonishingly, this is the first formal treatment of the Lord's Supper as a subject in its own right in the Western church. What were Radbertus's concerns? For one, he describes the Eucharist as a mystery that can be received only by faith. For another, he is more blunt than earlier treatments of the subject in equating the flesh and blood believers are offered in Communion with the body that was born of Mary.[5] This partaking happens through the Spirit. When God's flesh dwells in us, we are transformed into Him.[6] The flesh of Christ is prefigured in Old Testament meals; in the incarnation and its perpetuation in the Eucharist this flesh is literally consumed. And yet it can only be received spiritually.[7] So it is more than a physical eating. In the end, the majority reading of Radbertus is that he identifies the loaf and cup with the body and blood of the earthly Jesus. It is a case of mutual reinforcement. Equating the historical and sacramental

[3]See Elizabeth Saxon, "Carolingian, Ottonian and Romanesque Art and the Eucharist," in Levy, Macy, and Van Ausdall, *Companion to the Eucharist*, 251-326, esp. 258-93.
[4]Paschasius Radbertus, "The Lord's Body and Blood," in *Early Medieval Theology*, ed. George E. McCracken, Library of Christian Classics 9 (Philadelphia: Westminster, 1957), 94-107.
[5]Radbertus, "Lord's Body and Blood," 94.
[6]Radbertus, "Lord's Body and Blood," 96.
[7]Radbertus, "Lord's Body and Blood," 106.

Christ was already a habit of the medieval Christian mind. Radbertus's treatise gave the needed push for theological language to make this understanding more explicit and less guarded than it had heretofore been.

Debate ensued. The king requested another monk at Corbie, Ratramnus, to write a treatise on the Holy Supper.[8] His formulation is based on a separation of the modes of Christ's presence. Outwardly, we receive wine, "the *sacrament* of Christ's blood."[9] Inwardly, we receive Christ's blood. This wording is significant; it was commonplace by this time to speak of receiving the body and blood of Christ. Ratramnus asserts that we receive the sacrament, which mediates the body and blood of Christ, but the body and blood are not in the elements. It fits with a symbolic realism understanding: the wine is the means by which we receive the blood of Christ, but the two are not the same. Elsewhere in this document, Ratramnus talks about "physical appearances . . . as mysteries of Christ's body and blood."[10] The flesh that Jesus offers believers in John 6 is not that flesh that hung on the cross: it is the "*sacrament* of his flesh,"[11] "the body of the divine Spirit,"[12] "one thing in appearance and another thing in meaning."[13] In conclusion, Ratramnus makes two points. One, he cites Paul and Augustine on the subject of the church as the body of Christ. Two, he reminds his readers that the whole eucharistic action is what constitutes a memorial of the Lord's passion, not simply the elements of bread and wine.

In the end, Catholic tradition sided with Radbertus. Centuries later Protestant reformers sided with Ratramnus. In the imperial church after Charlemagne everyone had been made a Christian by baptism. Pastors and spiritual writers sought to draw people into faith as trust in Christ. But such existential faith and love could not be counted on in the communicants. Most problematic of all was the continuation of coerced baptisms of conquered peoples if they could not be won over by preaching.[14] To put the matter into

---

[8]Ratramnus of Corbie, "Christ's Body and Blood," in McCracken, *Early Medieval Theology*, 118-47.
[9]Ratramnus, "Christ's Body and Blood," 121.
[10]Ratramnus, "Christ's Body and Blood," 123.
[11]Ratramnus, "Christ's Body and Blood," 134, emphasis added.
[12]Ratramnus, "Christ's Body and Blood," 135.
[13]Ratramnus, "Christ's Body and Blood," 137. The modern term *transignification* comes to mind.
[14]Owen M. Phelan, *The Formation of Christian Europe: The Carolingians, Baptism, and the Imperium Christianum* (Oxford: Oxford University Press, 2014), 46, 53-54, 100-107, 144.

its simplest terms, theologians increasingly emphasized the objective nature of sacraments and the role of the presiding priest in bringing about what the sign signified. We remember from the previous chapter that the term *ex opere operato* (lit., from the work that is worked) was coined to express that. The instrumental (immediate rather than ultimate) cause of this transformation was the priest. He had the power of "consecration" to change the bread and wine into the body and blood of Christ. This power was the much-talked-about "miracle of the Mass." Unless communicants placed a severe moral impediment in the way, they would receive the saving grace of the body and blood of Christ. The effectiveness of this gift in them, however, depended on the extent of their faith. For this the term *ex opere operantis* was coined. It means "in virtue of the agent." In other words, there needs to be a good disposition on the part of the recipient for the sacrament to be fruitful. It was often placed side by side with *ex opera operato* to keep that claim from being misinterpreted as mechanical or automatic.

Throughout this evolution of thought, the meaning of "body of Christ" fell so heavily on what happened to the elements that the church lost sight of what happened to the congregation receiving them. The focus on the elements in and of themselves led to thinking about Christ's presence in terms of location, quantity, and dimensionality—terms we apply to physical matter.[15]

Two centuries later there was a major irruption of discourse on the Eucharist. One underlying reason for this was that the once-fluid movement between literal and metaphorical, material and spiritual, had hardened. Berengar of Tours, a monk and logician, questioned the increasingly dominant role Radbertus' thinking played in eucharistic thought and piety. Berengar took issue with the dominant assumption in theology and piety that flowed from this hardening of categories, that the sacramental body and the historical body of Christ were identical. Berengar relied on Augustine and Ratramnus in making his case but added to their thought. If, he argued, the sacramental body and the historical body of Christ are one, then the sacrament is dissolved. To put it into other words, then there is no longer bread and wine but only

---

[15]Two of the most influential leaders of the twentieth century liturgical movement, Yngve Brilioth (Lutheran) and Gregory Dix (Anglican), bemoan this development. Yngve Brilioth, *Eucharistic Faith & Practice: Evangelical & Catholic*, trans. A. G. Hebert (London: SPCK, 1934), 287; and Dix, *Shape of the Liturgy*, 630.

the physical body and blood. Against that interpretation, Berengar argued that we receive Christ truly, but not physically, through the consecrated elements. It is not our tongue but our mind that receives Christ, not our senses but the eye of faith.[16]

The abbot of the monastery in Bec (France), Lanfranc, responded to Berengar on the basis of Radbertus's arguments. But Lanfranc, as a representative of the dominant trend, qualified his mentor's argument by asserting a physical but not sensual (by means of the senses) partaking of Christ. Yet in the end Lanfranc and those like him forced Berengar to recant in a confession that bread and wine after the consecration "are truly, physically, and not merely sacramentally, touched and broken by the hands of the priests and crushed by the teeth of the faithful."[17]

Paths to the renewal of eucharistic spirituality and doctrine. The church spent the next century and a half retreating from the formulation forced on Berengar and other defenders of symbolic realism in the pursuit of a more profound confession of the real presence. (The church in the East was spared some of these tragic debates. It had a strong belief in the change of the elements, more like Ambrose than Augustine, but insisted that how this reality happened remained a mystery.) The renewal of monasticism in the eleventh century in the West produced a prolific, spiritual literature aimed at fostering personal piety, including the devout reception of Communion. Among the best known were Bernard of Clairvaux, Hildegard of Bingen, Julian of Norwich, Francis of Assisi, and Thomas à Kempis.

Similar reform movements, like the twelfth-century Waldensians[18] and the thirteenth-century Hussites,[19] went so far as to reformulate aspects of the doctrine of the Lord's Supper and were condemned for it. In the fourteenth century the highly esteemed English pastor and theologian John Wycliffe

---

[16]See Stephan Winter, *Eucharistische Gegenwart: liturgische Redehandlung im Spiegel mittelalterlicher und analytischer Sprachtheorie* (Regensburg: Pustet, 2002), 289. See pp. 222-319 for the unfolding of his argument. Winter, a Catholic theologian, depicts Berengar as one of the major dissenting figures in the history of Catholic eucharistic thought but one who made his case from within the received tradition.

[17]Owen F. Cummings, *Eucharistic Soundings* (Dublin: Veritas, 1999), 34.

[18]Malcolm Lambert, *Medieval Heresy: Popular Movements from the Gregorian Reform to the Reformation*, 2nd ed. (Malden, MA: Blackwell, 1992), 62-87, esp. 63-65. Lambert suggests the Waldensians were the precursors to the Franciscans.

[19]Lambert, *Medieval Heresy*, 302-11.

championed views similar to Berengar's. Wycliffe, in particular, was a careful and subtle thinker but refused to be bound by scholastic categories. He was clear that he believed in the true presence of Christ in the sacrament,

> which included neither the presence of the Galilean and risen body of Jesus nor the annihilation of bread and wine. Attention was shifted from the metaphysics of consecration and from the spectatorial focus of the Mass, with the rewards of attendance, to the faithful's reception of Christ, a shift that transformed the role of priests.[20]

The church's condemnation had its reasons. It believed that the dissenters' focus on the spiritual reception of Christ by means of bread and wine endangered the objective nature and power of the sacrament in a type of church in which the faith of the communicant could not always be called upon. The implication of Wycliffe's emphasis on the faithful reception of Christ in the Supper was that the congregation and each believer, along with the priest, were all agents of the dynamic of Christ's presence. This interpretation went squarely against the heightened role of the priest in the Gregorian reforms of the twelfth century. These reforms held to a more rigorous understanding of priesthood and the unique power of a priest to be the instrument of the Holy Spirit in "confecting" the presence of Christ.

Miri Rubin makes the case that the focus of the eleventh and twelfth centuries in Europe was not only on the nature of the Lord's Supper but on its increasing symbolic significance for the Christian social and political order: "A fragile, white, wheaten little disc" was given "the status of mediator between Christians and the supernatural. The Eucharist emerged as a unifying symbol of a complex world . . . a symbol which bound the essential narratives of incarnation, crucifixion, and the legacy of redemption."[21]

It makes for fascinating sleuthing to trace the evolution of language in the High Middle Ages to describe what is involved in the change that happens at the consecration of the elements in the Mass. There is the case of an anonymous mid-twelfth-century treatise in which the author seems to be trying out a new term, *transubstantiate*, to see if it better describes what the

---

[20] Aers, *Sanctifying Signs*, 32.
[21] Miri Rubin, *Corpus Christi: The Eucharist in Late Medieval Culture* (Cambridge: Cambridge University Press, 1991), 348.

church believes.[22] A few years later in the Paris School, Robert Mullen writes as if he is coining the term *transubstantiation* to describe what happens to the elements.[23] The fact that two philosophers, unknown to each other, arrive at the same concept suggests that there is a shared reasoning at work. *Transubstantiation* is not yet a technical, formal term but an expressive and experimental one.

In 1215 the Fourth Lateran Council declared transubstantiation to be the teaching of the Catholic Church. Its intention was to safeguard the belief that the substance of Christ's body and blood is received in Communion but not in a spatial or quantifiable way. A whole generation of Catholic theologians grappled philosophically with the meaning of this teaching.[24] Then the brilliant Thomas Aquinas formulated a theology of the Eucharist that addressed the issue at stake with particular rigor, ruling out materialism without giving up a belief in the presence of the "substance" of the body and blood of Christ.

Aquinas explains it this way:

> The body of Christ is in this sacrament as if it were just substance. But substance as such cannot be seen by the bodily eye, nor is it the object of any sense, nor can it be imagined; it is only open to the intellect, the object of which is the essence of things, as Aristotle says. Hence, properly speaking, the body of Christ according to the mode of existence which it has in this sacrament, can be reached neither by sense nor by the imagination; it is open only to the intellect, which may be called a spiritual eye.[25]

By this time, discord over the Supper was argued much more on philosophical than biblical grounds. At the time of the Reformation, that philosophical frame of reference was largely discarded by Protestants. Thus, it has not been easy for Protestants (or Eastern Orthodox) to grasp Aquinas's and similar attempts to describe how the body and blood of Christ could be present where the bread and wine had once been without having a location.

---

[22]Joseph Goering, "The Invention of Transubstantiation," *Traditio* 46 (1991): 148-50.

[23]Goering, "Invention of Transubstantiation," 155-58.

[24]For an insightful summary of this process, see Gary Macy, "Theology of the Eucharist in the High Middle Ages," in Levy, Macy, and Van Ausdall, *Eucharist in the Middle Ages*, 374-87.

[25]Thomas Aquinas, *Summa Theologiae* (New York: McGraw-Hill, 1963), 38:117, as quoted in Macy, *Banquet's Wisdom*, 135.

At stake for the medieval church was the "objective" presence of Christ as understood by the magisterium, not by individual theologians. To put the matter into short form, it saw the place of faith and experience in the Ratramnus lineage of eucharistic theology as subjectivism, that is, making the presence of Christ dependent on faith. The church accused people who thought like Ratramnus of undermining the very nature of a sacrament that, at the hands of a priest, brings about that which it signifies independent of the communicants' faith. Even though it was also claimed that the gift of Christ is effective only when received in faith, it was not part of the dynamic that actually made a sacrament. Popular piety seems not to have been greatly affected by either official or dissenting attempts at reform. The focus there was the physical miracle of bread and wine becoming body and blood.[26] Ironically, this herculean attempt to preserve and heighten the objective reality of the sacrament encouraged the subjective appropriation of Christ by gazing at him during and after mass rather than receiving him in the host.[27]

Because of the elaborate ceremonial and its focus on the act of consecration, there was less and less room in the Mass for a sermon. A separate preaching service called *Prone* emerged north of the Alps and Pyrenees to address this need. It was most widely practiced in the South German realm. It consisted of congregational singing, the reading of a lectionary text, a bidding prayer, and a sermon.[28] In some settings it became the liturgy preceding the Mass. In some Reformed and Anabaptist forms of Reformation, a slightly elaborated form of Prone (e.g., adding a pastoral prayer) with Communion on designated Sundays, became the weekly form of worship.

---

[26]For fascinating micro examinations of eucharistic piety in the late Middle Ages see Gabriella Erdélyi, "The Consumption of the Sacred: Popular Piety in a Late Medieval Hungarian Town," *Journal of Ecclesiastical History* 63, no. 1 (2012): 31-60, esp. 48-54; and Eamon Duffy, *The Stripping of the Altars: Traditional Religion in England 1400–1580*, 2nd ed. (New Haven, CT: Yale University Press, 2005), 91-130.

[27]Thomas Aquinas's formulation only gradually became Catholic orthodoxy. At the Council of Trent (1546) a Thomistic understanding of transubstantiation became official teaching. The council did not condemn doctrines of the real presence that did not contradict transubstantiation. In other words, it let them stand.

[28] Bradshaw, *Westminster Dictionary,* 59-60.

REFORMATION

Common protest, diverse alternatives. In the course of the fifteenth century,
reformers concluded that the church's problem extended beyond the need for
reform of eucharistic doctrine and piety. The nature of salvation and the church's
role in it were at stake. In the early sixteenth century the river of God burst its
banks and flowed in many directions. The Protestant Reformation had begun.
It started with acts that defied papal authority, but initially these acts were not
a repudiation of the Catholic Church. That came about gradually. At first, its
concern was to reground preaching, piety, and the moral life in keeping with
the teaching of Scripture and the early church. The most radical and rebellious
impulse toward reform and schism was a rejection of the sacerdotal system, the
church as the hierarchical institution of salvation. One of the crucial instances
under scrutiny was the power of the priesthood to act in the person of Christ
in forgiving sins and making Christ present in the Eucharist.

What occurred was the most profound and radical break in the continuity
of the Western church. Some scholars go so far as to say that this break was
nothing less than the rejection of Christendom's symbolic universe. Bernard
Cooke describes this shift as "a distancing of God." In his view this already
begins in late medieval thought and intensifies in the Reformation.[29] Lee
Palmer Wandel sees this distancing as happening in the Reformation. For
example, it rejects the identification of the Last Supper and the Mass. For
Catholics, the priest acts "in the person of Christ," and consecrated bread and
wine are identical with the body and blood of Christ at the Last Supper. Protestantism breaks this unity.[30] Researchers make their case on the basis of
popular and scholarly evidence. For example, on the popular level there were
Anabaptists who denounced Catholic sacramental claims as idolatrous.[31] On
a scholarly level there were Lutheran and Reformed theologians who decried
Catholic claims for the miraculous and the magical.[32] These developments

---

[29]Bernard Cooke, *The Distancing of God: The Ambiguity of Symbol in History and Theology* (Minneapolis:
Fortress, 1990), 178-208.

[30]Lee Palmer Wandel, "Introduction," in *A Companion to the Eucharist in the Reformation*, ed. Lee
Palmer Wandel, Brill's Companions to the Christian Tradition 46 (Boston: Brill, 2014), 9.

[31]Kat Hill, *Baptism, Brotherhood and Belief in Reformation Germany: Anabaptism and Lutheranism,
1525–1585* (Oxford: Oxford University Press, 2015), 140-41, 152-53.

[32]Carlos Eire, "Redefining the Sacred and the Supernatural: How the Protestant Reformation Really
Did Disenchant the World," in *Protestantism After 500 Years*, ed. Thomas Albert Howard and Mark
A. Noll (Oxford: Oxford University Press, 2016), 78-82.

spawned a worldview that eventually opened the door to the Enlightenment's disenchantment of the material world.

Certainly, magic and superstition were targeted as contrary to the gospel. Even the Council of Trent agreed with that concern. I am struck not only by the raw Catholic-Protestant division but also by the opposite reality, by the amount of tradition—both that of the dominant church and of dissenter movements—that was retained, consciously and unconsciously. In the popular imagination, the Reformation overthrew everything that had gone before it. In reality, the Reformation consisted as much in reform as in rejection. For instance, in Magisterial Protestantism, and even in several strands of Anabaptism, the teaching and practices of the patristic era were considered authoritative to the extent that they were in conformity with Scripture.

This double dynamic of rejection and reform was true in particular of the Eucharist. Gone was the priestly consecration; gone the adoration of the host. In its place was a vernacular liturgy of the Breaking of Bread modeled on how the Reformers interpreted the New Testament records, in which the whole congregation received the bread and wine presided over by a minister, not a priest. Yet some liturgical elements were widely retained and reformed without lasting controversy, the most important of which were the words of institution, which Protestants agreed were indispensable to a faithful Supper. On the pastoral level, the practices of reconciliation with one's neighbor and confession of sin before Communion were altered in form but retained in principle.

Each type of Protestantism took a different approach to tradition. For Reformed, Anglicans, and Anabaptists, attention was given not only to the dominant tradition but to the dissident one. For example, they acknowledged their indebtedness to Ratramnus and Berengar. All the movements were radical in some ways and conservative in others. Luther, for example, was most radical in his rejection of medieval spirituality by means of his understanding of justification by grace through faith. But in his theology of Communion he was at the conservative end of the early modern spectrum.

The social context of the Reformation included the more amorphous movement called the Renaissance. It contributed a novel status for the individual in the community, a rejection of the elaborate philosophical system known as scholasticism, and a passion to return to and translate the ancient sources, most importantly the Bible. This involved the discovery and study of liturgical texts from the patristic and early medieval eras in their simplicity and diversity. These discoveries led to the conclusion that the current forms of the Mass, in all their dogmatic and ritual complexity, were a departure not only from the New Testament but also from early tradition. All this ferment was broadly and quickly disseminated by the marvel of the printing press.

Protestant shifts. The return to the sources shaped every aspect of the Eucharist. To begin with, the Reformers wanted the Breaking of Bread to become a meal again. With that in mind, almost all of them called it the Lord's Supper rather than the Mass or Eucharist. Accompanying this shift was a radical development in ecclesiology: the priesthood was not the sole privilege of clergy but included all believers: they were also to be actors in the drama of the Breaking of Bread. They—the people—were, as Augustine and Chrysostom had taught, the body of Christ. This was expressed liturgically by bringing the Table from its hierarchical confinement in the sanctuary to the people so they could gather around it—and in some cases even sit around it. The orders of ministry (deacon, presbyter, bishop) were widely retained but made into a subset of the general priesthood of Christians.

The rejection of the sacerdotal priesthood opened the way to a rereading of New Testament images of the atonement and its enactment in the Holy Supper. A further, and related, rejection was that the Eucharist is a repetition of Christ's self-offering. At the heart of this reading of Scripture was the Supper as the memorial of the Lord's death and not its repetition. Christ's sacrifice had been "once for all" (Heb 9:26; 10:2); it need not and could not be repeated. Among some Reformers, room was made for the church to join Christ in offering ourselves with him to the Father.[33] This was based on the notion that that the Son's self-offering continues after his ascension. As those redeemed by his sacrifice on the cross, we join in Christ's ongoing self-offering and present our bodies as a living sacrifice (Rom 12:1).

Lee Palmer Wandel asserts that the Protestant return to the Supper's origin was at the same time the loss of a "sacramental proximity." The Protestant shift involved the severing of the human celebrant from divine agency. The

---

[33]Christopher Hancock, "Christ's Priesthood and Eucharistic Sacrifice," in *Essays on Eucharistic Sacrifice in the Early Church*, ed. Colin Buchanan (Bramcote, UK: Grove, 1984), 15-21.

presider no longer stood in Christ's place to make his body and blood present. Now no human actor, no set of mimetic acts, could represent Christ or replicate the Last Supper.[34]

Beyond the fundamental agreements among Protestant Reformers sketched out above, there were increasing disagreements as the implications of eucharistic reform became evident. The territorial churches and the Anabaptists had different understandings of the church but a common problem. By their act of rebellion against Rome, none of them retained the comprehensive dogmatic structure and process of decision-making vouched for by an unbroken succession, the papacy, and universal and regional councils of the church. Protestants had no universal and binding authority to appeal to. Thus, there was no way of arriving at a common structure of belief (what must be said, what cannot be said) about the Lord's Supper.[35] The Magisterial churches did have formal regional synods and the Anabaptists had informal ones, but none of them could claim universality.[36] And political rulers sponsored disputations that found modest levels of agreement. In spite of that, by the late 1520s the sacrament of the church's unity had become the mark of its disunity.

It remains baffling why the contending Reformation parties were unable to allow for a limited diversity in theologies of the Eucharist based on a shared faith, as is evident in the patristic and early medieval eras. The most famous attempt to accommodate two different views was the Marburg Colloquy in 1529 between Luther and Zwingli. The event was recorded verbatim by scribes. Luther argued that "this is my body" is a literal claim while Zwingli insisted that one signifies the other. Luther insisted that Christ is present in the Supper in both his natures whereas Zwingli argued that Christ is present in his divinity alone. Luther concluded that unless Zwingli agreed not only that Christ is spiritually present but also literally, they are not of the same faith.[37]

---

[34]Wandel, "Introduction," 9.

[35]Gerald Schlabach has written an insightful book-length treatment of this problem. Gerald W. Schlabach, *Unlearning Protestantism: Sustaining Christian Community in an Unstable Age* (Grand Rapids: Brazos, 2010).

[36]Strictly speaking, the Catholic Church couldn't claim a literal universality but only a universality of those who accept the pope's final authority. Among the Eastern Orthodox and Oriental churches, there was also no literal universality but only a universality of those who accept the final authority of bishops gathered in a council.

[37]Martin Luther, *Luther's Works,* vol. 38, *Word and Sacrament IV,* ed. Martin Lehmann (Philadelphia: Fortress, 1980), 3-89, esp. 56-59.

Two factors seem relevant to the matter. One, while Catholic theology of the Eucharist before the Reformation had diverse schools of thought, they were developed within a binding set of dogmatic boundaries. Two, universal ecclesial authority with its structures and processes was not possible in Protestantism. The alliance of territorial churches with territorial governments meant that theology was conflated with politics. Mutual churchly associations—and views of the Lord's Supper—were mostly limited to allies of the ruling prince.

Out of the theological and political ferment of the age, a broad spread of convictions concerning the Holy Supper arose. Martin Luther of Saxony, whose views soon held sway in many German territories, stood at one end of the eucharistic spectrum. He retained the belief that the body and blood of Christ are truly present. The Formula of Concord of 1577 summarized Luther's claim with the words "in, with, and under" the elements.[38] At the same time he separated this formulation from philosophical interpretations, like transubstantiation.[39] In emphasizing the weekly Communion of the whole congregation as well as a full sermon, he gave equal prominence to word and sacrament. In keeping with his core conviction of God's absolute initiative in salvation, Luther emphasized God as the sole actor in the Supper. This ruled out the medieval notion of the Eucharist as a sacrifice that the church offers to God. Rather, it is God's promise of forgiveness.[40] Luther remained ambivalent concerning the role of the believer's faith in Communion. He became increasingly emphatic in debates with other Reformers about the literal meaning of "this is my body."[41] He reinforced his understanding of Christ's presence with a Christology in which Christ's two natures were so closely tied together that Christ was present in the sacrament in his humanity as well as his divinity.

Almost at the other end of the spectrum stood Ulrich Zwingli of Zurich. Flowing from his emphasis on spiritual Communion, he concluded that the bread and wine were symbols in the modern sense of the word in which the

---

[38]Volker Leppin, "Martin Luther," in Wandel, *Companion to the Eucharist in the Reformation*, 55.

[39]Martin Luther, "A Prelude on the Babylonian Captivity of the Church," in *Three Treatises*, intro. and trans. Charles M. Jacobs, A. T. W. Steinhaeuser, and W. A. Lambert (Philadelphia: Muhlenberg, 1947), 137, 142.

[40]Luther, "Prelude on the Babylonian Captivity," 136-53.

[41]Leppin, "Martin Luther," 48-51.

symbol referred to something completely outside of itself. He invoked Berengar and the dissident medieval eucharistic tradition but went beyond it in separating the sign and the thing signified.[42] Parallel to the sharing of bread and wine was an inward feeding on Christ. In Zwingli's view, nothing happened to the elements, but the people were remade into the body of Christ.[43] Zwingli's most radical conclusion concerned the sentence "this is my body." Borrowing from late medieval spiritualists whose writings had been taken up by some Reformed thinkers, he interpreted the words figuratively. His Christology, in which the two natures of Christ were kept distinct meant that Christ's human nature was now confined to heaven. Zwingli's innovative way of sharing the loaf and cup gave concrete expression to the priesthood of believers. The minister gave the elements to the communicants, who passed them among themselves. This practice was taken over by Swiss Anabaptism.

Martin Bucer of Strasbourg, already noted as the most irenic figure in the discord over the Lord's Supper, stood between Zwingli and Luther. His via media was based "on a sharp distinction between the spiritual and material dimensions of the sacrament."[44] He sought an alternative to the dangers, as he saw them, of Luther's tendency toward materialism and Zwingli's tendency toward spiritualism. He held that Christ was present in the Breaking of Bread in "the same body given for us on the cross" but in a different mode.[45] Later Protestantism remained torn between the conciliatory terms of debate set forth by Bucer and the exclusive positions taken by others.

John Calvin, best known for his ministry in Geneva, left the defining imprint on French-speaking Protestantism. He gave prominence to the minister's role in doing what Christ did, that is, offer bread and wine. "God accomplishes *within* what the minister represents and attests by *outward* actions."[46] Distinctive to Calvin's eucharistic theology is the central role of

---

[42]Ulrich Zwingli, "On the Lord's Supper," in *Zwingli and Bullinger*, ed. G. W. Bromiley, Library of Christian Classics 24 (Philadelphia: Westminster, 1953), 188-97.

[43]This position has been variously interpreted. See Carrie Euler, "Huldrych Zwingli and Heinrich Bullinger," in Wandel, *Companion to the Eucharist in the Reformation*, 60-63.

[44]Nicholas Thompson, "Martin Bucer," in Wandel, *Companion to the Eucharist in the Reformation*, 75.

[45]Thompson, "Martin Bucer," 81.

[46]Nicholas Wolterstorff, "John Calvin," in Wandel, *Companion to the Eucharist in the Reformation*, 99, also 109, emphases added.

the Holy Spirit, the bond, the power, and the means of Christ's presence.[47]
The Holy Spirit is the agent of our union with Christ in his humanity as well
as his divinity in a particular way: in the Supper Christ descends to us so that
we can rise to heaven.

> But if we are lifted up to heaven with our eyes and minds, to seek Christ there
> in the glory of his Kingdom, as the symbols invite us to him in his wholeness,
> so under the symbol of bread we shall be fed by his body, under the symbol of
> wine we shall separately drink his blood, to enjoy him at last in his wholeness.
> For though he has taken his flesh away from us, and in the body has ascended
> into heaven, yet he sits at the right hand of the Father – that is, he reigns in the
> Father's power and majesty and glory. This Kingdom is neither bounded by
> location in space nor circumscribed by any limits.[48]

This ascent makes it unmistakable that Christ's presence is not mediated
by a priest or the elements but is the unmediated work of the Spirit.[49] Three
eucharistic motifs are typical of Calvin's thought. One is our "participation"
in the sacramental body of Christ (based on the older understanding of
symbol) through which we enter a relationship with him. Another of Calvin's
motifs, that of our souls feeding on the flesh of Christ, has its origin in Johannine mysticism. And, finally, the preached word and the offered sacrament
are parallel manifestations of Christ.

Anglican theologizing on the Supper is less indebted to one theologian
than is the case with Magisterial Reform movements on the Continent. The
outstanding figure, nevertheless, is Thomas Cranmer, not only for his theology but even more for his creation of the *Book of Common Prayer*. Because
the Reformation in England took form later than on the Continent, Cranmer
and his colleagues, like Nicholas Ridley, were influenced briefly by Luther
and more enduringly by Bucer and Zwingli. Cranmer retained much of the
liturgical structure of the medieval mass but drastically reinterpreted it. For
example, in the final version of his reform in 1552, the prayer for the Holy
Spirit is that it might come upon the people, not the elements. A strong
emphasis on the remembrance of Christ's sacrifice was combined with the

---

[47]John Calvin, *Institutes of the Christian Religion*, ed. John T. McNeill, trans. Ford Lewis Battles,
2.4.17 (Philadelphia: Westminster, 1960), 1405-7, 1416-21.

[48]Calvin, *Institutes*, 2.4.17, 1381.

[49]Calvin, *Institutes*, 2.4.17, 1370, 1393.

belief that as communicants received the bread and wine physically, they received the body and blood spiritually.[50]

One of the novelties of sixteenth-century Protestant eucharistic thought was a movement toward a modern understanding of the concept of the symbolic. As I have already noted, in this understanding a symbol is an external sign unrelated to the internal reality to which it points. What is meant by the term *sacrament* moves in the direction of metaphor. Zwingli, and with him some Anabaptists, came closest to this modern understanding. In his treatise "On the Lord's Supper" Zwingli is adamant that "this is my body" can only be figurative,[51] that feeding on Christ is an act of believing not one of sacramentally receiving Christ.[52] He rejects a mediating position that simply claims "partaking of the body of Christ takes place invisibly and imperceptibly."[53] When believers eat and drink together, "you signify thereby that you are one body and one bread, namely, the body which is the church of Christ."[54]

Some Anabaptists retained a realist reading of New Testament eucharistic texts and with Zwingli the germ of a mystical Communion. Other Anabaptists (notably Marpeck, as well as Cranmer, Bucer, and Calvin) remained closer to the classical understanding influenced by Augustine, with the Ratramnus tradition in the background. To illustrate that symbolic realism is quite different from mere symbolism, one can turn to many prayers of that age, like the prayer of preparation for Communion in the Anglican *Book of Common Prayer*.

We do not presume to come to this, thy table, O merciful Lord,

Trusting in our own righteousness,

But in thy manifold and great mercies.

We are not worthy

So much as to gather up the crumbs under thy table.

But thou art the same Lord,

Whose property is always to have mercy:

Grant us therefore, gracious Lord,

So to eat the flesh of thy dear Son Jesus Christ,

---

[50]James F. Turrell, "Anglican Theologies of the Eucharist," in Wandel, *Companion to the Eucharist in the Reformation*, 148.

[51]Zwingli, "On the Lord's Supper," in Bromiley, *Zwingli and Bullinger*, 191.

[52]Zwingli, "On the Lord's Supper," 198-205.

[53]Zwingli, "On the Lord's Supper," 219.

[54]Zwingli, "On the Lord's Supper," 237.

And to drink his blood,

That our sinful bodies may be made clean by his body,

And our souls washed through his most precious blood, and

That we may evermore dwell in him,

And he in us. Amen.[55]

To complete this sketch of innovation in the theology, piety, and practice of Holy Communion in the sixteenth century, the Council of Trent must be mentioned. Working from 1545 to 1563, it was the embodiment of Roman Catholic reform. The formal eucharistic theology (distinct from popular practice against which Protestant Reformers protested) was a synthesis of the work of Gabriel Biel and John Dun Scotus, two of the defining Catholic theologians of the fifteenth century.[56] Their thought, and that of their disciples, expressed the following concerning the Eucharist. One, the historical body of Christ is made present on the altar. Two, their thinking has characteristics of both symbolic realism and metabolic realism. Three, Christ's sacrifice on the cross is repeated in our imitation of him, not in a historical repetition.[57] Regarding pastoral practice, the council reformed the liturgy and devotional practices of the Mass. For example, the council combated superstition and forbad priests to take payment for the celebration of the Eucharist.

Concerning the disunity among Catholics and with Protestants concerning the sufficiency of Christ's "once for all" (Rom 6:10; Heb 7:27) sacrifice on the cross, Robert Daly, a Catholic theologian, points out the care with which these explosive questions were dealt with by Trent. He comes to the conclusion that Trent did not attempt to resolve the sacramental relationship between the historical sacrifice of Christ and its subsequent repetition in the Mass.[58] For Protestants, this unresolved question remained an open wound until Vatican II, when the notion of re-presentation, Christ's sole and sufficient self-offering made sacramentally present and active, yielded widespread ecumenical affirmation. Although the old uncomprehending antagonism

---

[55]*Book of Common Prayer* (Toronto: Anglican Book Centre, 1962), 83-84.

[56]Robert J. Daly, "The Council of Trent," in Wandel, *Companion to the Eucharist in the Reformation*, 161.

[57]Heiko A. Oberman, *The Harvest of Medieval Theology: Gabriel Biel and Late Medieval Nominalism* (Durham, NC: Labyrinth, 1983), 271-80.

[58]Robert J. Daly, "The Council of Trent," in Wandel, *Companion to the Eucharist in the Reformation*, 152-68.

concerning transubstantiation has been widely replaced with more under-standing by Protestants today, the fact that transubstantiation was made into a dogma at Trent still implies for Catholic doctrine that all other theologies of the Lord's Supper fall short of orthodoxy.

Transubstantiation was the most sophisticated attempt to describe the changing of bread into the body of Christ. It was the most audacious incar-national claim made for sacramental reality: that the natural could bear—and even become—the supernatural. George Hunsinger, a Reformed theologian, makes the astonishing assertion that Protestants must be able to make a completely parallel claim to that of transubstantiation in order to have taken the incarnation seriously. He summarizes his detailed approach: "At the level of first order discourse, the liturgical use of 'This is my body' would need to be affirmed by all without equivocation."[59] This challenge sets a very high bar for any ecumenical theology of the Supper.

Conclusions. The diversity of eucharistic thought and practice in the sixteenth century is troubling and inspiring in equal portions. The passion to confess, to know, to be transformed by the surpassing presence of Christ in the Holy Supper was profound and tenacious, from Trent's transub-stantiation to Zwingli's memorialism. All of them braided together strands of New Testament thought and early tradition. In my judgment, none of them wove all of the strands together. The tragedy of the late Middle Ages, which carried over into early modern time, was the insistence that there could be only one true theology of the Eucharist. This stands in contrast with the patristic and early medieval era. To be sure, there were borrow-ing and negotiating in the sixteenth century but little reciprocity and mutual acceptance.

---

[59]George Hunsinger, *The Eucharist and Ecumenism* (Cambridge: Cambridge University Press, 2008), 72. For his larger argument, see pp. 52-81 and 95-186. I address his call for a Protestant parallel in John D. Rempel, "Jesus' Presence in the Meal He Gave Us: A Free Church Inquiry," in *Proceedings of the North American Academy of Liturgy*, ed. Richard E. McCarron (Notre Dame, IN: North American Academy of Liturgy, 2014), 107-17. See also the symposium on Hunsinger's book in the journal *Pro Ecclesia* 19, no. 3 (2010): Will Cohen, "The Thing of It: An Orthodox Response to Hunsicker's not-so-High Sacramental Theology," 247-54; Mark McIntosh, "Christ the Word Who Makes Us: Eucharist and Creation," 255-59; Margaret O'Gara, "Reformed and Catholic: Welcom-ing George Hunsinger's Eucharistic Theology," 260-66; Risto Saarinen, "Fire, Iron and the Eucha-rist: Some Questions for George Hunsinger," 267-72; George Hunsinger, "Widening the Circle of Acceptable Diversity: a Reply to My Ecumenical Friends," 273-84.

My tentative observation is that the Reformed tradition, broadly speaking—including Anglicanism at one end of the spectrum and Anabaptism at the other end—was most able to abide secondary differences of belief and interpretation. This was the case because its focus was more on a corporate and personal participation in Christ and less on a dogmatic interpretation of that reality. Ironically, the Lutheran and Roman Catholic eucharistic theologies were as adamant as they were because they believed the other reform movements lacked a sacramentality robust enough to safeguard the objective nature of such an evangelical feeding on Christ.

This criticism raises the fundamental question as to what extent doctrinal formulations are sufficient to grasp the mystery of Christ's presence in the Supper. This was the question the Reformed tradition, broadly speaking, asked of the Catholic and Lutheran traditions. But Lutherans and Catholics would be equally justified in asking a parallel question of the Free Church offspring of the Reformed tradition, whether its alleged biblicism on the subject is in fact a modern reductionist reading of the eucharistic texts. All three of the historic streams can be accused of lapses into a kind of rationalism that is unreceptive to the paradoxical thinking the presence of mystery calls for or the moral implications of being part of the body of Christ.

This leaves us with a question: What is the role of doctrinal formulation in establishing faithful eucharistic belief and practice? None of the traditions would claim that we can fully grasp the mystery of Christ's presence in the Supper. They would say, in varying degrees, that only a certain doctrine and liturgical form of the Supper can safeguard its mystery. At what point does rational discourse suppress paradox? At what point does debate about the fine points of receiving the body of Christ suppress becoming the body of Christ? Why has so little weight been placed on what the Eucharist does to the people who receive it? Supposedly, it makes them one with Christ, their neighbor, and their enemy. If that is so, the following question (which comes in many guises) needs to be taken seriously: When German and French, Russian and British Christians—all fellow members of the body of Christ—went to war with one another in 1914, did their destruction of the body of Christ on the battlefield invalidate their doctrine and liturgy of the Eucharist?

8

THE MEAL JESUS GAVE US

ANABAPTISM, FREE CHURCHES,
AND PEACE CHURCHES

AS WE HAVE SEEN, the Reformation brought about tectonic shifts in the theology and practice of the Lord's Supper. Lutherans and Catholics were drawn to John's language (consuming Christ) as their major point of reference. Other Protestants gravitated to Paul's understanding (participating in Christ). These preferences both arose from and led to different understandings of Holy Communion. Catholics and Lutherans identified transformed bread and wine with Christ's body and blood; this ingestion was the surpassing form of encounter with Christ. To put their view into a phrase one might say that Christ is received "by means of" the objects of bread and wine. Other Protestants saw the Supper more as an action, a sharing and reception of the elements as the dynamic that mediates the encounter. To put their view into a phrase one might say that Christ is received "by an act of faith with" the bread. Those Protestants with leaner liturgies, who even then were moving toward a modern understanding of symbol, would have said that the outward element of bread signifies the inward presence of Christ. On the one hand, Catholics and Lutherans bound the presence of Christ so closely to the elements that the personal nature of the encounter remained undeveloped. On the other hand, other Protestants put the weight so strongly on union with Christ that the emphasis fell on subjective experience more than on objective reality.

There was a further division within Protestantism concerning the nature of the church, which bears directly on our focus. The Magisterial Reformers remained in continuity with the medieval church in their retention of the

Christendom model of church. We remember from the previous chapter the conceptual shift in the Middle Ages in which the patristic notion was that the church is the *sacramental* body of Christ, its visible, historical manifestation. By contrast, the Eucharist is the *mystical* body, invisible yet outwardly manifested. Catholics retained one aspect of the church as the sacramental body, that is, its hierarchical structure. Because Magisterial Protestants rejected a sacerdotal priesthood, they rejected this last aspect of a visible church. For them, the true church was invisible; its outward forms were not part of its essence. For both churches, baptism was the door into the mystical body of Christ, the invisible church.

For Anabaptists, the essence of the church was the visible congregation and networks of visible congregations as they gathered around the Lord's Table and scattered to bring the message of the kingdom. To put their thinking into our concepts, one might say Christ is the primal sacrament, the church is the extension of this sacramental reality, and specific ritual acts, like baptism and the Lord's Supper, are the extension of the body of Christ on earth.

Anabaptism arose from the conviction that the church is made up of those who make an existential confession of allegiance to Christ and his body. It came into being when Zurich radicals to the left of Zwingli defied the authorities. In carrying out celebrations of baptism and the Lord's Supper, they became a visible community. Similar irruptions took place across German- and Dutch-speaking Europe. One historian describes the liturgical outworking of this shift. The Lord's Supper in early Anabaptism was a movement from the self-communication of a priest without a congregation to the self-communication of a congregation without a priest.[1]

VISIBLE AND INVISIBLE CHURCH

The counterpoint to the establishment of mass churches was a church whose members had personally professed God's grace and heeded his call to discipleship. Anabaptism retained the Catholic teaching of the outward, visible church as the true church but radically redefined it not as the magisterium but as the priesthood of all believers. A comparison might be helpful in

---

[1] J. F. Gerhard Goeters, in *Studien zur Geschichte und Theologie der Reformation: Festschrift für Ernst Bizer*, ed. Luise Abramowski and J. F. Gerhard Goeters (Neukirchen-Vluyn: Neukirchner Verlag, 1969), 270.

clarifying the difference between ecclesiologies. Both Zwingli and several streams of Anabaptism made much of Augustine's teaching that the final goal of the Supper is the transformation of the congregation. For Zwingli, the congregation is a representation of the visible church, a mixed multitude of the elect and the damned. The body of Christ is the invisible community of the elect. By contrast, for Anabaptists it was the visible community of the baptized.[2] Thus, two different understandings of the body of Christ were enacted in the Lord's Supper.

Early in the Radical Reformation this near equation of the gathered church and the true church was challenged from within. The spiritualists (God's presence is in the soul; the created order cannot mediate this presence) made the case that the true church is invisible and that in the realm of Spirit no outward measurements apply. The outstanding spiritualist, who continued a debate with the Austrian Anabaptist Pilgram Marpeck over more than two decades, was the German Caspar Schwenckfeld. The movement toward an inward and often mystical Christianity was hastened by disgust with Rome and with all the Protestant Reformers for making the love feast of Jesus into a battlefield. The conclusion of the spiritualists was that outward signs are not necessary for truly spiritual persons: they meet Christ in their souls. In this conviction the spiritualists were cut from the same cloth as the Quakers, who came after them. Behind this conclusion about the inward nature of spiritual reality lay a unique understanding of the incarnation with monumental consequences. It was best articulated by Schwenckfeld. One part of it was his "celestial flesh" Christology: rather than taking on fallen flesh, Christ brought with him unfallen flesh from heaven.[3] Schwenckfeld argues, "Christ has his own flesh; he did not take on human lineage. Rather he, as the Word, took on his own flesh."[4] Another dimension of this view was that the incarnation as an ongoing medium of God's work in the world ended with Jesus' ascension and the coming of the Spirit.

---

[2] A nuance: since most Mennonites have believed, along with most other Christians, that only God can see into someone's soul, they have generally held that the church is made up of those who confess a living faith in Christ in baptism without claiming ultimate knowledge of who is a Christian.

[3] Pilgram Marpeck, *Pilgram Marbecks Antwort auf Kaspar Schwenckfelds Beurteilung*, trans. Johann Loserth (Vienna: Carl Fromme, 1929), 285-88.

[4] Marpeck, *Pilgram Marbecks Antwort*, 285.

The most important consequence of this position was that the fallen flesh of the creation was too marred by sin to bear and mediate spirit.[5] This meant that only the human spirit could receive the divine Spirit. This, in turn, meant that feeding on Christ, as set forth in John 6, was a mystical encounter beyond all earthly mediation. The consequence of this was an invisible church with no visible ceremonies or bonds. For almost all Anabaptist streams, this view of the spiritual was the insurmountable difference between the two emerging tendencies of the Radical Reformation. Anabaptism ultimately cast in its lot with an orthodox understanding of the incarnation, but spiritualism left an enduring mark on its mindset.

Alongside their differences, there were several similar eucharistic traits among the major first-generation Anabaptist thinkers centered on their common view of the church. The first of these was restoring the meal character of the Supper and using it as the interpretive key to the words of institution. This, in turn, led to an understanding of being the body of Christ as the primary mode of sacramental participation in Christ, the place where the incarnation is prolonged and Christ dwells. Receiving the body of Christ in Breaking of Bread itself was a secondary (and sometimes spiritualized) form of sacramental participation. Their preoccupation was with the fruit of the Supper: having partaken of Christ becomes evident in a life of love for neighbor and enemy.

Anabaptists stood with the other Reformers in their emphasis on the once-for-all death of Christ for the salvation of the world. They made a great deal out of our self-offering that is enabled by Christ's self-offering. We will see below how this comes to liturgical expression: participants in the Holy Supper make a pledge of love to lay down their lives for others just as Christ laid down his life for us. The Breaking of Bread enacts this paradigm. An emphasis on Christ's and our willingness to take evil upon ourselves and bear it away is the dominant motif. The Anabaptist teaching and practice of nonretaliation was derived as much from the atonement and its enactment in the Supper as

---

[5]Menno Simons (and some other Dutch Anabaptists) was deeply influenced by this celestial flesh Christology but rejected the consequences spiritualists drew concerning the nature of the church. Simons's teaching on the incarnation was uniformly rejected in German-speaking Anabaptist communities.

from the Sermon on the Mount.[6] There are references to God's wrath that suggest something like a penal substitution theory, but it is not the dominant motif, as was the case with Luther and Calvin.

KEY ANABAPTIST WRITINGS ON THE BREAKING OF BREAD

Balthasar Hubmaier was a matriculated German Catholic theologian who was attracted to Anabaptism. He is a paradoxical figure in that he made believer's baptism the door to church membership yet understood the church as a public institution protected by the state. This arrangement prompted him to create liturgical forms for baptism, the Lord's Supper, and the ban (excommunication).[7] Zwingli was a formative influence on Hubmaier, both in emphasizing an inward feeding on Christ prior to or during the outward ceremony and in locating the change that happens in Communion as the transformation of the congregation. Hubmaier's "Pledge of Love" just before partaking is the response of obedience to that gift. The pledge asks all believers, before Communion, if they are willing to lay down their lives for their neighbor in the power of Christ who laid down his life for us.[8]

> If you will love God before, in, and above all things . . .
> If you will love your neighbor and serve him . . .
> If you will practice fraternal admonition toward your brethren and sisters . . .
> If you will also love your enemies and do good to them . . .

The most significant and enduring theology of the Lord's Supper in Dutch Anabaptism comes from Dirk Philips, the fellow bishop of Menno Simons. There is a deep spirituality with late medieval roots in his writing focused on remembering Christ's death on our behalf. The celestial flesh Christology is at work here, channeled toward a mystical union with Christ as in John 6, of which the bread and wine are signs. Philips describes this union as

---

[6]John Driver applies this thinking to the mission of the church in the twentieth century: John Driver, *Understanding the Atonement for the Mission of the Church* (Scottdale, PA: Herald Press, 1986), esp. 129-46, 243-53.

[7]Michele Zelinsky Hanson, "Anabaptist Liturgical Practices," in *A Companion to the Eucharist in the Reformation*, ed. Lee Palmer Wandel, Brill's Companions to the Christian Tradition 46 (Boston: Brill, 2014), 252-56.

[8]Balthasar Hubmaier, "A Form for Christ's Supper," in *Balthasar Hubmaier: Theologian of Anabaptism*, trans. and ed. H. Wayne Pipkin and John H. Yoder (Scottdale, PA: Herald Press, 1989), 403.

"divinization."[9] The Supper is an action initiated by the Spirit and completed by the Communion of the people. There is no explicit teaching of the transformation of the congregation, but it is suggested by the possibility of mutual footwashing as the culmination of the service.

The most original and incarnational eucharistic theology in Anabaptism is that of Pilgram Marpeck, whose ministry was in southern German-speaking territories from Moravia to the Alsace. A unique contribution of Marpeck to the Radical Reformation is that he found a language with which to critique spiritualism without dismissing its desire for intimacy with God. If outward signs are only obstacles to the true believer, Marpeck countered, then ultimately there is no need for the Bible and the visible church, to say nothing of its rituals. Marpeck went to the heart of this theological debate, to the incarnation itself.[10] In it God in Christ condescended to become one with the creation, one with us as creatures of flesh and blood.[11]

Through the fires of controversy, Marpeck arrived at a coherent sacramentality that was congruent with a believer's church. His foundation was twofold. The first part was biblical: God's will in Christ is revealed in the commands and examples of the New Testament. For example, the church is commanded to baptize.

The second part was theological, the meaning of the incarnation for the church and its ceremonies. Marpeck tried to persuade those who wanted to put aside a visible church and focus on individual, inward participation in Christ that a visible church with visible signs is spread across the pages of the New Testament. These mediations of spirit in no way lessen being indwelled by Christ in the power of the Spirit. This indwelling does not come about by putting aside the body and transcending the world; it happens through the body, through the Bible, through the church.[12]

---

[9]Dirk Philips, "The Supper of Our Lord Jesus Christ," in *The Writings of Dirk Philips*, ed. Cornelius J. Dyck, William E. Keeney, and Alvin J. Beachy (Scottdale, PA: Herald Press, 1992), 120, 127.

[10]Pilgram Marpeck, "Pilgram Marpeck's Response," in *Later Writings by Pilgram Marpeck and His Circle*, vol. 1, *The Exposé, a Dialogue, and Marpeck's Response to Caspar Schwenckfeld*, trans. Walter Klaassen, Werner O. Packull, and John D. Rempel (Scottdale, PA: Herald Press, 1999), 82-85, 110-19, 124-31.

[11]Hebrews 2:14-18 was one of Marpeck's signature passages.

[12]The principal of incarnation is true not only of the spiritual life narrowly considered but of its expression in cultural creativity. Rembrandt's shapes mediate beauty through the eye; Bach's musical notes mediate beauty through the ear.

As Marpeck grappled with the implications of the Word becoming flesh, it dawned on him that the most profound of outward realities were the Bible and the church. He thought of the Bible as the physical Word of God speaking spiritual truth, the most profound medium of God's revelation, given to guide the church and the believer in everyday faithfulness. Marpeck turned to trinitarian language to describe God's inward and outward working, to demonstrate the enduring nature of the incarnation. One of his formulations was that God the Father works inwardly through the Spirit while God the Son works outwardly through the church.[13] The church is the extension of Christ's humanity. To amplify Marpeck's image: if the church is the body of Christ, its ceremonies, like footwashing, are the hands and feet of the Lord's body. Thomas Finger reinforces this train of thought by noting that "the elements function outwardly, as did Jesus' historical humanity, to mediate the Spirit to us inwardly."[14]

None of these notions were original with Marpeck, or even the Reformation. The element of originality was how they were brought together in this new setting. Marpeck understood a sacrament to be the meeting point of grace and faith. He had a sure place for God's prevenient grace. But his idea of ceremonies, as he called sacraments, was that in the dynamic nature of a sacrament the human response is inseparable from the divine initiative. Further, he had a trinitarian reason for the argument that outward things are capable of participating in inward realities. When they are inhabited by the Spirit, the outward becomes one with the inward. In baptism, for example, water becomes God's seal of his saving work in the presence of Spirit and faith. Similarly, when bread is broken and shared, those who eat it are made one with Christ and the body of Christ, the church. Marpeck's greatest feat of originality was to fuse foundational claims of classical theology with a believer's church ecclesiology.

For Marpeck and other Anabaptists (like Hubmaier), the presence of Christ in a ceremony was not the end point but the starting point of the Spirit's work.

---

[13]Pilgram Marpeck, "A Clear and Useful Instruction," and "The Admonition of 1542," in *The Writings of Pilgram Marpeck*, trans. and ed. William Klassen and Walter Klaassen, Classics of the Radical Reformation 2 (Harrisonburg, VA: Herald Press, 1978), 76-79, 186-87, 195-98, 226-32.

[14]Thomas N. Finger, *A Contemporary Anabaptist Theology: Biblical, Historical, Constructive* (Downers Grove, IL: InterVarsity Press, 2004), 191.

The believers who had gathered were united with Christ; in the sway of the Spirit they became what they had eaten. They turned from the table of the church to spread a table for the world. Just as Jesus Christ had offered up his life for them, they would now offer up their lives for others—sisters and brothers, neighbors, and even enemies. Because of that dynamic, the Lord's Supper was the densest actualization both of God's grace and of our obedience. In Marpeck's understanding of the incarnation, the spiritual and the ethical were inseparable.

Much of what he believed was implicit in other Anabaptist ways of talking about the gospel and its enactment in the Breaking of Bread. Marpeck's distinctive contribution was that he made explicit what was implicit in most Anabaptist thinking. This was especially the case in incorporating the classical three meanings of "body of Christ" (Rom 7:4; 1 Cor 10:16-17; 1 Cor 11:24, 27; 1 Cor 12:12, 27) into his theology. The first one is the historical body of Jesus whom we meet in worship in a kind of living memory. The Spirit draws us into the event of Christ's suffering and death to redeem us.

The second meaning of "body of Christ" is that we receive the One who died and came back to life. A Marpeckian description would say that the action of sharing bread in the sway of the Spirit makes us one with Christ and one another, not just in feeling but in being. Christ has inhabited us.[15]

The third meaning of "body of Christ" is that we become what we have received. When we leave the Table, we return to the world as members of Christ and one another, offering ourselves for our neighbors as Christ offered himself for us.

DEVELOPMENTS IN THE THEOLOGY OF THE SUPPER: MODERNITY

Anabaptism was a movement that uneasily straddled the long church tradition and an early modern form of restorationism, the notion that the church could be returned to its original apostolic purity. On the one hand, in its continuity with orthodoxy, most especially trinitarianism, Anabaptism

---

[15]Neal Blough has an insightful treatment of Marpeck's Christology but insists that "participation in divine reality occurs at the level of meaning not substance." Neal Blough, *Christ in Our Midst: Incarnation, Church, and Discipleship in the Theology of Pilgram Marpeck* (Kitchener, Ont.: Pandora, 2007), 175.

belonged to the Catholic tradition, as did other streams of the Reformation. On the other hand, in its radical critique of Catholic and Protestant ecclesiologies, it broke away from the *corpus christianum*, the medieval and Reformational unity of church and society. One of the reasons for this rupture was the Anabaptist belief in an inaugurated eschatology in which the church already participates in the kingdom. A church that was not conformed to the state had a utopian impulse: it was marked by baptism on confession of faith and pacifism, based on the Sermon on the Mount as well as Jesus' love of enemies to the point of death. Another mark of its restorationism was Anabaptism's charismatic worship. Its liturgical forms were lean and open to improvisation. Its community was marked by an existential covenant, one that was freely given and mutual. The consequence of this quest for integrity of belief and practice was that Anabaptism gave the subjective side (the human response) of the church's identity disproportionate emphasis. The objective side (the divine initiative), especially where it concerned the church and its practices, was overshadowed. As we have seen, this stance had consequences for Anabaptism's sacramental life.

This paradigm, with its strengths and weaknesses, was the beginning of the Free Church tradition and its subsets, believers churches (who baptized only upon confession of faith) and peace churches (for whom nonviolence was constitutive of their identity).[16] These were dissenting faith communities in Britain and the Continent who freed themselves from an alliance with the state. Membership was by the confession of faith of the believer, whether by infant or believer's baptism. They included Mennonites, Separatist Puritans, Baptists, Methodists, and their offspring in North America. The place of individual faith and competence before God was central. These sacramentally lean movements (except for Methodism) originated in Europe, thrived in North America, and were later

[16]See David W. Bebbington, *Baptists Through the Centuries: A History of a Global People* (Waco, TX: Baylor University Press, 2010); Hans-Jürgen Goertz, *The Anabaptists*, trans. Trevor Johnson (New York: Routledge, 1995); Ted Campbell, Ann K. Riggs, and Gilbert W. Stafford, eds., *Ancient Faith and American-Born Churches: Dialogues Between Christian Traditions*, Faith and Order Commission Theological Series (New York: Paulist Press, 2006); D. H. Williams, *Evangelicals and Tradition: The Formative Influence of the Early Church* (Grand Rapids: Baker Academic, 2005); and John H. Yoder, *The Royal Priesthood: Essays Ecclesiological and Ecumenical*, ed. Michael G. Cartwright (Grand Rapids: Eerdmans, 1998).

passed on across the Global South. We will trace an outline of this trajectory. Two distinct post-Reformation formulations of the theology and
practice of the Lord's Supper, Baptists and Disciples/Churches of Christ,
need to be mentioned to complete the whole of the eucharistic tradition
out of which Christians in the West live. We will also make mention of
Quakers, Methodists, and Plymouth Brethren, denominations whose
identity only partially fits the Free Church model but who have distinctive
understandings of the Breaking of Bread.

Baptists emerged from the underground dissent in England at the turn of
the seventeenth century.[17] Those who fled to Amsterdam were influenced
by Mennonites, but the larger influences, especially in their view of the Lord's
Supper, were Zwingli (to whom General Baptists turned) and Calvin (the
authority for Particular Baptists).[18] Both groups spoke of communion with
Christ, in the sense of John 6, and wrote hymns expressing these convictions.[19]
It was in their hymnody more than in their prose that the symbolic realism
understanding of sacraments still found a place. Their concern was clearly
with the subjective integrity of the communicant and the congregation but
also dwelt on the objective reality of Christ's presence.

> Here at thy table, Lord! we meet
> To feed on food divine:
> Thy body is the bread we eat,
> Thy precious blood the wine.
>
> His body, torn with rudest hands,
> Becomes the finest bread;
> And with the blessing He commands,
> Our noblest hopes are fed.

---

[17]See Roger Hayden, *English Baptist History and Heritage* (Oxfordshire, UK: Baptist Union of Great Britain, 2005); and Stephen Wright, *The Early English Baptists, 1603–49* (Rochester, NY: Boydell, 2006).

[18]Shawn Wright makes the case that for Calvin there is "the real presence" of Christ in the Supper in the historic sense of that term and that it shaped Baptist thought through the Westminster Confession. Shawn D. Wright, "The Reformed View of the Lord's Supper," in *The Lord's Supper: Remembering and Proclaiming Christ Until He Comes*, ed. Thomas R. Schreiner and Matthew B. Crawford (Nashville: B & H Academic, 2010), 254-78.

[19]Michael Walker, *Baptists at the Table* (Didcot, UK: Baptist Historical Society, 1992), 17; and Joseph Stennett, *Hymns in Commemoration of the Sufferings of Our Blessed Saviour Jesus Christ, Compos'd for the Celebration of his Holy Supper*, n.p., n.d.

His blood, that from each opening vein
In purple torrents ran,
Hath filled this cup with generous wine,
That cheers both God and man.[20]

The language of presence is more evident in the first centuries of Baptist life than in the twentieth century. Some theologians affirmed that Christ's presence was given through but not as the elements.[21] Others added that this participation was a sealing of the covenant. This reflected the higher sacramentality of writers like Thomas Grantham,[22] but even less sacramentally inclined writers like Benjamin Keach spoke of a mystical conveyance of Christ's merits in the ordinance.[23] The Second London Confession of 1677 makes the following claim:

> Worthy receivers, outwardly partaking of the visible Elements of this Ordinance, do then also inwardly by faith, really and indeed, yet not carnally and corporally, but spiritually receive and feed upon Christ crucified and all the benefits of his death: the Body and Blood of Christ, being then not corporally or carnally, but spiritually present to the faith of Believers.[24]

Emphasis was also laid on the body of Christ as the congregation. In light of this conviction, the practice arose to hold Communion immediately before or after a congregational meeting to remake its unity. The words of institution were spoken as the narrative out of which the Supper grew, followed by a prayer of thanksgiving.

The covenant of believer's baptism was understood as the door to the covenant of the Lord's Table until the mid-nineteenth century. Since then many Baptist churches have welcomed Christians baptized as infants, with the argument that the Eucharist is the sign of the unity and catholicity of the body of Christ.[25] In this ecumenical notion the mainstream of British

---

[20]Walker, *Baptists at the Table*, 22.

[21]Paul S. Fiddes, *Tracks and Traces: Baptist Identity in Church and Theology* (Milton Keyes, UK: Paternoster, 2003; repr., Eugene, OR: Wipf & Stock, 2007), 160-64, 171.

[22]Thomas Grantham, *Christianismus Primitivus or the Ancient Christian Religion*, book 2 (London: Francis Smith, 1678), 81-98, Open Library, https://archive.org/stream/christianismuspr00gran?ref=ol#page/n2/mode/2up.

[23]Fiddes, *Tracks and Traces*, 165-67.

[24]William Lumpkin, ed., *Baptist Confessions of Faith* (Valley Forge, PA: Judson, 1980), 293.

[25]Lumpkin, *Baptist Confessions of Faith*, 175-79.

Baptists was ahead of all Christian bodies except the Disciples of Christ (see below), who came later.

Quakerism emerged out of the earlier seventeenth-century dissenter ferment in England as a distinct movement about 1640. Its earliest leaders, like George Fox and Margaret Fell, reacted against their experience of Anglicanism as a religion of external forms and beholden to the state. The Society of Religious Friends was a quest for the unmediated experience of the living Christ, who spoke to his people now with the same mystical power as he had after his resurrection. This allegiance to Christ relativized their allegiance to all human institutions. Among these institutions was the official church. This allegiance to Christ was the basis of their pacifism. Together with Mennonites and the German Brethren movement (like the Church of the Brethren) of the late eighteenth century, these three communities form a subset of the Free Church called peace churches.[26]

Early Friends piety was both charismatic and mystical. The term *Quaker* was originally a nickname to describe the ecstasy that might come upon the gathered congregation. By the same principle, those gathered might also be led into collective, mystical silence. An onlooker might say that the very act of gathering is a mediation of the Spirit. For Quakers, traditional Christian rituals had, at most, a metaphorical significance. For example, the Lord's Supper was an image of unmediated communion with Christ. The Gospel of John, and especially the eucharistic John 6, were Quaker staples. Traditional Quakers placed great weight on the Bible but studied it outside their Sunday meeting. It was the outer Word of God that pointed beyond itself to the inner Word.

David Johns, a Quaker scholar, uses liturgical categories to talk about Friends' worship. He speaks about the ambiguity of communal silence and that this silence allows for the experience of the absence of God. It is the illuminated ground from which words emerge.[27] He takes a critical stance toward Quaker "spiritualization of sacraments."[28] Some Quakers have

---

[26]Donald F. Durnbaugh, *The Believers' Church: The History and Character of Radical Protestantism* (London: Macmillan, 1968); and Douglas Gwyn, *The Covenant Crucified: Quakers and the Rise of Capitalism* (Wallington, PA: Pendle Hill, 1995).

[27]David L. Johns, *Quakering Theology: Essays on Worship, Tradition, and Christian Faith* (Burlington, VT: Ashgate, 2013), 17-25.

[28]Johns, *Quakering Theology*, 43-45.

adopted "programmed meetings" with a Free Church style of planned worship but without sacraments. Quakerism is unique in the body of Christ in putting outward signs completely aside in relation to the spiritual life.[29]

Almost a century later John Wesley, a minister in the Anglican Church in England, came to a new and profoundly personal faith in Christ through the ministry of the Moravian Church, an heir of pietism. Wesley was also a patristics scholar. His distinctive contribution to sacramental practice was the marriage of ancient liturgy and evangelical spirituality. The originality of Wesley's thought and practice arises from his commitment to hold together his Anglican identity, including infant baptism, his study of the life and practice of the early church, and his passion to help people come to an intensely personal experience of God's grace. Gayle Carlton Felton observes, "Because he believed that the grace of baptism was usually lost, Wesley affirmed the need for a subsequent experience of regeneration without denying the validity of sacramental rebirth."[30] He was indebted to Moravian and other German pietists for this belief.

Wesley's evangelistic ministry led tens of thousands to life in Christ. His own Anglican Church was inhospitable to these converts so Wesley prepared catechetical and liturgical resources for them. In the end, he prepared a book of prayer with a Sunday service of Holy Communion that was both liturgical and evangelical.[31]

When Wesleyan missionaries took the movement to the thirteen colonies just before the American Revolution, they found a popular culture in the process of separating itself from European political and religious order. The fusion of the evangelical and liturgical dimensions of worship did not speak to the people they had come to minister to. Consequently, they left most of the prayer book behind but kept the Lord's Supper in the form of a quarterly love feast, which they placed at the center of church life.[32] In his study of this

---

[29]The Salvation Army began as a mission made up largely of Anglicans. Initially, its worship included no sacramental acts because the Church of England was counted on to provide them. Nonsacramental practice became the norm when the Army became a denomination in its own right.

[30]Gayle Carlton Felton, *This Gift of Water: The Practice and Theology of Baptism Among Methodists in America* (Nashville: Abingdon, 1992), 41.

[31]James F. White, ed., *John Wesley's Prayerbook* (Akron, OH: Order of St. Luke, 1995), 125-39.

[32]Lester Ruth, *A Little Heaven Below: Worship at Early Methodist Quarterly Meetings* (Nashville: Abingdon, 2000), 103-45.

period, James White, the great historian of Christian worship, notes that despite the radical reshaping of Protestant worship after the American Revolution, there was still a sacramental dimension to it. The origin of camp meetings and revivals lay in their preparatory role for receiving Communion. Because of the rugged roads on the frontier and the dispersal of colonists across wide spaces, the only time many of them were in reach of the Lord's Supper was at the yearly camp meetings and revivals. In the course of the nineteenth century they lost this sacramental foundation.[33] This is a stunning turn of events, a case of amnesia that sacramentally lean Protestants are not aware they have.

Alexander Campbell was an early nineteenth-century Presbyterian minister educated in the prevailing philosophy of the common-sense realism of his native Scotland. Its most influential thinker was the Scottish philosopher Thomas Reid.[34] This was a school of thought that arose as a response to the philosophical skepticism of the day. It taught that the practice of factual, rational thinking allows anyone to understand a text. To the clear-headed reader, its meaning is obvious. It left little room for paradox. Campbell was representative of a movement applying this broad philosophy to the study of the Bible. He was an early advocate of church unity because he was convinced that a common-sense reading of Scripture would overcome ancient antagonisms. He believed that the Old and New Testaments contained instructions for the structure and practices of a restored church. Because of this belief, he left the Presbyterian Church to build a movement that would bring all Christians into one body. The Disciples of Christ and Churches of Christ emerged from his labors. He was impatient with "speculation" and "abstract notions," in which categories he included the creeds.[35]

Campbell's mindset was typical of much educated theology in nonliturgical Protestant churches in the United States in the nineteenth century. It made little room for mystery. This approach has been imbibed by many Free Church

[33]James F. White, *Protestant Worship: Traditions in Transition* (Louisville, KY: Westminster John Knox, 1989), 171-91, esp. 172-75.

[34]Thomas Reid wrote *An Inquiry into the Human Mind on the Principles of Common Sense* in 1764, *Essays on the Intellectual Powers of Man* in 1785, and *Essays on the Active Powers of Man* in 1788. The titles are suggestive of the content. See Thomas Reid, *Essays on the Active and Intellectual Powers of Man*, Microtexts ESTC reel 2529, no. 3, University of Toronto Libraries; and Reid, *An Inquiry into the Human Mind on the Principles of Common Sense*, ed. Derek R. Brookes (State College, PA: Penn State University Press, 2000).

[35]Alexander Campbell, *The Christian System* (New York: Arno, 1960), 109-14.

people until today.[36] Campbell held that all believers are priests and have the calling to preside at the Lord's Table. The only requirement is a prayer of thanksgiving for the loaf and then for the cup. There "all have communion with the Lord and one another in eating the broken loaf."[37] On the basis of early Christian gatherings recorded in the book of Acts, Campbell concluded that the heart of worship is the Breaking of Bread every Lord's Day. This practice, he noted, was preserved in the Western church for two centuries and in the Eastern one for six centuries. Campbell adds that weekly Communion ended when the church lost her first love (Rev 2:4). He quotes Calvin and Wesley in support of his appeal for weekly Communion.[38] Taking Communion every Sunday was a novelty in the nineteenth century. For Catholics and Eastern Orthodox and Orientals of the era, the liturgy was considered to be complete when the priest alone communed.

The Brethren Assemblies (also known as Plymouth Brethren) originated under John Nelson Darby as an offshoot of Anglicanism in Ireland in the 1820s. They deserve mention because they are another restorationist movement that observes a weekly Lord's Supper because Christ commanded it. To the outside observer it is evident that they have an ambivalent relationship to ritual. On the one hand, their practice suggests the importance they attach to the founding ordinance of the church. On the other hand, the Breaking of Bread is related to personal piety and not to the unity of the church. The Supper is the occasion on which all believers turn inward to reflect on their redemption in a disciplined way. Only a Christian who is "right with the Lord," that is, faithfully living the gospel in every way, is welcome at Communion. Such participation is unrelated to baptism, which is understood as the believer's testimony to his conversion and is unrelated to church membership. The form of their Sunday morning worship is very simple, with prayers and testimonies framing the Breaking of Bread. Traditionally, teaching is done in the Sunday school hour and the evening service.[39]

---

[36] See Jennifer L. Woodruff Tait, *The Poisoned Chalice: Eucharistic Grape Juice and Common-Sense Realism in Victorian Methodism* (Tuscaloosa: University of Alabama, 2011), esp. 3-8, 101-7.

[37] Tait, *Poisoned Chalice*, 309.

[38] Tait, *Poisoned Chalice*, 323.

[39] Daniel Smith, *Worship and Remembrance*, vol. 3 (Vancouver: self-published, n.d.). In these Sunday morning meditations, the atoning work of Christ and intimate experiences of him are the focus. I am grateful to Ken Reid for his nuanced understanding of Brethren practices.

These post-Reformation developments reached a high point in the middle of the nineteenth century. They mark the completion of a history of the Lord's Supper in its Anglo-American appropriation of Mediterranean and European liturgical origins. The broadest and most populous movement of new churches that came into being outside European tradition was Pentecostalism. The charismatic gifts, such as speaking in tongues, have never been entirely lost. But as a formal movement, Pentecostalism arose in the United States at the beginning of the twentieth century. It has many kindred movements on other continents, like African Initiated Churches. Some of them consider themselves to be postdenominational or post-Protestant. All these churches are historically removed from the established as well as the dissident expressions of the long Western tradition. Their connection to the sacramental life of the historic denominations varies greatly.

UNSCIENTIFIC POSTSCRIPT

There is an aspect of post-Reformation sacramental understanding and practice, almost never discussed, that illuminates the malaise of liturgically lean churches. It has to do with the intriguing and little-explored influence of modern science, as popularly interpreted, on the Protestant and especially the Free Church worldview. This shift has already been introduced in chapter one under the subhead "Enchantment and Disenchantment" as well as in this chapter's references to the Disciples of Christ. Now I would like to give those concepts a historical context and theorize on the unforeseen but enormous effect of this shift on Protestant understandings of sacramentality.

In the wake of the Enlightenment, the Catholic Church gradually accepted the shift to a new science but opposed certain of its prerequisites. It saw that a mechanistic model of nature was in direct conflict with the Christian teaching of the incarnation. The mainline Protestant churches were of two minds. On the one hand, their very identity was based on a providential God. On the other hand, the place of the individual, whose status before God the Protestant Reformation had exalted, appealed to them as did the freedom of the mind to explore the world by means of the scientific method. For a time Protestantism hovered between an enchanted and a disenchanted universe, but it increasingly belonged to the disenchanted world, one in which the material and spiritual realms were completely separate. The material realm was rational, objective, and subject to its own laws; the spiritual realm was nonrational, subjective, and unprovable. This mindset fueled the existing suspicion of sacramentality in some Reformed and Free Church settings, the outcome of which was a further reductionism in which sacraments were human pedagogical enactments rather than divine ones.

Specific aspects of this Enlightenment worldview, in a popularized form, were surprisingly attractive to two similar forms of church life, Pietism/ Evangelicalism and Free Churches. The place of individual faith and competence before God was central. Although the church as the body of Christ and the Holy Spirit as the giver of faith still mattered to them, both movements discovered a kinship with the Enlightenment belief that human beings can come to God on their own, without the mediation of the institutional church. This notion tapped into the suspicion Free churches had had of Protestant and Catholic national churches all along and made the Free churches susceptible to ways of thinking that went against the grain of their own assumptions.

Two illustrations of this Free Church susceptibility follow. Some strands of those denominations bought into the Enlightenment scientific assertions that ritual, in its broadest sense, belongs to a "primitive stage" of human understanding. This is how the argument went: before humanity had a rational grasp of nature, it resorted to practices like offering sacrifices to unknown gods to appease them. This argument resonated with the Old Testament judgment on pagan practices and the New Testament teaching that Christ's death on the cross was the final sacrifice. In the light of science and with the aid of philosophy, inhabitants of modernity have learned to think abstractly. More and more we can explain why the world functions as it does. Rationality has replaced the mythic potency of ritual as a way of coping with the immensity of the world and the depth of our experience.

Thus, two very different and often hostile worldviews, the Free Church concern for the individual's inward decision in the light of revelation and the secular concern for the individual's action in the light of reason, came together in popular forms to push aside the world of symbols. Other Free Church thinkers went even further: they agreed with the rationalists that nothing of

God could be found in the outward world of matter.[40] We have already seen this in the writings of Alexander Campbell. In thinking this way, theologians crossed the final bridge from an enchanted to a disenchanted cosmos. Nature was no longer God's creation. It became a place in which sacrament and mystery have no dwelling. It is hard to resist the conclusion that this dismissive view of the creation is a major factor in the disdain for ecological ethics found in strands of American fundamentalist culture.

Further, rationalistic Bible exegetes went on to impose this modern worldview on the Bible. Of relevance to the pilgrimage onto which this book invites the reader is the logic according to which cardinal New Testament passages concerning sacraments were read. For example, in Romans 6, Paul is presumed to rule out the possibility that God could use elements of creation as a medium of grace. Thus, these exegetes argued that in baptism believers declare their faith, making the ritual of baptism an entirely human undertaking. Such a reading of texts like this goes against the grain of Paul's claim that God the Spirit acts in baptism: "all of us who have been baptized into Christ Jesus were baptized into his death" (Rom 6:3).

To conclude, Catholicism and all forms of Protestantism were affected by the scientific mindset.[41] But the Free churches were affected most negatively because they lacked the encompassing dogmatic and liturgical structures of the established churches in Europe, and their mainline sibling churches in North America, as a buffer. With limited resources of systematic theology, the Free churches could not fully grasp the consequences of a disenchanted worldview. In addition, their ever-diminishing memory of historic ritual and symbolism left them with fewer intimations of an enchanted universe.

Without always knowing what they were getting into, and sometimes in spite of their opposition to theories like the evolution of species, nonliturgical churches mistakenly embraced popularized scientific thinking because it

---

[40]The Scottish philosophy of common-sense realism (crudely: what you see is what you get) became one basis for theological arguments against a sacramental universe. Sydney E. Ahlstrom, "The Scottish Philosophy and American Theology," *Church History* 24, no. 3 (1955): 257-72, www.jstor.org/stable/3162115.

[41]Brad Gregory gives an insightful overview of the rise of modern science and its unforeseen consequences for religion. Brad S. Gregory, *The Unintended Reformation: How a Religious Revolution Secularized Society* (Cambridge, MA: Belnap Press, 2012), esp. 332-58.

seemed close to that of the dissenting churches in two ways.[42] First was their attraction to the disenchantment of the world that science championed. The most radical Free Church voices joined the disenchanters in condemning a sacramental worldview as *magical*. By this term some voices in both camps meant *superstition*. But what was superstition? Was it a credulous belief in physical manipulation of the spiritual world for private gain? Or was what they called superstition simply the belief that God communicates with us through the material world?

The disenchanters had a second commonality. Like religious dissenters, advocates of the Enlightenment experienced highly sacramental and hierarchical churches with public status as alien and oppressive structures. What attracted Free Church radicals to the Enlightenment project was its rejection of imposed religious norms, its emphasis on experience, its separation of spirit and matter, and its insistence on religious tolerance.

The separatistic stance of some Free churches toward the dominant culture limited the direct influence of the Enlightenment on them in the eighteenth and nineteenth centuries. Those who remained at home in a premodern worldview, like Old Order Brethren, Baptists, and Mennonites, still inhabited an enchanted universe. But everyone else was affected by this revolutionary worldview in which nature replaced creation through intellectual osmosis. Scientific thinking relegated the divine from the natural outward order to the realm of inward experience. Religion became the private, subjective pursuit of individuals. This outcome, of banishing God from his creation, was not the intention of Protestant theology, mainline or Free Church, but it became an unintended consequence of the viewpoints sketched above.

Thus the last remaining bond between spirit and matter in Free Church sacramental thought, the church as the visible body of Christ in the world, was endangered. Their last foothold in a sacramental universe no longer had a coherent theological rationale. Parallel to this development, in countries like the Netherlands and the United States, unofficial (that is, nonstate) entities were all placed in the category of "voluntary associations." In their earlier

---

[42]It is impossible to avoid oversimplification in summarizing this topic. For example, there were both liberal and evangelical church leaders who accepted the claims of science, like evolution, and those who rejected them. The latter were the fathers of fundamentalism. Yet even they agreed with much scientific thought in its separation of the material and spiritual worlds.

history, these liturgically lean churches had not thought of themselves as such. For them the church was not simply an association of people who had common interests; it was not merely the sum total of its adherents. It was a community called into being by the grace of God that prolonged Christ's incarnation on earth.

Because of this imposed (and later accepted) reductionism, there was little left of a sacramental ecclesiology. It became harder and harder to think in terms of the incarnation. And so the already lean Free Church theology of the incarnation continued to unravel: eventually there was no place for grace in the material world. And so the world became detached from its enveloping skin of religious references. This meant that all experience of God—if one believed in God—was unmediated. In the New Testament, the evangelical dimension of faith (Paul's, "It is no longer I who live, but it is Christ who lives in me," Gal 2:20) was embedded in a communal and sacramental reality. If any church relinquishes these two pillars, in my view, all that remains of that identity in this novel age of individualism is the solitary believer, reliant solely on the intensity of private experience.

There were, however, Free Church and evangelical leaders who saw what was unfolding and sought to reclaim incarnational and sacramental thinking.[43] This book is my attempt to apply their insights to the present condition of the lean Protestant traditions.

Where do we go from here? Those listed in the previous footnote are only an inkling of a vast movement of Christians in the Western world engaged in the same project. You will have noticed that many of my sources have been from liturgically stout traditions—churches that have cultivated worship inspired by the long tradition. The liturgically lean ones can learn much from them. Yet in some ways we all face today's challenges together. The world we

---

[43]In the past generation they have included George Beasley-Murray, *Baptism in the New Testament* (Grand Rapids: Eerdmans, 1973); Hans Boersma, *Heavenly Participation: The Weaving of a Sacramental Tapestry* (Grand Rapids: Eerdmans, 2011); Scott W. Bullard, *Re-membering the Body: The Lord's Supper and Ecclesial Unity in the Free Church Traditions* (Eugene, OR: Cascade, 2013); Neville Clarke, *An Approach to the Theology of the Sacraments* (London: SCM Press, 1958); T. W. Coleman, *The Free Church Sacrament and Catholic Ideals* (Toronto: Dent & Sons, 1930); Geoffrey Wainwright, *Eucharist and Eschatology* (New York: Oxford University Press, 1981); Robert E. Webber, *The Complete Library of Christian Worship*, 8 vols. (Nashville: Star Song, 1994); and James F. White, *Sacraments as God's Self Giving: Sacramental Practice and Faith* (Nashville: Abingdon, 1983).

live in is disenchanted—with fewer and fewer signs of the transcendence and immanence of God. The two types of church can be a gift to each other. In many places the "stout" ones[44] are no longer established churches but minorities with a more intense sense of faith and community. Here the dissenting churches have something to offer.

In addition, our perception of tradition has changed. As I have already said, Protestants are reclaiming respect for and ownership of the whole Christian narrative while Catholics since Vatican II have immersed themselves in the Bible.[45] Recent research into the origins of Christian worship has discovered that in the early centuries there was enormous diversity even though the church developed liturgical forms almost from the beginning. There seems to have been as much trust in the extemporaneous movement of the Holy Spirit as in the structures of worship. Some aspects of this continued into the medieval church—longer than earlier scholarship had detected. So the stereotype of established churches as ritually rich but with no room for improvisation no longer holds. Similarly, the stereotype of dissenting churches, as open to the Spirit but formless in their worship, no longer holds.

At a recent reception I attended, a group of Catholics from the same parish let me eavesdrop on their conversation. They had just completed a course for readers in the liturgy. One person spoke appreciatively of their pastor's explanation of what happens in the Eucharist. Someone else brusquely interrupted, "Why on earth did I have to wait until I was sixty to find out that Catholics believe the transformation in the Eucharist is not only of the elements but also of the congregation?"

If I have heard one person in the Reformed tradition say the inverse of what the Catholics said, I have heard a dozen: "Zwingli taught us that the transformation in the Lord's Supper is of the congregation. Why on earth have we had to wait so long to realize that the transformation is also of the elements?"

---

[44] I'm deliberately using unconventional names for the two types of churches because they are not static and can complement each other.

[45] It needs to be said that ultimately the circle of mutuality needs to be enlarged to include the Eastern Orthodox and Oriental churches, on the one hand, and post-Protestant nondenominational churches, on the other hand.

Christians in the West are rightly troubled by the decline of the church. Many are on a quest for new ways to be church. One of the ways has not been given its due. It is the coming together of Christians in two converging ways. One is that *church* increasingly means being gathered into communities where all are on the path of discipleship. The other is that they have entered a sacramental universe whose center is the water bath and the eucharistic meal.

9

THE MEAL OF COVENANT

WHAT IS THE NATURE of the community that enacts its identity through the water bath and the eucharistic meal?[1] How does a church in mission hold onto two sides of its identity, openness and boundedness, vulnerability and covenant? There are many dimensions to this question and responses to it. They are expressed concretely in who has a place in the Breaking of Bread. Does the growing practice of Communion without baptism undermine the sacramental and covenantal character of the church? Or is it the practice of freedom given by the Spirit to improvise? Here is my reflection on this cluster of questions.

ABUNDANCE OR SCARCITY?

There are two kinds of table fellowship. For one of them a shared meal is an elemental expression of hospitality: the offer of food is an opening of hand and heart to a stranger. For the other kind of table fellowship a shared meal is an expression of covenant: the offer of food seals an alliance of common purpose. Lack of clarity about this difference is at the root of the current debate about open Communion.

This debate is raging in Protestant denominations and post-Protestant movements concerning the nature of Communion: Is it an inclusive or a covenantal meal?[2] This inquiry has spawned a rich study of the meals that

---

[1]Most of this chapter is lightly adapted from an article by the author: John D. Rempel, "Understanding the Lord's Meals and the Lord's Supper in Relation to Baptism and Communion," *Canadian Mennonite*, vol. 18, issue 2, January 20, 2014, https://canadianmennonite.org/articles/bread-acceptance -and-covenant. Used by permission.

[2]John Hammett, "Baptism and the Lord's Supper," in *Baptist Faith and Message 2000: Critical Issues in America's Largest Protestant Denomination*, ed. Douglas K. Blount and Joseph D. Wooddell (Lanham: Rowman & Littlefield, 2007), 71-81; Thomas Breidenthal, "The Festal Gathering: Reflections on Open Communion," *Sewanee Theological Review* 54, no. 2 (2011): 142-57; and Sarah Miles, *Take This Bread: A Radical Conversion* (New York: Ballantine, 2008).

Jesus shared in the Gospels, in addition to the Last Supper and the post-Easter Breaking of Bread.[3] To address this question let us pursue, first of all, a biblical inquiry and then a theological one. Following that comes a pastoral proposal. First, I shall look at both types of meals and their implications for the church's table ministry. Then I want to ask whether it is the Lord's Supper or baptism that is the proper sacrament of initiation. Finally, I will conclude that several "Lord's Tables" are called for to fully express Jesus' meal ministry.

Before we proceed, two prior considerations need to be taken into account. One, are we clear about the terms of the debate? We often talk about open or inclusive and closed or bounded Communion. *Open* can refer to inviting unbaptized Christians, on the one hand, or all who desire to come, on the other hand. *Closed* can mean only those who belong to the covenant of a specific congregation, on the one hand, or all who have been baptized as believers (or confirmed upon their baptism as infants), on the other hand.

I have two caveats concerning this language. First, I think the term *inclusive* has too many meanings to be helpful. "Openness to outsiders" is a better description of what Jesus demonstrates in the Gospels. His invitation is an act of hospitality to guests. In the current debate hospitality is often equated with belonging. Yet these are quite different social gestures. Hospitality is care for wayfarers—neither host nor guest thinks that a single meal together is a binding arrangement. Belonging, on the other hand, comes about through identifiable markers by means of which a community claims someone as a member through a birth ritual or a later initiation rite. With belonging comes accountability.

There is a second, and different, linguistic problem. It sets baptism as the absolute marker of belonging when not all the baptized might be living in the Spirit, and, conversely, people who are not baptized might be doing so. At issue here is whether a sacramental act in and of itself is an adequate marker of the presence of grace and faith. For that reason the sentence of invitation in the order of service for Holy Communion in appendix one has been expanded: "all who are baptized *and seek the way of Christ* are invited to it."

A subtopic of the question of who is invited concerns children of the church. They are not outsiders but faith novices in the sense that they have

---

[3]See Eugene LaVerdiere, *Dining in the Kingdom of God: The Origin of the Eucharist in the Gospel of Luke* (Chicago: Liturgy Training, 1994); and LaVerdiere, *The Breaking of the Bread: The Development of the Eucharist According to Acts* (Chicago: Liturgy Training, 1998).

a home in the congregation because they were raised in it. They might well "live in the Spirit but lack the maturity for covenant making."[4] Their relationship to Christ and the church is different from children or adults who do not know the gospel. One way of affirming the relationship of children in the care of the church to the gospel is to invite them to come forward for a blessing during Communion.

The overarching consideration that needs to be taken into account is the question of whether Jesus' message is one of abundance or scarcity. The greatest of human fears, underlying all others, is the fear that there will not be enough love to go around. This is how we argue: if I, my family, my church, my country give away too much love, we shall not have enough for ourselves. This surpassing fear needs to be transformed if we are to turn from being hoarders of love and all the blessings of life to being givers of love and life.

The fear of scarcity has often made the church into a defensive and selfish community bent on guarding what it has. Those like myself, who make the case that baptism initiates one into a covenant that is renewed in every celebration of the Eucharist, have sometimes been motivated by a fear of scarcity. The heart of the Gospel and Epistle meal narratives is the confidence that bread that is shared never runs out. We see this in Jesus' astonishing act of making five loaves and two fishes into a feast for five thousand (John 6 and parallel passages in all the other Gospels). The motivation for covenantal Communion cannot be hoarding; it must be vulnerability and generosity.

Finally, there is a need for pastoral discretion because the Holy Spirit is not bound to the church's order. In chapter 5, on baptism, I noted that in the book of Acts the sequence of laying on of hands, receiving the Spirit, and being baptized in water is not always the same. Gradually the church arrived at a normative pattern while confessing that God is not bound to it. There needs to be room for a pastorally discerned exception. But the norm remains. For example, in Acts 10:44-48, the Spirit came upon the seekers before they were baptized. Someone like that, for whom the Holy Spirit is clearly a living presence, might be invited to take Communion. But participating in the covenant meal would imply readiness to fully enter the covenant through the

---

[4]Personal correspondence with Elsie Rempel on April 7, 2013, then director of worship for Mennonite Church Canada.

act of baptism. Similarly, people who are baptized but not at all living in the Spirit of Christ might be challenged to live the loyalty to which they once committed themselves. Further, there are countries in which the baptism of converts to Christ is punishable by the state and by one's family because, strikingly, baptism is seen by them as an act of initiation into another community. In that case, the believer's *desire* for baptism is already a declaration of loyalty. God's initiative, the believer's faith, and the church's confirmation of that faith are all present, accomplishing what baptism with water does under normal circumstances. Should the opportunity to gather around the Lord's Table come to these underground believers, they would clearly be seen as members of the covenant.[5]

Covenanted Communion, then, is not a law but a practice that builds the integrity of the community. It makes provision for exceptional circumstances, such as those described above.

TABLES OF JESUS IN THE GOSPELS

In Luke 15:1-2 Jesus is accused of preferring outsiders to insiders as his table companions. Those to whose social and religious circle Jesus belongs scorn him for welcoming sinners and eating with them. Like most of us, Jesus' peers insist that dinner parties are occasions for insiders, for people like themselves who carefully invite one another in order to keep abundance within safe confines. There's an echo in this story of the laws of neighborliness found in Deuteronomy 24:17-22, where special mention is made of aliens, people without a home or status who need food and company but can't return the favor.

It is significant that all four Gospels include an account of feeding the five thousand. Mark tells us that Jesus comes ashore and stands face to face with a throng of people (Mk 6:34). Jesus is moved with compassion for people who are like sheep without a shepherd. He teaches them many things. Late in the

---

[5]There are at least two approaches to belonging. One of them is exemplified by William A. Dyrness, *Insider Jesus: Theological Reflections on New Christian Movements* (Downers Grove, IL: IVP Academic, 2016). Dyrness deals with Christians in other religious settings. Another approach is exemplified by Richard Rohr, *Everything Belongs: The Gift of Contemplative Prayer*, rev. ed. (New York: Crossroad, 2003); and Rohr, *The Universal Christ: How a Forgotten Reality Can Change Everything We See, Hope for, and Believe* (New York: Crown/Convergent, 2019). Rohr posits a cosmic Christ who is incarnate in every particle and being in the universe. In that sense everyone already belongs.

day, the Lord's disciples urge him to send the crowds away before dark so they can still scrounge for food. The disciples are baffled when Jesus insists that they feed the multitude! As they stand helpless, Jesus takes the five loaves and two fish a child has brought, looks up to heaven, blesses and breaks the food, then gives it to his disciples for the crowd. "All ate and were filled" (Mk 6:42).

Most of us have only recently related the meals of Jesus' ministry to the church's mission. We are struck by their unconditional welcome in contrast to the conditions that are set for the Last Supper. For that reason some people want to substitute the meals of Jesus' ministry for the Last Supper as the model for Communion. But if we go back through history to the early church, we see that it developed a range of bread rituals that carried on these aspects of the Lord's meal ministry. In the apostolic and early patristic era, the Lord's Supper was often celebrated within a larger meal, as had been the case with the Passover. Between the second and fourth centuries this love feast (*agape*) was separated from the Eucharist but was still tied to Jesus' table ministry.

Saying grace over a meal is a remnant of the *agape*. When we pray, "Come, Lord Jesus, be our guest," we invoke his presence at our sharing of food. Later, another bread ritual echoing the *agape* was practiced in monasteries as an act of hospitality for guests. In the East, bread as a sign of Jesus' presence was given to worshipers at the end of the Sunday Orthodox liturgy. After the Reformation, the Moravians and Church of the Brethren practiced (and still practice) the love feast.

Since the Middle Ages, symbolic breads have accompanied the celebration of the church year. The symbolic pastry for German Christianity is Stollen, an Advent bread; for Italian Christianity, panettone, a Christmas bread; and for Russian Christianity, paska, an Easter bread. Funeral meals have a spiritual, a more than literal, meaning: we break bread in solidarity with those who grieve; we also eat with them in the hope of the resurrection. Wedding meals have a similar symbolic density: we break bread with those who have made the covenant of love; our festivity anticipates the marriage supper of the Lamb.

All these breads recall Jesus' table ministry, in which all who gather in Jesus' name are invited to eat together. The most common meal of this type is the church potluck gathering in which those who can bring enough food to feed all who are present. At the same time, a potluck often lacks this symbolic density. Such a meal could easily be framed by specific association with bread references in the Old Testament, in Jesus' ministry, and in tradition. For example, at a potluck meal during Advent, a single loaf of Stollen could be cut into enough pieces that everyone participates in the same loaf. It could also be a time when food is gathered or money collected for a local shelter.

THE TABLE OF JESUS AT THE LAST SUPPER
AND AFTER THE RESURRECTION

Symbolically, the densest meal recorded in the New Testament is the Last Supper. There is a continuing dispute over whether it was a Passover feast.[6] In any case, there is a Passover spirit to the story: it is hard to miss the implication that Jesus himself is the unblemished Lamb (Mt 26:26-29). Here the implicitly religious gestures and words of Jesus' earlier table fellowship become explicit. The covenant established in Egypt is remade. This sacred meal seals a mutual pact between the master and his disciples (Lk 22:24-30). By means of this venerable custom of a covenantal bread and cup, Jesus gives himself to his companions. This feast is the culmination of his life.

At this point we encounter a surprising dimension to Jesus' table fellowship that has significance for the church's practice. There is a unique dimension to the Last Supper in comparison to Jesus' other shared meals. It consists of two aspects. The first is that this ritual is recognizably religious, even in the reinterpretation of its gestures, that is, understanding Jesus as the Passover Lamb. Second, this time the company is made up only of people whom Jesus is entrusting with his mission, however fainthearted they turn out to be.

Judas is one of them. In fact, there are scholars today who see Judas's handing over of Jesus as an attempt to force his hand but not to desert him. When Jesus is arrested, all the other men but John abandon Jesus. Only John and the two Marys are faithful. This shocking outcome does not lessen the fact that Jesus intended this meal only for those with whom he has entered a covenant. Ultimately, all but Judas return to keep the pledge they have made. It is this covenantal aspect of the Last Supper that led the early church to set baptism and holiness of life as conditions for participation in Communion.

---

[6]Willard M. Swartley, *John*, Believers Church Bible Commentary (Harrisonburg, VA: Herald Press, 2003), 316-17.

This practice is already evident in the Didache, a church order dated well within the first century: "But let no one eat or drink of your thanksgiving but those who have been baptized in the name of the Lord."[7]

Two final historic meal references from the early church expand further on what the gospel means by covenantal table fellowship. At the feast of Pentecost in Jerusalem, three thousand people have welcomed the message of the apostles, been baptized, and added to the household of faith. They devote themselves to the apostles' teaching and fellowship, the Breaking of Bread and prayer (Acts 2:29-42). The meal's logic of intimate fellowship is intensified at this point; it has immediate economic consequences. For the Jerusalem church the sharing of bread was a rehearsal for the sharing of possessions (Acts 2:43-46).

A CASE OF MISTAKEN IDENTITY?

Are people reacting to the principle of bounded Communion or to its misuse? Self-satisfaction and self-righteousness quickly create insiders and outsiders. The past generation of Christians has worked hard to become humbler about our faithfulness, wiser about our judgments, less reliant on class and denomination-based stereotypes of goodness. Being a church member is not at all a claim that one has found the key to living a consistently altruistic life. In fact, it is the opposite! Putting our trust in God's boundless love in Christ allows us to face the many ways in which we fall short of the life we have chosen.

This cluster of concerns has led to a tendency to err on the side of making everyone an insider. God's grace is like that; so should ours be. But is this truth most profoundly expressed by inviting everyone to the Lord's Table? On the one hand, "while we were enemies, we were reconciled to God" (Rom 5:10). On the other hand, "do you not realize that God's kindness is meant to lead you to repentance?" (Rom 2:4). Putting all the weight on inclusion and none on confession runs the danger of pushing evangelism to the side. There comes a time for declaring one's loyalty. This happens through changes of belief and behavior. Each of us grows into loyalty to Christ in different ways, some dramatic, others so quiet as to be hardly measurable.

---

[7]"Didache," in *Prayers of the Eucharist: Early and Reformed*, by R. C. D. Jasper and G. J. Cuming, 3rd ed. (Collegeville, MN: Liturgical Press, 1990), 23.

Baptism condenses and equalizes these different paths: it enacts our change in loyalty by means of the universal sign of initiation. It is big enough to include all our paths to Christ. Acting in God's name, the church confirms the inward and invisible working of grace with an outward and visible sign. Confusion in the meaning of the two foundational symbols of the gospel is at work here. The push to make Communion the unconditional ritual of acceptance forgets that the gospel already has a sacrament of initiation and inclusion: it is baptism.

If the New Testament intends baptism to be the sacrament of initiation and inclusion, have we misused baptism and set conditions for it that misrepresent the good news? The faith that readies us to be brought into the body of Christ is not mastery of doctrine and maturity of discipleship. In the simplest terms, the faith that conversion and baptism call for is surrender to God's work of letting us die to our old life and raising us to a new life. It is the confession that Christ has made a claim on my life and that by his grace I intend to live out this claim in the company of other believers. This suggests that most faith formation should follow baptism. There we discover what entering the covenant entails—worship, prayer, Bible study, and concrete acts of charity and justice. Thomas Breidenthal suggests, "If baptism is the sacrament in which we are being pushed out into God's world, then Eucharist is the sacrament in which we are drawn ever further into formation."[8]

Baptism is the sign that God has claimed us and that we have said yes to his claim. It is initiation into an apprenticeship with Jesus and those who have answered his call. We are not better than others, but we love much because we have been forgiven much (Lk 7:36-50). Members of Christ's body have been baptized not because they are good but because they know they are loved. In our encounter with Christ and our sisters and brothers in the Breaking of Bread, this love reclaims us and sets us on the path of vulnerability and generosity. Without counting the cost, we share with the world the bread we receive at the Lord's Table.

PASTORAL PRACTICE

What light do all of these meal encounters of Jesus shed on the much-asked question, "Who is invited to the Lord's Table?" To begin with, I venture the following thoughts to those who stand on either side of the debate.

---

[8]Breidenthal, "Festal Gathering," 152.

First, a word to those who see the Supper as a sacred meal of renewal for the covenant made in baptism. The unguardedness of Jesus' meal encounters with outsiders is so emblematic of his person and message that it cannot but shape the great ritual of those who follow him. The meals in Jesus' ministry are a metaphor for the message of grace, but they are also the medium of that grace. They are a metaphor for Christ's offer and our acceptance, our dying and rising with him in conversion and baptism (Rom 7:4). But they are also the medium of his offer: in Holy Communion the Lord offers himself with bread and wine. To be true to the practice of Jesus, doesn't our Breaking of Bread need to be open to "intruders"? When we resist intruders, are we in the grip of the fear that there will not be enough love to go around?

Second, a word to those who see Communion as the unconditional offer of acceptance to either unbaptized believers or to all who come without regard to their response. Is their plea for the inclusion of outsiders based more on human rights logic than on the spirit and practice of Jesus? By that I mean that in liberal democracies inclusion now has absolute status: everyone has the right to be included. Equal rights is a profound moral value, but that is not what is at stake in coming to the Lord's Table. At issue here is a freely given response to God's grace, which makes me one with the body of Christ, enacted in joining a congregation.

To people who lift up God's unconditional love, I would say that encounter always makes a claim. Jesus was able to be both lavishly accepting and passionately engaged in making relationships right. He called those who knew they were loved to love others. Jesus' table fellowship at the Last Supper and in the post-Easter accounts is with people who had already entered the covenant of love, however frayed their loyalty. The early church saw the meals in Jesus' ministry as a metaphor for the invitation to outsiders, and the church was soon filled with them (Eph 2:11-22). But the Breaking of Bread itself was reserved for those who had responded to the claim Christ had made on their lives in baptism.

A paradox is at work here. On the one hand, Jesus' way of meeting people involved the overthrow of convention, the disregard for merit, status, or the ability to return the favor. On the other hand, his presence announced God's reign and called for commitment to it. True, it is only when I know that I am invited "just as I am" that the call of grace and cost of discipleship win me over. "Just as I am" is the beginning, not the outcome, of the encounter. Offer and claim, openness and call condition each other.

This paradox is expressed in the two types of table fellowship Jesus practiced. One is an open table where nothing other than a willingness to meet is asked for. The other is a covenantal meal where those who have entered a pact promise one another solidarity. The decisive factor is not whether one is an insider or an outsider but whether one is willing to be changed. Jesus' openness to be with those whom religious people shunned is remarkable. But out of this encounter came a decision for or against him. Mary Magdalene said yes; the rich young ruler said no. The gospel offers us the gesture by which we enact Christ's initiative and our response: it is baptism.

There are those who would agree with the preceding paragraph up until the final sentence, that is, that those who come to Communion must have become Christ's disciples but they need not be baptized. In that case, aren't such new believers setting their own terms for coming to Christ? Aren't they coming to the meal of a covenant community they have not yet joined by means of the sign Christ gave the church?

How can we do justice both to the openness with which Jesus encountered people and the claim that this encounter made on them? If we follow the dominant exegetical and dogmatic tradition of the church, the Last Supper is the defining source of the Lord's Supper and the basis of bounded Communion. At the same time, other dimensions of Jesus' table sharing are no less part of the gospel. It is a profound loss that their place in Christian tradition has been marginalized. Earlier I mentioned the *agape* meal, the love feast, the monastic and liturgical bread rituals. My hope is that taken collectively they might extend Jesus' table ministry to people at every stage of encounter with him. How might we life-givingly reclaim these symbols of Jesus' self-offering?[9]

Two expressions of Jesus' tables of generosity and fellowship in the feeding of the multitudes might be the potluck meal after church and in shelters where homeless people gather. The place of such meals in the life of the church could be deepened by framing the table fellowship with references

---

[9]See Eleanor Kreider, *Communion Shapes Character* (Scottdale, PA: Herald Press, 1997), 75-96.

to Jesus' feeding of the crowds, by inviting people we often forget to join in, by giving children a prominent place, by reminding one another that bread is always a gift to be shared.

If there is a higher level of intentionality, such as Christians gathering in small study groups, environmental projects, or peace education, the language and gestures could be more explicit with an invoking of Jesus' presence and a place for intercessory prayer. Another example might be a meal for people exploring Christian faith: there they will meet an unseen guest waiting to be recognized.

A yet higher level of intentionality might be an *agape* meal for candidates for baptism with their mentors, spouses, or best friends.

All these meals would gain in focus with the provision of seasonal breads from cultures of the people present, like panettone at Christmas and paska at Easter.

These forms of table fellowship all point beyond themselves to Jesus, the Bread of Life, whom we receive in the shared bread and cup of the Holy Supper. At the same time, the Supper points beyond itself to all those who are hungry. For them the Eucharist is the sign of eating and drinking in the kingdom, whose promise—even now—is that bread that is shared never runs out.

10

SERVICE OF
THE LORD'S SUPPER

GATHERING AROUND CHRIST'S TABLE has taken many forms through the centuries. It began as an improvisation on Jewish Passover practice and an evocation of Jesus' meals with "insiders" and "outsiders" in the course of his ministry. In the first century after Jesus' ascension, aspects of these meals were linked and stylized in different ways in different cultural settings. This usually included Jesus' fourfold action of taking, blessing, breaking, and giving bread (Mt 14:19; Mk 14:22; Lk 24:30). Matthew, Mark, Luke, and Paul preserve local adaptations of Jesus' words of institution at the Last Supper.[1] They were the interpretive key of the Supper and increasingly the center point of its enactment.

Liturgies. In most places the Breaking of Bread soon became the normal Lord's Day service or perhaps, better said, the culmination of the service. Visitors and those being prepared for baptism participated in singing (largely of psalms), reading of Scripture, and preaching. Then they left the service, which continued with intercessions, self-examination, and Communion. There was no single form of worship, but there was an emerging pattern for the liturgy on which the presider improvised. It was shaped differently in East and West, but the pattern was recognizable from liturgy to liturgy.

The high point of the service was the Communion prayer (also called the Great Thanksgiving and the eucharistic prayer). It began as an expansion of Jewish prayers of blessing (bərākāh) in which an aspect of God's goodness was lifted up and praised. The prayers of the Last Supper were of this type.

---

[1] John preserves the Passover meal but with a most striking innovation, the act of footwashing (Jn 13:1-17).

Over time this prayer came to include a narrative of salvation history from the giving of the Law to the coming of the Messiah. In some settings it also included thanksgiving for the goodness and beauty of creation. In time the eucharistic prayer also encompassed a remembrance of the dead and intercessions for church leaders.

Here is an outline of the core of the service to which various prayers and ceremonial acts were added in the course of the patristic era:[2]

+ confession of sin / Kyrie

+ passing the peace

+ eucharistic prayer

+ preface praising God for redemption

+ Sanctus (Holy, holy, holy, Lord God of hosts)

(The order of the following is not always the same.)

+ words of institution

+ *anamnesis* (the living memory of Jesus' death for us)

+ *epiclesis* (prayer for the Spirit to come upon the congregation so that it might receive and become the body of Christ; soon this prayer was extended to the bread and wine that they might be a communion of the body and blood of Christ)

+ Agnus Dei (Lamb of God)

+ receiving the bread and cup

+ praising God for his gifts

After Christianity became the religion of the empire, worship became a public event in a public building, increasingly performed only by clergy. Its ceremonial became increasingly elaborate. The congregation had less and less of a role in worship. Infant baptism was obligatory but did not necessarily issue in a life of faith. Thus, many worshipers were not ready to come to

---

[2]Everett Ferguson, *Early Christians Speak* (Austin, TX: Sweet, 1971), historic texts with interpretive comments; Edward Foley, *From Age to Age: How Christians Have Celebrated the Eucharist* (Chicago: Liturgy Training, 1991), esp. 2-42, liturgical, musical, and architectural details; and Herman Wegman, *Christian Worship in East and West: A Study Guide to Liturgical History*, trans. Gordon W. Lathrop (Collegeville, MN: Liturgical Press, 1990), esp. 1-51, historic and cultural shaping of worship.

the Lord's Table (1 Cor 10:14-22). Gradually the devotion of churchgoers became focused on the words of institution (thought to be the moment when the bread and wine became the body and blood) and the elevation of the host. But the congregation itself did not normally take Communion. That took place once a year, usually during Holy Week in preparation for Easter Sunday, after confession and making amends for having wronged others.

In the Reformation, the Lord's Table was brought from the east wall of the church into the midst of the congregation. Most Reformers wanted frequent Communion in which grace, and not worthiness, had the final word. Much of the inherited ceremonial was removed from the service to make the central act of the liturgy accessible to the people. For this reason the whole service was to be in the vernacular. The most significant aspect of this process of simplification was the eucharistic prayer. The elaborate narrative was shortened to make its focus, the once-for-all sacrifice of Christ, unmistakable. Prayers for the dead and clergy were removed. Some Anabaptists and later Free churches added two specific prayers of thanks before the reception of bread and wine in imitation of Jesus' two blessings at the Last Supper. Some historic Mennonite services added in the invitation a sentence that invited all those willing to give up their lives for Jesus' sake to take Communion. The reference here is to martyrdom. This invitation is included in brackets in the order of service presented in appendix one.

As to the service as a whole, the New Testament fragments of how the Supper was first celebrated were given pride of place in many Protestant liturgies.[3] Early patristic practices were improvised upon in different denominations and under the influence of different Reformers.[4] Almost all Protestant liturgies added an explicit invitation to the Table. It urged worshipers who accepted God's forgiveness not to be shy in coming to the Lord's Table but also warned people not to commune unworthily. Frequent repetition of the Kyrie was removed, and a single confession of sin was added. In the eucharistic prayer the *epiclesis* was sometimes omitted. The omission

---

[3]Meal-related images like the "Lord's Table" and the "Breaking of Bread" were used. The Communion of the "blood of Christ" and "the body of Christ" (1 Cor 10:16) was favored over later and more philosophical terms to evoke the presence of Christ.

[4]Lutherans, Reformed, and Anglicans kept early liturgical pieces like the Kyrie, Gloria, and Agnus Dei, in varying degrees.

of the *epiclesis* easily led to a contradiction. On the one hand, the more radically reformed churches wanted to be absolutely clear that they did not hold to the physical transformation of the elements. But without a prayer for the Spirit they were in danger of ending up with a "real absence." Most of them did believe that through the Spirit the Lord Jesus was present in a surpassing way in the Breaking of Bread, but, ironically, they found it hard to pray for that presence.

As post-Reformation Free churches came into being, this improvising and simplifying continued. By that time the sense of connection with patristic practice had been lost. In the course of the twentieth century, movements within Free churches sought to reclaim the longer liturgical tradition without simply imitating the practices of those denominations. They also wanted to remedy the confusion that had led in some settings to omission of an epicletic moment, that is, a request for the Spirit to make Christ present to us in the meal he gave us. The service described in appendix one expresses this twentieth-century recovery of a fuller eucharistic worship in a Free Church key. Justifications for the inclusion of certain aspects or how they are worded are found in the footnotes.

Sometimes called "the lost sacrament," the rite of footwashing is attached to the service as it has been practiced, usually twice a year, in Brethren, Baptist, and Mennonite circles. Other churches have reclaimed this ancient rite and practice it on Maundy Thursday. It is striking that this rite has never had a fixed home in the church's ritual life, though it keeps appearing.[5] This suggests to me that once people have participated in it they are persuaded of its meaningfulness. Throughout church history there is a sprinkling of references to its use. In Milan, newly baptized members had their feet washed as part of their initiation. Various monastic orders practiced it as an act both of hospitality and of mutual commitment. Because it is such a striking act of humility, monarchs in various countries washed the feet of beggars each Maundy Thursday. Late medieval dissenting movements intuitively included footwashing in their revised set of rituals. In the Reformation numerous Anabaptists taught and practiced the rite. It has been carried on in a number

---

[5]John Christopher Thomas, *Footwashing in John 13 and the Johannine Community* (Sheffield: JSOT, 1993); and Thomas O'Loughlin, *Washing Feet: Imitating the Example of Jesus in the Liturgy Today* (Collegeville, MN: Liturgical Press, 2015).

of denominations, often as the culmination of Holy Communion, symbolizing the belief that in the Supper the people are transformed.

Because of its intimacy, people are shy about practicing footwashing. It is hard to participate in it often. The most evocative times for it are occasions like Holy Week, as an act of reconciliation before the Lord's Supper, and in Communion services where there is a special emphasis on covenant and community. In a setting of warmth and serenity, it is a gesture of love that words stammer to express. In the congregation I am part of, concern was raised about the difficulty it presents for people with physical limitations. We agreed that we should offer them the gesture of handwashing as entirely appropriate but also make clear for able-bodied people that handwashing is not an alternative if the reason for choosing it is to avoid the vulnerability of washing someone's feet.

Frequency. The frequency of Communion has varied greatly across the centuries. The meaning of this term in Roman Catholicism and Eastern and Oriental Orthodoxy is different from its use in Protestantism. For Catholics and Orthodox the Sunday liturgy is always the Eucharist. That the bread and wine have been consecrated is the high point of the service even if none of the laity receive them. The term *frequency* concerns how often worshipers take Communion. For Protestantism, historically, the service of the Word is a full act of worship on the Lord's Day. At the same time the Lord's Supper is the most complete act of the church's worship. In Protestant churches *frequency* refers to how often a Eucharistic service is held.

From the records we have of the postapostolic church, it is clear that in most settings there was a weekly Breaking of Bread in which those who were baptized and sought the way of Christ participated. Later on, nominal adherents feared that their mere conformity to the dominant religion made them unworthy to commune. This fear of unworthy reception was exaggerated by the growing emphasis on the bread and the cup as the physical body and blood of Christ. If one dropped a crumb or spilled a sip, their Communion would be unworthy. In addition, it was widely held that the miracle of the real presence was accomplished by the consecration whether or not anyone other than the priest actually took Communion. Most people opted for "spiritual Communion," that is, gazing reverently upon the host at the moment of consecration. At the Fourth Lateran Council of 1215, sacramental Communion at least once a year, preferably at Easter, was mandated.

At the time of the Reformation, many Reformers wanted more frequent sacramental Communion. Some of them made the case for a weekly Breaking of Bread. In a desire to reclaim the meal character of the Supper, private Communion (of the priest alone) was rejected; in its very nature, the Eucharist was intended to be a corporate event. In most parts of most denominations, the norm that emerged was quarterly Communion with acts of preparation and reconciliation (with God as well as one's neighbor) in the week before the Lord's Supper. Communion Sundays were usually the most solemn and reverent assemblies of the year.

However, in both the lean and the rich liturgical traditions, movements arose in the early nineteenth century to celebrate the meal Jesus gave us at least monthly if not weekly. In the second half of the twentieth century, weekly Communion became more and more common across a range of denominations. In the Catholic Church the shift was a different one. The Mass was celebrated every Sunday, but now the whole congregation communed every Sunday.

In my judgment the two strongest arguments for weekly Communion are the following. One, it was the dominant pattern in the patristic era. Two, it centers the service on God's initiative. It offers worshipers the thickest liturgical symbol, the tangible presence of Christ, as the basis and culmination of the liturgy. Of course the reading and proclaiming of Scripture happen on God's initiative as well. But proclaiming also has a subjective side, the personality and gifts of the preacher. Other aspects of the service, like singing and praying, are our offerings to God. By contrast, encountering God in Christ around the Lord's Table is an objective reality.

At the same time, I have two cautions about weekly Communion. One is that its habitual nature easily loses the solemnity appropriate to the occasion. One dimension of this loss is vertical—the awesomeness of God's love in Christ's self-offering on the cross. The other dimension is horizontal—the awesomeness of our belonging to the body of Christ. Self-examination is the gateway to transformation by the encounter with Christ and the body of Christ. My impression from conversations with clergy and attendance at services in churches that practice weekly Communion is that it is hard to sustain reflectiveness among worshipers week to week. By that I mean worshipers asking themselves, Have we taken Christ's love for us for granted? Have we become indifferent to that love in sister, brother, neighbor, and enemy? To be sure, Christ's presence in the Eucharist does not depend on the intensity of our faith and love. But without contrition and amendment of life, do we close ourselves off to the transformation intended by the gift we have just received?

Coming from a denomination that allows for congregational discernment regarding the frequency of the Breaking of Bread, my pastoral practice has been to encourage monthly Communion (plus Good Friday). The act of preparation takes place at the end of the previous Sunday's service so that people have time to make good on their intentions. The preparation always begins with God's grace and invitation and then asks what stands in the way of each member and of the congregation receiving that grace.

Authority/ordination. Who presides at a congregation's sacred events, most importantly, baptism and the Eucharist? To some churches the answer to this question is completely clear. But to churches with a certain way of interpreting the priesthood of all believers and the Spirit's giving of gifts to all believers, the answer is less clear. There is a tension between the giftedness of all and the particular gift of leadership, which has traditionally been set apart by ordination. Ordination designates persons who the church believes have been called by God to that ministry and who the wider church and the congregation trust and respect. Ordination makes this designation clear within a denomination and to other denominations.

Historically (both in the early church and after the Reformation), one of the roles of leadership is to preside over the community's core rituals. In this role the minister acts on behalf of the people before God and on behalf of God before the people. Therefore, in my judgment, the Lord's Supper should normally be presided over by a pastor assisted by other designated leaders, like deacons and elders. I find the comparison with baptism helpful here. Normally, the gift of the Spirit precedes water baptism, but in God's freedom it can happen afterwards. The Anabaptist Strasbourg Order of 1568 illustrates both the norm and the freedom to improvise. The 1568 order was composed in the midst of persecution. Normally a bishop presides at sacramental occasions, but there is a procedure for exceptions: "Anyone who has been appointed, who has a good testimony, and is in the confidence of the people, such an one may take charge of communion, baptism, marrying, punishing and expelling, if no ordained bishop should be on hand, who might have been hindered for cause."[6]

These provisions allowed for the real possibility that leaders or members of the community might be arrested or killed, but the celebration of the sacrament could continue.

---

[6]Harold Bender, "The Discipline Adopted by the Strasburg (sic) Conference of 1568," in *MQR*, vol 3, October 1927, 66.

AFTERWORD

I HAVE WRITTEN THIS BOOK to entice people into looking a second time when they participate in a community's ritual.[1] I want them to discover that there is more going on than meets the eye. I wish them the unexpected and also unmistakable joy of encountering the presence of the transcendent in a particular time and place, in the Breaking of Bread, the pouring of water, the laying on of hands, and the sanctifying of time. I invite them to get ready to see a burning bush, whether they come from ritually drenched traditions or ritually parched ones that are no longer life-giving for them.

My goal has been to take a fresh look at the history of Christian worship in the West on the basis of my research over the past four decades. The first influence on my spiritual formation was the Mennonite congregation in which I grew up. It was there that I first realized there is more than we have words for in the rituals that embrace us. I was blessed by participation in various Christian movements for church unity during my undergraduate and semi-nary years. This involved worshiping with friends across the denominational spectrum. These ties to the worship life of other communities were deepened during further studies in Berlin and a year's teaching in the Philippines. My doctoral studies in an ecumenical consortium involved books of worship and the theologies behind them, as well as a calendar year of residence at an Anglican college in which I attended evening prayer every day in order to inhabit the skin of a liturgical tradition.

The core of my inquiry became sacramental gestures, both narrowly and broadly understood, as doors to the sacred. Bit by bit I pieced together litur-gical sources and their developments. As someone from a sacramentally lean

---

[1] This material was originally published in *The Conrad Grebel Review* and appears here with per-mission of the publisher: John Rempel, "On False Distinctions: The Body of Christ, Mystical and Sacramental," *The Conrad Grebel Review* 24, no. 3 (Fall 2006): 95–104, https://uwaterloo.ca/grebel/publications/conrad-grebel-review/issues/fall-2006/false-distinctions-body-christ-mystical-and-sacramental.

background, I was astonished on two counts. One of them was that my study of the dominant Catholic and Protestant traditions showed the extent of their rootedness in the Bible and the early church. The other source of my astonishment was the discovery that tradition was not a monolith. This was the case both within the dominant tradition as well as within dissident movements. The latter appeared throughout the church's story in which certain characteristics kept appearing. Among them was profound concern for the unity of the inward and outward dimensions of a practice. This sometimes involved a bias toward a freely chosen baptism and toward a dynamic of the Lord's Supper in which both grace and faith are essential. At the same time, these same dissenter movements ran the danger of reductionism in sacramental theology and practice.

In order to gain access to "what the church thought it was doing," I have ventured a theological as well as a pastoral hypothesis. Theologically, the incarnation is the essential grounding for the claim that matter can bear spirit. We have sampled the development of the doctrine of the incarnation in Scripture and tradition and how it was used by both the dominant and dissident traditions. We have also followed the incarnation trajectory. In doing so, it has become evident that physical enactments are as innate to the gospel as verbal articulations. The church speaks both "oral" and "sign" language. In the wake of secularism and pluralism, the language of signs often communicates a first impression of God's self-disclosure prior to any oral communication.

It goes without saying that the incarnation is possible only if God is triune. The incarnation is not a general metaphor for God's nearness to the creation; it is the specific claim that God entered the world he had fashioned and made himself known to it in the person of Jesus Christ.

I went on from there to make a crucial historical observation about the shift of meaning in the word *symbol* in and after the Reformation. Patristic and medieval thought categories are complex and belong to a distinct intellectual past; summarizing or distilling them requires great care. Bearing that in mind, I think that "symbolic realism" and "mere symbolism" are adequate—though not definitive—ways of distinguishing two thought patterns that have had enormous influence in post-Reformation conceptions of the sacramental. To use the example of the Eucharist once again, in symbolic realism Jesus offers us a participation in his body and blood, his very person, through the shared meal of bread and wine. Bread and wine bear the promise that Christ is present in their sharing, that we are made one with him and his body, the church, in a surpassing way. In mere symbolism there is no real presence: bread and wine are only signs of the body and blood; they do no more than signify a reality in which they have no part. Taken to an extreme, they are the sign of a "real absence."

One can make the case for Ulrich Zwingli and those Anabaptists who followed in his sway, that they had to put forth a radical corrective because the church faced a radical problem, that is, the popular view that Jesus of Nazareth's body and blood were physically consumed at the Lord's Table. It took the jarring dislocation we call the Reformation to compel a reconsideration of what the real presence of Jesus means. Because of their radical corrective to a radical problem, the Zwinglians shifted all the meaning of Jesus' presence to the belief that in the Breaking of Bread it is the congregation that is transformed. They allowed for the possibility that in the liminal space Holy Communion creates, there could be a mystical encounter with Christ. In other words, they did make (precarious) provision for something beyond our acts of remembrance happening to us.

Historically speaking, however, this formulation of sacramental thought was so unstable that it could not withstand reductionism. The Supper ended up as less than Zwingli, and the Anabaptists who agreed with him, intended: a merely human act of remembrance from which all mystery was shorn. Many theologians, ministers, and denominations have inherited this mere symbolism. Wanting to remain loyal to their church's historic reading of the New Testament, the heirs of the Reformation in Zurich have not opened themselves to another understanding of the emblematic realm—like symbolic realism— that could open doors to the sacred for them, consistent with their understanding of the church. It has been my intention to make this case convincingly.

The dominant sacramental tradition of Orthodox, Catholics, and liturgical Protestants is well known; it is the subject of most books on liturgy. Until recently its practitioners have more or less assumed that there is a straight line from the early church to the thirteenth century, the peak of Catholic sacramental development, by way of what I have called metabolic realism. By this

I mean the belief that the bread and wine become the body and blood of Christ through a sacramental act that accomplishes what it signifies. This view was modified in the sixteenth century but continued by Lutherans and later by High Anglicans. Other churches, like Reformed and Mennonites, took two paths. The more-traveled path was grounded in the New Testament, made modest reference to the patristic era, and went from there straight to the Reformation. The less-traveled path also began with the New Testament and age of the Fathers. It went on to identify with symbolic realism as an understanding of the sacramental realm that had had equal status with metabolic realism in the Western church until the ninth century. It was then marginalized and became a dissenting interpretation carried forward by theologians, like Berengar, the Waldensians, and Wycliffe, into the Protestant Reformation.

As we saw in the first chapter on the Eucharist, chapter six, both the metabolists and the symbolists, or more broadly Catholic and Protestant, viewpoints have changed in the course of the twentieth century, the age of liturgical rediscovery and reappraisal. To cite only one aspect of the shift, the metabolists realized that they had imposed sacramental views of much later generations on the early church. The symbolists, in turn, realized that the Reformation had brought along more than they were aware of from the age of the Fathers and had lost more than they were aware of in subsequent centuries.

It is this gradual realization, that there was a second sacramental tradition in the Western church that had normative status into the ninth century and then lived on as a dissident tradition until the close of the Middle Ages, to which I have tried to draw attention. I have tried to show that there is a kind of apostolic succession—a persistent way of doing theology and liturgy across the generations—that believed it was orthodox as deeply as did the dominant strand. Of enormous significance is the fact that this standpoint was not a departure from the sacramental universe. It too was grounded in a trinitarian confession of God, the Word becoming flesh and its implications for the world of matter and for the church as the prolongation of the incarnation.

This dissident tradition further developed its character traits after the Reformation, starting with Baptists and concluding with Plymouth Brethren. Missionary zeal took those as well as older denominational identities into the Global South. With the advent of Pentecostalism, there was a reclamation of ancient charismatic worship. At the same time, Pentecostalism burst the bounds of historic Protestantism. For it, and current movements like it, the historic dissident position is at best a dotted and not a solid line between Christian origins and the present.

After a century of liturgical ferment and a half century of changed understandings of the church (established churches are less established; sectarian churches are less sectarian), we might be ready to critically engage the whole tradition, dominant and dissident, in pursuit of a sacramentality and ecclesiology in which divine initiative and human response, grace and faith, will each be given its due. This challenge stands at the heart of the search for Christian unity.

In conclusion, taking the Lord's Supper as the richest case study of sacramental worship as a whole, I want to name the danger that sacramental worship, even when it is steeped in tradition and open to the Holy Spirit, carries with it. Its peril is to confine the bread of life and the cup of salvation to the sacred time and space in which it is given. The watching world wonders whether the gospel has anything to offer it. The question before us is this: Is the church willing to make the bread of Christ into bread for the world, offering it with words of witness and deeds of compassion?

Christians with a passion for peace and justice worry that people who are drawn to the spiritual and sacramental dimensions of the gospel never get around to changing the world. I'm one of the culprits. By nature I choose silence and music, social and religious ritual, as settings in which I find a heightened sense of presence and encounter. I am caught up in a profound harmony that stands over and against the noisiness of life. I prize the transcendent moment precisely because its sacredness participates in a plane of reality removed from everyday life. I end up wanting to confine God to these "holy places" because I fear that this treasured reality is too fragile to make a mark on the disordered world.

People like me are in danger of making the Eucharist into a holy ritual that gathers people from the messiness of ordinary time into a tidy sacred symmetry but forgets to send them back to embrace the joys and sorrows of everyday life. Yet the whole point of sacraments as unequivocal gestures of blessing is to take them with us and live out of them in the ambiguities of worldly existence. That possibility follows from an incarnational understanding of mission. Yet too often we fear that there will not be enough love to go around in this broken world. In time our fear becomes not only a momentary faltering but a way of life. We reluctantly conclude that there is no bridge between religious and secular moments. In time, how we live depends on this separation: we give God his due on Sunday but have no place for him in the midst of our everyday dealings. Yet the whole point of devouring God's love in the sharing of bread and wine is to go forth in the confidence that there will be enough—to testify to the truth that love expands when it is shared and shrivels when it is hoarded.

The Bible is full of warnings against making such false distinctions between the holy and the profane. The prophets and psalmists talk about the inseparability of worship and justice. The preacher Amos is the bluntest. He talks about ritual without discipleship. The Lord says, "I hate, I despise your festivals, and I take no delight in your solemn assemblies" (Amos 5:21). For the prophets and Jesus, the sacramental moment is not the end of the encounter with grace but the means to its realization—not the abandonment of the ordinary but its transformation.

Suppose that one Sunday I am in the same service as a colleague I can't get along with at work. At the confession of sin I am able to release my resentment, and during the passing of the peace I offer sincere acceptance to my estranged coworker. Of course, when we meet at work the next day, we still need to come to terms with the fact that our personalities grate on each other. But in two ritual gestures, confessing sin and passing the peace, we have cleaned the slate and taken the freedom to deal with each other in a new way. We have been delivered from the lie that nothing can be done to overcome our conflict, that we are stuck being enemies. Think of the significance this revelation can have for overcoming strife between classes, races, and nations.

Wholeness of life, rather than its division into secular and sacred, grows out of the rhythm of the church in its gathering and scattering. Liturgy is the drama of gesture and recitation we create to give time and place to the presence we are promised we will encounter. Whether a congregation celebrates the Lord's Supper every Sunday or not, the Supper embodies the implicit point of reference for all Christian worship; it is the sign that the circle of reconciliation around the Lord's Table is what God intends for all creation.

The core of the recital is always God's self-giving love in creation and redemption. It gathers and then scatters those who have been drawn into its orbit.

Part of the problem is that we pit the personal and communal aspects of love's orbit against each other. Personal encounter with Christ becomes private encounter. Yes, of course, Christ died, not only for the whole world but also for me. But this is not a private encounter: I can't belong to Christ without belonging to his body; I can't belong to his body without living for the world.

The transformation that happens in worship, of which the Breaking of Bread is the densest manifestation, is not so much its immediate experiential effect as the mark it leaves on our hearts and wills. The encounter with Christ and our sisters and brothers makes us into different people over the long haul. Think of the daring but consistent development in the early church for it to move from sharing meals to creating an economic community, as we find in the Jerusalem church (Acts 2:41-47).

In worship we are remade into Christ's body; through worship we become people who are convinced, bit by bit, that there will be enough love to go around. We give to others what we have been given—forgiveness, joy, freedom, and outrage at injustice. We who have been inhabited by the Bread of Life become bread for hungry people. Sacramental living is both the concentrated moments when the cup of salvation is held and drunk and the dispersed moments when it is poured out for the world.

William Crockett delineates "ideological" ritual (legitimizing the existing order) and "utopian" ritual (embodying an alternative).[2] Ideology is commonly understood as the sum total of concepts, assumptions, and practices that legitimate—or put into question—the existing order of things. In order to not be conscripted by political ideologies of the left and right, people are tempted to think of worship and piety as having to do only with spiritual community and, therefore, apolitical. But the effect of confining religion to church, if not always the intention, is for it to bless the web of unjust social relationships as they are.

Over the years I have tried to alert people to this problem. "Take for instance, the political situation in the Deep South of the United States early in the civil rights movement. African Americans were demanding full admission to US

---

[2]William Crockett, *Eucharist: Symbol of Transformation* (New York: Pueblo, 1990), 247.

society, inclusion in the social and religious institutions that existed for the benefit of the white majority. Black people started attending white churches. In some, they were shunned and frozen out with silence. In others, the police were called in to remove these intruders on the grounds that the sacred assembly could proceed only when the impediments to its ritual purity had been removed. The ideological role of segregated worship in hallowing the status quo is too plain to miss."[3]

I once learned a maxim that was attributed to the Russian Orthodox philosopher Nicholas Berdyaev: bread for me is a material matter; bread for my neighbor is a spiritual one. Berdyaev meant by this that when I go to a bakery to buy bread for myself, it is a physical act for a physical need, hunger. But to see my neighbor without bread, and to take that neighbor to the bakery to buy bread, is an act of discipleship.[4]

I have used another historical example of blindness to one's own prejudices that takes the Lord's Supper as its case study. Enrique Dussel, a Latin American ethicist, presents Bartolomé de las Casas, the sixteenth-century Roman Catholic missionary to the Caribbean, as a model for just eucharistic fellowship.[5] He ultimately found himself unable to celebrate the Mass because the bread it used was ill-gotten. Las Casas realized that his slaves labored not for their own gain but for that of their master. His response to the injustice of the situation was twofold. First was to put a symbolic moratorium on the celebration of the Eucharist, and the second was to literally set his own slaves free. The goal of both actions was to liberate people to reap the fruit of their labor."[6]

> What he saw was the identity between the bread-product of everyday work, changed and exchanged, respected or stolen, and the bread of the altar. The bread contains the objectified life of the worker . . . and . . . what was being done was taking this bread from him unjustly and offering it to God. For this bread to become the very "body" of the lamb that was slain, it has to be . . . the bread of justice.[7]

---

[3]John Rempel, "On False Distinctions: The Body of Christ, Mystical and Sacramental," in *The Conrad Grebel Review*, Fall 2006, 97-98.
[4]See Nicolas Berdyaev, *The Destiny of Man*, trans. Natalie Duddington (New York: Harper & Row, 1960; first published in 1931), 187-95.
[5]Enrique Dussel, "Bread . . . as a Sign of Justice," in *Can We Always Celebrate the Eucharist?*, ed. Mary Collins and David N. Power (New York: Seabury, 1982), 56-65.
[6]Rempel, "On False Distinctions...," 98.
[7]Dussel, "Bread . . . as a Sign of Justice," 61.

William Cavanaugh's rightly praised book, *Torture and Eucharist*, is built on Las Casas's pregnant insight. Cavanaugh is an American Catholic ethicist who lived in Chile in the 1980s. He turned to such a provocative and revealing interpretation as a desperate attempt to make sense of the awful reality that the torturers of the Pinochet regime were members of the same church, sometimes the same congregation, as the tortured.

Cavanaugh posits an identity between the victim's body and Christ's body, both mystical and sacramental. He makes the case that "in the Eucharist . . . Christ Himself, the eternal consummation of history, becomes present in time."[8] In my article "On False Distinctions," I summarize Cavanaugh's thesis: "Essential to his case is the patristic use of *corpus mysticum* (the Supper) and *corpus verum* (the church). Christ's ritual and literal presence are two manifestations of the same reality. In the view of this Catholic theologian, the tragedy of his church in Chile was its failure to live out this indivisible reality."[9] The literal or historical body of Christ is by nature visible. It cannot but identify itself with the victims of torture: it suffers these afflictions with Christ in its own flesh (Col 1:24). The disappeared re-appear as members of the body of Christ. They still remain members of the communion of saints, the solidarity of Christians in heaven and on earth and part of the visible church.[10] And this body of Christ must excommunicate the perpetrators of torture. By torturing they exclude themselves. If the church fails to do both of these, it forfeits its very nature.[11]

Cavanaugh's case depends on the patristic understanding of Holy Communion as the form of Christ's mystical presence and the church community as his sacramental presence. As we have seen, in the Middle Ages these references were reversed. This reversal led to a preoccupation with a localized presence of the historical body of Christ in the elements of the Eucharist. All the while, the church relinquished the body of Christ as his sacramental presence in the world, that is, the community of believers who prolong his incarnation. This theological inversion was a watershed in the ritual and

---

[8]William T. Cavanaugh, *Torture and Eucharist: Theology, Politics, and the Body of Christ* (Hoboken, NJ: Wiley-Blackwell, 1998), 223.

[9]Cavanaugh, *Torture and Eucharist*, 233.

[10]Cavanaugh, *Torture and Eucharist*, 277.

[11]Cavanaugh, *Torture and Eucharist*, 243; Rempel, "On False Distinctions," 99.

missionary life of the church. Cavanaugh argues that this switch allowed Pinochet loyalists in deeply Catholic Chile to conclude that the presence of Christ in the elements has nothing to do with his presence through the church in the world.

This false distinction between what we do when we gather and when we scatter again is the heart of the church's problem. To repeat it one final time, the ritual moment is not the end of the encounter with grace but the means to its realization, not the abandonment of the ordinary but its transformation.

AN ORDER OF SERVICE FOR THE LORD'S SUPPER

I AM INCLUDING HERE this order of service for the Lord's Supper that I created as the fruit of my ministry. For over forty years I have studied liturgies ancient and modern and participated in communities that worshiped through them, from a black Baptist church in Philadelphia to a Chaldean church in Basra, Iraq. I have had the privilege of writing and adapting worship resources for congregations in which I ministered and for our denomination.

A purist might think that such an order of service is neither fish nor fowl. I would protest that it is both fish and fowl. I have used the ancient form of the Breaking of Bread as it was improvised upon in the Reformation and in the outburst of liturgical creativity in many denominations beginning in the 1960s. I have used language that falls between traditional and inclusive. I have given the service a posture: the bread we receive at the Lord's Table is the bread we share with the world. We turn to and then from the Table. I have broadened *confession* to include the good we confess as well as the bad. I have included an invitation to Communion, which was a Reformation innovation both to persuade people to partake of God's offer and to examine themselves. I have left a few places for improvisation, that is, to write words for this occasion beforehand or to reflect deeply beforehand such that one's extemporaneous words truly suit this occasion. I was explicit about this gathered community worshiping with the whole body of Christ on earth and in heaven. I have included a petition for the Spirit to make Christ present, using Paul's words in 1 Corinthians 10, hoping that it has enough breadth to speak for a range of beliefs about the nature of Christ's presence in the Eucharist. I hope that it is a blessing to you.

AN ORDER OF SERVICE FOR THE LORD'S SUPPER

For testing in congregations

Communion usually follows the service of the Word.

Music and/or singing can be included throughout according to local custom.

INTRODUCTION

(Words prepared for this occasion or the following may be used.)

> M: (*Minister*) Being invited to the Lord's Table is the greatest honor we can receive. At times we come to it with joy for God's goodness in creation and redemption. At other times we gather in sorrow for our own sins and the sins of the world. Always we come because Jesus promises to be present.

CONFESSION

> M: In the silence let us confess what is ours to confess: the good we have given and received, the bad we have given and received.[1]

(Silence of at least one minute.)

> M: To those who have brought what is life giving, Jesus says, "The kingdom is among you!" To those who have brought what is life taking, Jesus says, "Your sins are forgiven you!"

> M: God forgives us in Christ;

> P: (*People*) by God's grace let us forgive others.

> M: God restores us in Christ;

> P: with God's help let us restore others.

> M: God reconciles us in Christ;

> P: in God's peace let us reconcile others.[2]

> M: In the name of Jesus Christ, Teacher, Healer, Redeemer. Amen.

---

[1] There is a concern abroad that a disproportionate emphasis on sinfulness does not take seriously the promise that we can grow in grace. Hence, space is given to confess what is good in our lives and world as well as what is bad. For this awareness I am indebted to my fellow committee members in a study of the misuse of religious language and gestures when sexual abuse takes place in religious settings.

[2] I thank Darrin Snyder Belousak for this formulation.

CHRIST'S PEACE

M: Hear the words of Jesus: "Peace I leave with you; my peace I give to you. I do not give to you as the world gives. Do not let your hearts be troubled, and do not let them be afraid" (Jn 14:27). As a sign of our reconciliation, let us pass the peace of Christ to those around us.

INVITATION TO THE LORD'S TABLE

M: Sisters and brothers, it is right that we should call to mind the meaning of this Holy Supper. It is a remembrance of Christ's self-offering for the healing of the world. It is a communion with the Risen One and with his body the church, a sharing in the bread of life, and an offering of bread to the world in anticipation of the day when all shall eat and be filled.

It is the Lord's Table: all who are baptized and seek the way of Christ are invited to it. [Let whoever is willing—by God's grace—to give up life, limb, and possessions for Jesus' sake, come and eat.][3]

Come to Christ and never be hungry; trust in him and you will not thirst.

COMMUNION PRAYER

M: Lord of the cosmos, at your command all things came to be. Where once there was nothing, your love brought into being countless galaxies with countless stars.[4] And, finally, you made us in your own image. Through the ages you cared, like a mother, for all you had created. You made us stewards of the earth, yet we betrayed your trust. Through the prophets you called us to return to you. In the fullness of time you sent us your Son, our Messiah, to teach us the law of love, to heal our infirmities, and mend your torn creation.[5] When evil arose against your Beloved, he lived what he had taught and loved his enemies to the end.[6]

---

[3]This is Jesus' breathtaking appeal as found in the Gospels and repeated in early Mennonite invitations to Communion. It is an expression not of law but of costly grace. It is in brackets, however, because it could be misunderstood as setting a standard that only the strongest can meet. It is included for experimentation.

[4]These images are intended to bring to mind recent scientific discovery of the vastness of God's creation.

[5]*Mend* is a response to a concern that a disproportionate emphasis has been placed on salvation and not enough on transformation.

[6]In Jesus' willingness to die for us, his enemies, he lived out his teaching in the Sermon on the Mount and made it a model for his followers.

In awe and wonder we remember Jesus' death for us, who caused his shame. In his dying you reconciled us, and the whole creation, to yourself. In his rising you opened your covenant with Israel to all humanity.[7] In the company of all the saints in heaven and on earth we gather around this Table to praise you for his life lived, laid down, and taken up again for us.[8]

Send now your Spirit upon us so that the bread we break and the cup we share might be a communion of the body and blood of Christ.[9] Send now your Spirit upon us so that we, and all who bear his name, might live lives conformed to Christ.

Hear us for his sake, (in whose name we pray, Our Father . . .) Amen.

The words of institution and prayer of thanks may be said separately for bread and wine, as below, or together. The words of institution from Matthew, Mark, or Luke may be used instead of these from 1 Corinthians.

WORDS OF INSTITUTION FOR THE BREAD

M: For I received from the Lord what I also handed on to you, that the Lord Jesus on the night when he was betrayed, took a loaf of bread, and when he had given thanks, he broke it and said, "This is my body that is for you. Do this in remembrance of me."

PRAYER OF THANKS FOR THE BREAD

(As is or a prayer prepared for this occasion, traditionally offered by a deacon, elder or other caregiver in the congregation.)

Blessed are you, abundant God. You made bread to strengthen us; you gave us this bread as a sign of your Beloved's broken body. Let our sharing in it be a foretaste of the bread that feeds the whole world. Amen.

(Distribution during music or silence.)

---

[7]In Romans 9–11 and Ephesians 3 Paul writes that the "mystery of Christ" is his bringing outsiders into the covenant God had made with the Jews.
[8]See John 10:17. God's redemption of the world in Christ happened inseparably through his life, his death, and his resurrection. It is important to name them all at Communion.
[9]See 1 Corinthians 10:16-17.

WORDS OF INSTITUTION FOR THE CUP

M: In the same way he took the cup also after supper, saying, "This cup is the new covenant in my blood. Do this as often as you drink it in remembrance of me." For as often as you eat this bread and drink the cup, you proclaim the Lord's death until he comes.

PRAYER OF THANKS FOR THE CUP *(as with the bread, spoken by a deacon, elder, or other caregiver in the congregation)*

Blessed are you, bountiful God. You made the fruit of the vine to nourish us; you gave us this cup as a sign of your Beloved's shed blood. Let our sharing in it be a foretaste of the wine we shall drink in your kingdom. Amen.

(Distribution during music or silence; a suitable silence is kept after all have received.)

FOOTWASHING

Read all or part of John 1:1-17 with a short commentary prepared for the occasion or as follows.

M: When Jesus washed the disciples' feet, he set an example for us to follow. Jesus, the Ruler and Teacher, emptied himself, taking the form of a slave. In kneeling before one another we practice serving sister and brother, neighbor and enemy. As we return to daily life, let us recall the posture we have taken here. Come and renew the covenant of the upside-down kingdom.

Chairs are set up beforehand in circles of not more than eight people with an opening in the circle for people to enter. It is less disruptive if the chairs are beside the worship space or in another room. A basin of warm water (large enough for a foot to be covered with water) is set down at the opening in the circle. A towel is draped across the nearest chair.

Participants are invited to join a circle. In some congregations women and men go to separate circles; in others they simply choose the nearest seat. All are seated. They remove footwear and socks. The person who has sat down in the first chair drapes the towel across her shoulder. She places the basin in front of the person to her left. She takes one foot and places it in the basin, cupping water over it once or twice. She lifts the first foot and dries it and does the same with the second foot. Both people arise and give each other a sign of peace. The towel is passed to the person whose feet have been washed. The person who has washed feet returns to her seat. Then the person whose feet have been washed turns to the person to her left and repeats the ritual. There may be singing, instrumental music, or silence. At the end people return to where they had been sitting for the closing of the service.

All: Lord Jesus, we have knelt before each other as you once knelt before your disciples, washing another's feet. We have done what words stammer to express.

Accept this gesture of love as a pledge of how we mean to live our lives. Bless us, as you promised, with joy and perseverance in the way of the cross. Amen.

POST-COMMUNION PRAYER

M: Blessed are you, God our Father, Source of Life. Through this holy meal you have made us partakers of Christ and of one another.

Blessed are you, Lord Jesus Christ, Word Made Flesh. You have put your life into our hands; now we put our lives into yours.[10]

Blessed are you, Holy Spirit, Indwelling Presence. As we go forth, set us free to live what Jesus taught and did. Amen.

MUSIC

---

[10]The phrase, "You have put . . . lives into yours" comes from *Bridgefolk Double Eucharist, Sunday Liturgy*, July 30, 2017, Seattle, WA.

LITURGY FOR FOOTWASHING
AND AGAPE MEAL
(LOVE FEAST)

THIS SERVICE IS INCLUDED with three uses in mind. The first is to provide a sacred meal, grounded in the Gospels, for ecumenical settings in which some participants might not be able to share Holy Communion with other denominations. The second use is to provide a meal for baptized believers to share with new Christians as part of their preparation for baptism. The third use is as a congregation's preparation (can be done in small groups) for the Lord's Supper, which will happen in a subsequent service. Music accompanies the service.

OPENING

Greeting and opening prayer by presider

Opening song

First reading: 1 John 4:7-16

Psalm 78:13-25, antiphonally

Gospel: John 13:1-20

Commentary by one or several people

Invitation to and preparation for footwashing

Words of institution: John 13:3-5, 14

FOOTWASHING

See the footwashing instructions in Appendix I.

Well-known songs such as "Ubi Caritas" and "Will You Let Me Be Your Servant?" may be sung.

Participants give each other a sign of peace when they have finished washing.

PRAYERS OF PRAISE AND PETITION

The minister (M) opens and closes the time of prayer.

Participants offer brief prayers of thanks and aspiration. After each one:

M: We pray to the Lord.

P: (*People*) Lord, hear our prayer.

AGAPE MEAL

Grace is said or sung.

Someone lights the candle at each table.

THANKSGIVING FOR THE LIGHT

M: Blessed are you, Sovereign God.

You sent us the Messiah to shine on all you have created:

light for the path of discipleship;

light to reveal the dignity of all people;

light of teaching, healing, and forgiveness;

light to show the power of love that does not retaliate on the cross.

Send your Spirit to guide us to this light.

Let us be its reflection to others.

In the name of Jesus. Amen.

BLESSING OF THE BREAD

M: Blessed are you, Lord our God. You sustain the universe; you bring forth bread from the earth.

P: Amen.

M: Just as the bread we break was once scattered over hills and prairies, but now has been gathered and made one, so let your church be gathered from the ends of the earth and be made one.

P: For the power and glory are yours forever.

Bread is broken and shared at each table.

BLESSING OF THE CUP

Reading of John 15:1-8, 16-17

Wine is poured into glasses and held up for the blessing.

M: Blessed are you, Lord our God, Creator of the fruit of the vine, which you have given us to drink anew in your reign.

P: Amen.

The meal continues.

FINAL BLESSING

M: We bless you, heavenly Father, that the Word became flesh. And being found in human form, he humbled himself and washed his disciples' feet. Let our participation in these sacraments of love strengthen us to serve you with words of witness and deeds of justice.

P: Come, Lord Jesus!

M: God of every gift, rain down your Spirit on us:

Protect us from harm,

Strengthen us in love,

Send us forth with courage and joy.

From the four winds gather all your disciples

into communion with you, Triune God,

into the reign you have prepared.

All: Come, Lord Jesus![1]

CLOSING SONG

---

[1]Written by Mary Schertz, with adaptations. Used by permission.

EMMAUS COMMUNION

THIS SIMPLE SERVICE for the Breaking of Bread is especially suited for informal settings. It is drawn from Luke (22:19-20; 24:13-35). Music can open and close the service.

SELF-EXAMINATION

Silence

M: (*Minister*) God of patience, God of surprises, it is hard to keep on believing that Jesus will come into our lives. We no longer expect him; we live life on our own.

P: (*People*) By your Spirit open our senses to recognize the Risen One in the Breaking of Bread. By your Spirit, help us to recognize him in our daily lives. Through Jesus, the One who returned from the dead. Amen.

NARRATION

NARRATOR: On the third day after Jesus' execution, two disciples, sad and confused, were going home to a village called Emmaus, about seven miles from Jerusalem, and talking with each other about all the things that had happened concerning the arrest and crucifixion of Jesus. Another walker, a stranger, drew near and asked,

STRANGER: What are you discussing with each other as you walk along?

FIRST DISCIPLE: The things about Jesus of Nazareth, who was a prophet mighty in deed and word before God and all the people. Our chief priests and leaders handed him over to be condemned to death and crucified him. But we had hoped that he was the one to redeem Israel. It is now the third day since these things took place.

STRANGER: Do you not remember what the prophets have declared? Was it not necessary that the Messiah should suffer these things and then enter into his glory?

NARRATOR: Then, beginning with Moses and all the prophets, he interpreted to them the things about the Messiah in all the Scriptures. As they came near the village to which they were going, he walked ahead as if he were going on. But they urged him strongly, saying,

SECOND DISCIPLE: Stay with us, because it is almost evening, and the day is now nearly over.

NARRATOR: So he went in to stay with them. When the stranger was at the table with them, he took bread, blessed and broke it, and gave it to them. Then their eyes were opened, and they recognized him.

FIRST DISCIPLE: It is the Lord!

NARRATOR: And he vanished from their sight. The disciples said to each other:

SECOND DISCIPLE: How our hearts burned within us while he was talking to us on the road, while he was opening the Scriptures to us! And then we recognized him in the Breaking of Bread.

Silence

M: Almighty, merciful, mothering God, in tender love your Word became flesh, full of grace and truth. Taking the form of a servant, your Beloved lived our life and died our death, disarming the power of sin on the cross. Christ rose again, victorious over death, and met disbelieving friends in the Breaking of Bread. Send your Holy Spirit on us now as you did of old so that as we receive this bread and cup Christ might be made known to us. Through and with Christ we pray (Our Father . . .). Amen.

M: "Then [Jesus] took a loaf of bread, and when he had given thanks, he broke it and gave it to them, saying, 'This is my body, which is given for you. Do this in remembrance of me.' And he did the same with the cup after supper, saying, 'This cup that is poured out for you is the new covenant in my blood'" (Lk 22:19-20).

M: (addressing the congregation)

And so now we break the bread (*lifts and breaks*)

and raise the cup (*lifts cup*).

Our hearts, too, burn within us as we remember Jesus' words.

He stands here among us and comforts us:

M: Peace be with you!

P: And also with you.

M: Do you recognize him in the Breaking of Bread?

P: The Risen One is here!

The bread and cup are shared.

CLOSING PRAYER

M: Bountiful God, you have fed us with the bread and cup of eternal life. Send us forth now to be bread for the world so that all might taste your goodness. Amen.

The readers should rehearse the narrative beforehand to better convey the drama of the encounter.[1]

---

[1] Written by Eleanor Kreider, with adaptations. Used by permission.

BIBLIOGRAPHY

Abbott, Walter M., ed. *Documents of Vatican II*. New York: American Press, 1966.

Abramowski, Luise, and J. F. Gerhard Goeters, eds. *Studien zur Geschichte und Theologie der Reformation: Festschrift für Ernst Bizer*. Neukirchen-Vluyn: Neukirchener Verlag, 1969.

Abrams, M. H., ed. *The Norton Anthology of English*. 1st ed. Vol. 2. New York: Norton, 1962.

Aers, David. *Sanctifying Signs: Making Christian Tradition in Late Medieval England*. Notre Dame, IN: University of Notre Dame Press, 2004.

Ahlstrom, Sydney E. "The Scottish Philosophy and American Theology." *Church History* 24, no. 3 (1955): 257-72. www.jstor.org/stable/3162115.

Aldwinckle, Russell Foster. *More than Man: A Study in Christology*. Grand Rapids: Eerdmans, 1976.

Aquinas, Thomas. *Summa Theologiae*. Question 38. New York: McGraw-Hill, 1963.

Arendt, Hannah. *The Human Condition*. Garden City, NY: Doubleday, 1959.

Auden, W. H. *Selected Poetry of W. H. Auden*. New York: Vintage, 1977.

Augustine. *An Augustine Reader*. Edited by John J. O'Meara. Garden City, NY: Doubleday Image, 1973.

Barrett, C. K. *The First Epistle to the Corinthians*, second edition. London: Adam Black, 1968.

Barth, Karl. *Church Dogmatics*. Vol. 4, pt. 2, *The Doctrine of Reconciliation*. Edited by G. W. Bromiley and T. F. Torrance. Edinburgh: T&T Clark, 1967.

Beachy, Alvin J. *The Concept of Grace in the Radical Reformation*. Nieuwkoop: De Graaf, 1976.

Beasley-Murray, G. R. *Baptism in the New Testament*. Grand Rapids: Eerdmans, 1973.

———. *Jesus and the Kingdom of God*. Grand Rapids: Eerdmans, 1986.

Bebbington, David W. *Baptists Through the Centuries: A History of a Global People*. Waco, TX: Baylor University Press, 2010.

Berdyaev, Nicolas. *The Destiny of Man*, trans. Natalie Duddington. New York: Harper & Brothers, 1960. First published in 1931.

Bernier, Paul. *Bread Broken and Shared: Broadening Our Vision of Eucharist*. Notre Dame, IN: Ave Maria Press, 1981.

Blough, Neal. *Christ in Our Midst: Incarnation, Church, and Discipleship in the Theology of Pilgram Marpeck*. Kitchener, Ont.: Pandora, 2007.

Boers, Arthur, Barbara Nelson Gingerich, Eleanor Kreider, John Rempel, and Mary Schertz. *Take Our Moments and Our Days: An Anabaptist Prayer Book Advent Through Pentecost*. Vol. 2. Scottdale, PA: Herald Press, 2010.

Boersma, Hans. *Heavenly Participation: The Weaving of a Sacramental Tapestry*. Grand Rapids: Eerdmans, 2011.

Boersma, Hans, and Matthew Levering, eds. *The Oxford Handbook of Sacramental Theology*. Oxford: Oxford University Press, 2015.

Bonhoeffer, Dietrich. *Ethics*. Translated by Neville Horton Smith. New York: Macmillan, 1960.

Book of Alternative Services of the Anglican Church of Canada. Toronto: Anglican Book Centre, 1985.

Bradshaw, Paul F. *The Search for the Origins of Christian Worship: Sources and Methods for the Study of Early Liturgy*. 1st ed. New York: Oxford University Press, 1992.

Breidenthal, Thomas. "The Festal Gathering: Reflections on Open Communion." *Sewanee Theological Review* 54, no. 2 (April 2011): 142-57.

Brilioth, Yngve. *Eucharistic Faith & Practice: Evangelical & Catholic*. Translated by A. G. Hebert. London: SPCK, 1934.

Bromiley, G. W., ed. *Zwingli and Bullinger*. Library of Christian Classics 24. Philadelphia: Westminster, 1953.

Brown, David. "A Sacramental World: Why It Matters." In Boersma and Levering, *Oxford Handbook of Sacramental Theology*, 603-15.

Brown, Raymond E. *The Gospel According to John I–XII*. Anchor Bible 29. Toronto: Anchor Bible, 1966.

Buc, Philippe. *The Dangers of Ritual: Between Early Medieval Texts and Social Scientific Theory*. Princeton, NJ: Princeton University Press, 2001.

Buchanan, Colin. *A Case for Infant Baptism*. Bramcote, UK: Grove Books, 1973.

Bullard, Scott W. *Re-membering the Body: The Lord's Supper and Ecclesial Unity in the Free Church Traditions*. Eugene, OR: Cascade, 2013.

Calvin, John, *Institutes of the Christian Religion*. Edited by John T. McNeill. Translated by Ford Lewis Battles. 2 vols. Philadelphia: Westminster, 1960.

Campbell, Alexander. *The Christian System*. New York: Arno, 1960.

Campbell, Ted, Ann K. Riggs, and Gilbert W. Stafford, eds. *Ancient Faith and American-Born Churches: Dialogues Between Christian Traditions*. Faith and Order Commission Theological Series. New York: Paulist Press, 2006.

Cavanaugh, William T. *Torture and Eucharist: Theology, Politics, and the Body of Christ*. Hoboken, NJ: Wiley-Blackwell, 1998.

Clarke, Neville. *An Approach to the Theology of the Sacraments*. London: SCM Press, 1958.

Coleman, T. W. *The Free Church Sacrament and Catholic Ideals*. Toronto: Dent & Sons, 1930.

Commission on Faith and Order. *Baptism, Eucharist and Ministry*. Geneva: World Council of Churches, 1982.

Confession of Faith in a Mennonite Perspective. Scottdale, PA: Herald Press, 1995.

Cooke, Bernard J. *The Distancing of God: The Ambiguity of Symbol in History and Theology*. Minneapolis: Fortress, 1990.

Crockett, William. *Eucharist: Symbol of Transformation*. Collegeville, MN: Liturgical Press, 1990.

Cross, Anthony R. "Baptismal Regeneration: Rehabilitating a Lost Dimension of New Testament Baptism." In *Baptist Sacramentalism 2*, edited by Anthony R. Cross and Philip E. Thompson, 149-74. Eugene, OR: Wipf & Stock, 2008.

Cross, Anthony R., and Philip E. Thompson, eds. *Baptist Sacramentalism*. Studies in Baptist History and Thought 5. Waynesboro, GA: Paternoster, 2003.

Cummings, Owen F. *Eucharistic Soundings*. Dublin: Veritas, 1999.

Daly, Robert J. "The Council of Trent." In Wandel, *Companion to the Eucharist in the Reformation*, 159-83.

Dix, Gregory. *The Shape of the Liturgy*. 1945. Reprint, London: Dacre, 1975.

Driscoll, Michael. "The Conversion of the Nations," in Geoffrey Wainwright and Karen Westerfield Tucker, eds., *The Oxford Dictionary of Christian Worship*. Oxford: Oxford University Press, 2006, 175-215.

Driver, John. *Understanding the Atonement for the Mission of the Church*. Scottdale, PA: Herald Press, 1986.

Driver, Tom F. *The Magic of Ritual: Our Need for Liberating Rites That Transform Our Lives and Our Communities*. San Francisco: Harper, 1991.

Duffy, Eamon. *The Stripping of the Altars: Traditional Religion in England 1400–1580*. 2nd ed. New Haven, CT: Yale University Press, 2005.

Durnbaugh, Donald F. *The Believers' Church: The History and Character of Radical Protestantism*. London: Macmillan, 1968.

Dussel, Enrique. "Bread . . . as a Sign of Justice." In *Can We Always Celebrate the Eucharist?*, edited by Mary Collins and David N. Power, 56-68. New York: Seabury, 1982.

Dyck, Cornelius, William E. Keeney, and Alvin J. Beachy, eds. *The Writings of Dirk Philips*. Scottdale, PA: Herald Press, 1992.

Dyrness, William A. *Insider Jesus: Theological Reflections on New Christian Movements*. Downers Grove, IL: IVP Academic, 2016.

Egeria. *Egeria: Diary of a Pilgrimage*. Translated by George E. Gingras. Ancient Christian Writers 38. New York: Newman, 1970.

Eire, Carlos. "Redefining the Sacred and the Supernatural: How the Protestant Reformation Really Did Disenchant the World." In *Protestantism After 500 Years*, edited by Thomas Albert Howard and Mark A. Noll, 75-97. Oxford: Oxford University Press, 2016.

Eliot, T. S. "Four Quartets." In *Collected Poems 1909–1962*, 173-210. London: Faber & Faber, 1977.

Erdélyi, Gabriella. "The Consumption of the Sacred: Popular Piety in a Late Medieval Hungarian Town." *Journal of Ecclesiastical History* 63, no. 1 (2012): 31-60.

Euler, Carrie. "Huldrych Zwingli and Heinrich Bullinger." In Wandel, *Companion to the Eucharist in the Reformation*, 57-74.

Felton, Gayle Carlton. *This Gift of Water: The Practice and Theology of Baptism Among Methodists in America*. Nashville: Abingdon, 1992.

Ferguson, Everett. *Early Christians Speak*. Austin, TX: Sweet, 1971.

Fiddes, Paul S. *Tracks and Traces: Baptist Identity in Church and Theology*. Milton Keyes, UK: Paternoster, 2003. Reprint, Eugene OR: Wipf & Stock, 2006.

Finger, Thomas N. *A Contemporary Anabaptist Theology: Biblical, Historical, Constructive*. Downers Grove, IL: InterVarsity Press, 2004.

Finley, James. *Christian Meditation: Experiencing the Presence of God*. New York: HarperCollins, 2004.

Finn, Thomas M., ed. *Early Christian Baptism and the Catechumenate: West and East Syria*. Collegeville, MN: Liturgical Press, 1992.

Fisch, Thomas J., ed. *Primary Readings on the Eucharist*. Collegeville, MN: Liturgical Press, 2004.

Foley, Edward. *From Age to Age: How Christians Have Celebrated the Eucharist*. Chicago: Liturgy Training, 1991.

Funck, Heinrich. *A Mirror of Baptism*. Mountain Valley, VA: Joseph Funk, 1851. First published 1744 in German.

Ganoczy, Alexandre. *Becoming Christian: A Theology of Baptism as the Sacrament of Human History*. New York: Paulist Press, 1976.

Gilmore, Alec, ed. *Christian Baptism: A Fresh Attempt to Understand the Rite in Terms of Scripture, History, and Theology*. London: Lutterworth, 1959.

Goering, Joseph. "The Invention of Transubstantiation." *Traditio* 46 (1991): 147-70.

Goertz, Hans-Jürgen. *The Anabaptists*. Translated by Trevor Johnson. New York: Routledge, 1996.

Grantham, Thomas. *Christianismus Primitivus or The Ancient Christian Religion*. Book 2. London: Francis Smith, 1678. Open Library, https://archive.org/stream/christianismuspr00gran?ref=ol#page/n2/mode/2up.

Gregory, Brad S. *The Unintended Reformation: How a Religious Revolution Secularized Society*. Cambridge, MA: Belknap Press, 2012.

Guzie, Tad W. *Jesus and the Eucharist*. New York: Paulist Press, 1974.

Gwyn, Douglas. *The Covenant Crucified: Quakers and the Rise of Capitalism*. Wallingford, PA: Pendle Hill, 1995.

Hammett, John. "Baptism and the Lord's Supper." In *Baptist Faith and Message 2000: Critical Issues in America's Largest Protestant Denomination*, edited by Douglas K. Blount and Joseph D. Wooddell, 71-81. New York: Rowman & Littlefield, 2007.

Hancock, Christopher. "Christ's Priesthood and Eucharistic Sacrifice." In *Essays on Eucharistic Sacrifice in the Early Church*, edited by Colin Buchanan, 15-21. Bramcote, UK: Grove, 1984.

Hanson, Michele Zelinsky. "Anabaptist Liturgical Practices." In Wandel, *Companion to the Eucharist in the Reformation*, 251-72.

Härdelin, Alf. *The Tractarian Understanding of the Eucharist*. Uppsala: Almqvist & Wiksell, 1965.

Hayden, Roger. *English Baptist History and Heritage*. Oxfordshire, UK: Baptist Union of Great Britain, 2005.

Heim, S. Mark. "Baptismal Recognition and the Baptist Churches." In *Baptism and the Unity of the Church*, edited by Michael Root, 150-63. Geneva: World Council of Churches, 1998.

Heller, Dagmar. *Baptized into Christ: A Guide to the Ecumenical Discussion on Baptism*. Geneva: World Council of Churches, 2012.

Heschel, Abraham Joshua. *The Sabbath: Its Meaning for Modern Man*. New York: Farrar, Straus, & Giroux, 1978. First published in 1951.

Hill, Kat. *Baptism, Brotherhood and Belief in Reformation Germany: Anabaptism and Lutheranism, 1525–1585*. Oxford: Oxford University Press, 2015.

Holland, Scott. "Signifying Presence: the Ecumenical Sacramental Theology of George Worgul." *Louvain Studies* 18 (1993): 38-55.

Hopkins, Gerard Manley. "God's Grandeur." In *The Poems of Gerard Manley Hopkins*, edited by W. H. Gardner and N. H. MacKenzie, 66. 4th ed. Oxford: Oxford University Press, 1970.

Hubmaier, Balthasar. "On the Christian Baptism of Believers." In Pipkin and Yoder, *Balthasar Hubmaier*, 95-149.

Hunsinger, George. *The Eucharist and Ecumenism*. Cambridge: Cambridge University Press, 2008.

———. "Widening the Circle of Acceptable Diversity: A Reply to My Ecumenical Friends", in *A Book Symposium on George Hunsinger's The Eucharist and Ecumenism: Let Us Keep the Feast*, in *Pro Ecclesia* 19, no. 3 (2010): 273-284.

Hymnal: A Worship Book. Elgin, IL: Brethren Press; Newton, KS: Faith and Life Press; Scottdale, PA: Herald Press, 1992.

International Theological Commission. "The Hope of Salvation for Infants Who Die Without Being Baptized." January 19, 2007. Vatican document. www.vatican.va/roman_curia/congregations/cfaith /cti_documents/rc_con_cfaith_doc_20070419_un-baptised-infants_en.html.

Jasper, R. C. D., and G. J. Cuming, eds. *Prayers of the Eucharist: Early and Reformed*. 3rd ed. Collegeville, MN: Liturgical Press, 1990.

Jeschke, Marlin. *Believers Baptism for Children of the Church*. Scottdale, PA: Herald Press, 1983.

Johns, David L. *Quakering Theology: Essays on Worship, Tradition, and Christian Faith*. Burlington, VT: Ashgate, 2013.

Johnson, Lawrence, and Mark Searle, eds. *The Church Gives Thanks and Remembers: Essays on the Liturgical Year*. Collegeville, MN: Liturgical Press, 1984.

Johnson, Maxwell E. *The Rites of Christian Initiation: Their Evolution and Interpretation*. Collegeville, MN: Liturgical Press, 2007.

Johnson, Maxwell E., ed. *Living Water, Sealing Spirit: Readings on Christian Initiation*. Collegeville, MN: Liturgical Press, 1995.

Jones, Joe R. *A Grammar of Christian Faith: Systematic Explorations in Christian Life and Doctrine*. Vol. 2. New York: Rowman & Littlefield, 2002.

Jung, Carl. *Psychology and Religion*. New Haven, CT: Yale University Press, 1960.

Kalantzis, George, and Marc Cortez, eds. *Come, Let Us Eat Together: Sacraments and Christian Unity*. Downers Grove, IL: InterVarsity Press, 2018.

Kaufman, Gordon D. *In Face of Mystery: A Constructive Theology*. Cambridge, MA: Harvard University Press, 1993.

Knox, David Broughton. *The Lord's Supper from Wycliffe to Cranmer*. Exeter, UK: Paternoster, 1983.

Kreider, Alan. *The Patient Ferment of the Early Church: The Improbable Rise of Christianity in the Roman Empire*. Grand Rapids: Baker Academic, 2016.

Kreider, Eleanor. *Communion Shapes Character*. Scottdale, PA: Herald Press, 1997.

LaCugna, Catherine Mowry. *God for Us: The Trinity & Christian Life*. San Francisco: Harper, 1973.

Lambert, Malcolm. *Medieval Heresy: Popular Movements from the Gregorian Reform to the Reformation*. 2nd ed. Malden, MA: Blackwell, 1992.

Lathrop, Gordon. *Holy People: a Liturgical Ecclesiology*. Minneapolis: Fortress, 1999.

LaVerdiere, Eugene. *The Breaking of the Bread: The Development of the Eucharist According to Acts*. Chicago: Liturgy Training, 1998.

———. *Dining in the Kingdom of God: The Origins of the Eucharist in the Gospel of Luke*. Chicago: Liturgy Training, 1994.

Lears, T. J. Jackson. *No Place of Grace: Antimodernism and the Transformation of American Culture 1880-1920*. New York: Pantheon, 1981.

Leenhardt, F. J. "This Is My Body." In *Essays on the Lord's Supper*, by Oscar Cullmann and F. J. Leenhardt, 24-85. Cambridge, UK: Lutterworth, 1958.

Léon-Dufour, Xavier. *Sharing the Eucharistic Bread: The Witness of the New Testament*. New York: Paulist Press, 1987.

Leppin, Volker. "Martin Luther." In Wandel, *Companion to the Eucharist in the Reformation*, 39-56.

Levering, Matthew. "The Eucharist, the Risen Lord, and the Road to Emmaus: A Road to Deeper Unity?" In Kalantzis and Cortez, *Come, Let Us Eat Together*, 150-69.

Levy, Ian Christopher, Gary Macy, and Kristen Van Ausdall, eds. *A Companion to the Eucharist in the Middle Ages*. Boston: Brill, 2011.

Lewis, C. S. Introduction to *On the Incarnation*, by Saint Athanasius. London: Mowbray, 1975.

Lichty, Richard J. *Meetinghouse on the Plain: Plains Mennonite Congregation Remembering 250 Years*. Harleysville, PA: Plains Mennonite Church, 2015.

Lightman, Alan. *Searching for Stars on an Island in Maine*. New York: Pantheon, 2018.

Lubac, Henri de. *Corpus Mysticum: The Eucharist and the Church in the Middle Ages*. Translated by Gemma Simmonds. Notre Dame, IN: University of Notre Dame Press, 2007.

Lumpkin, William, ed. *Baptist Confessions of Faith*. Valley Forge, PA: Judson, 1980.

Luther, Martin. *Luther's Works*. Vol. 38, *Word and Sacrament IV*, edited by Helmut T. Lehmann and Martin E. Lehman. Philadelphia: Fortress, 1980.

———. "A Prelude on the Babylonian Captivity of the Church." In *Three Treatises*, introduced and translated by Charles M. Jacobs, A. T. W. Steinhaeuser, and W. A. Lambert, 115-248. Philadelphia: Muhlenberg, 1947.

Macy, Gary. *The Banquet's Wisdom: A Short History of the Theologies of the Lord's Supper*. 2nd ed. Ashland City, TN: OSL, 2005.

———. "Theology of the Eucharist in the High Middle Ages." In Levy, Macy, and Van Ausdall, *Companion to the Eucharist in the Middle Ages*, 365-98.

Mantel, Hilary. "The Magic of Keith Thomas." *New York Review of Books*, June 7, 2012, 38-39.

Marpeck, Pilgram. *Pilgram Marbecks Antwort auf Kaspar Schwenckfelds Beurteilung*. Translated by Johann Loserth. Vienna: Carl Fromme, 1929.

———. *The Writings of Pilgram Marpeck*. Translated and edited by William Klassen and Walter Klaassen. Classics of the Radical Reformation 2. Harrisonburg, VA: Herald Press, 1978.

Marpeck, Pilgram, et al. *Later Writings by Pilgram Marpeck and His Circle*. Vol. 1, *The Exposé, a Dialogue, and Marpeck's Response to Caspar Schwenckfeld*. Translated by Walter Klaassen, Werner O. Packull, and John D. Rempel. Scottdale, PA: Herald Press, 1999.

Martos, Joseph. *Doors to the Sacred: A Historical Introduction to Sacraments in the Catholic Church*. Garden City, NJ: Doubleday, 1982.

McCracken, George E., ed. *Early Medieval Theology*. Library of Christian Classics 9. Philadelphia: Westminster, 1957.

McDonnell, Kilian, and George Montague. *Christian Initiation and Baptism in the Holy Spirit: Evidence from the First Eight Centuries*. 2nd, rev. ed. Collegeville, MN: Liturgical Press, 1994.

McGinn, Bernard. *The Harvest of Mysticism in Medieval Germany*. New York: Herder & Herder, 2012.

Meyer, Hans. "Anthropological Notes on Liturgical Time." *Studia Liturgica* 14 (1982): 8-13.

Miles, Sara. *Take This Bread: A Radical Conversion*. New York: Ballantine, 2008.

Mitchell, Nathan. *Real Presence: The Work of Eucharist*. Chicago: Liturgy Training, 2001.

Mitchell, Nathan. "Reforms, Protestant and Catholic," in Geoffrey Wainwright and Karen Westerfield Tucker, eds., *The Oxford Dictionary of Christian Worship*. Oxford: Oxford University Press, 2006, 307-50.

Niemöller, Martin. *Dachau Sermons*. Translated by Robert H. Pfeiffer. New York: Harper & Brothers, 1946.

Oberman, Heiko A. *The Harvest of Medieval Theology: Gabriel Biel and Late Medieval Nominalism*. Durham, NC: Labyrinth, 1983.

O'Loughlin, Thomas. *Washing Feet: Imitating the Example of Jesus in the Liturgy Today*. Collegeville, MN: Liturgical Press, 2015.

Paris, Arthur E. *Black Pentecostalism: Southern Religion in an Urban World*. Amherst: University of Massachusetts Press, 1982.

Phelan, Owen M. *The Formation of Christian Europe: The Carolingians, Baptism, and the Imperium Christianum*. Oxford: Oxford University Press, 2014.

Philips, Dirk. "The Congregation of God." In *The Writings of Dirk Philips*, edited by Cornelius J. Dyck, William E. Keeney, and Alvin J. Beachy, 350-82. Scottdale, PA: Herald Press, 1992.

———. "The Supper of Our Lord Jesus Christ." In Dyck, Keeney, and Beachy, *Writings of Dirk Philips*, 112-33.

Pipkin, H. Wayne, and John H. Yoder, trans. and eds. *Balthasar Hubmaier: Theologian of Anabaptism*. Scottdale, PA: Herald Press, 1989.

Placher, William C. "Three in One: Believing in the Triune God." *Christian Century*, April 17, 2007, 28.

Polanyi, Michael. *Personal Knowledge: Towards a Post-Critical Philosophy*. Corrected ed. Chicago: University of Chicago Press, 1962.

Polkinghorne, John. *The Faith of a Physicist*. Minneapolis: Fortress, 1996.

Quoist, Michel. "Lord, I Have Time." In *Prayers*, 96-99. New York: Sheed & Ward, 1963.

Radbertus, Paschasius. "The Lord's Body and Blood." In McCracken, *Early Medieval Theology*, 90-108.

Ratramnus of Corbie. "Christ's Body and Blood." In McCracken, *Early Medieval Theology*, 109-47.

Reid, Thomas. *Essays on the Active and Intellectual Powers of Man*. Microtexts ESTC reel 2529, no. 3. University of Toronto Libraries.

———. *An Inquiry into the Human Mind on the Principles of Common Sense*. Edited by Derek R. Brookes. State College, PA: Penn State University Press, 2000. Originally published in 1764.

Rempel, John D. "Critically Appropriating Tradition: Pilgram Marpeck's Experiments in Corrective Theologizing." *Mennonite Quarterly Review* 85, no. 1 (2011): 59-76.

———. "Jesus' Presence in the Meal He Gave Us: A Free Church Inquiry." In *Proceedings of the North American Academy of Liturgy*, edited by Richard E. McCarron, 107-17. Notre Dame, IN: North American Academy of Liturgy, 2014.

———. "Sacraments in the Radical Reformation" in Hans Boersma and Matthew Levering, eds., *The Oxford Handbook of Sacramental Theology*. Oxford: Oxford University Press, 2015, 298-312.

Rempel, John D., ed. *Jörg Maler's Kunstbuch: Writings of the Pilgram Marpeck Circle*. Kitchener, ON: Pandora Press, 2010.

———, ed. *Minister's Manual*. Newton, KS: Faith and Life Press, 1998.

Riedemann, Peter. *Hutterite Confession of Faith*. Translated and edited by John J. Friesen. Scottdale, PA: Herald Press, 1999.

Riley, Hugh M. *Christian Initiation*. Washington, DC: Catholic University of America Press, 1974.

Rohr, Richard. *Everything Belongs: The Gift of Contemplative Prayer*. Rev. ed. New York: Crossroad, 2003.

———. *The Universal Christ: How a Forgotten Reality Can Change Everything We See, Hope for, and Believe*. New York: Crown/Convergent, 2019.

Roy, Kevin. *Baptism, Reconciliation, and Unity*. Carlisle, UK: Paternoster, 1998.

Rubin, Miri. *Corpus Christi: The Eucharist in Late Medieval Culture*. Cambridge: Cambridge University Press, 1991.

Ruth, Lester. *A Little Heaven Below: Worship at Early Methodist Quarterly Meetings*. Nashville: Abingdon, 2000.

Sattler, Michael. "The Schleitheim Articles." In *The Radical Reformation*, edited by Michael G. Baylor, 172-80. Cambridge: Cambridge University Press, 1991.

Saxon, Elizabeth. "Carolingian, Ottonian and Romanesque Art and the Eucharist." In Levy, Macy, and Van Ausdall, *Companion to the Eucharist in the Middle Ages*, 251-326.

Schillebeeckx, Edward. *The Eucharist*. London: Sheed & Ward, 1968.

Schlabach, Gerald W. *Unlearning Protestantism: Sustaining Christian Community in an Unstable Age*. Grand Rapids: Brazos, 2010.

Schmemann, Alexander. *The Eucharist*. Translated by Paul Kachur. Crestwood, NY: St. Vladimir's Seminary Press, 1988.

Schmidt, Orlando, ed. *Sing and Rejoice: New Hymns for Congregations*. Scottdale, PA: Herald Press, 1979.

Schnackenburg, Rudolph. *Gottes Herrschaft und Reich: Eine biblische-theologische Studie*. Freiburg: Herder, 1963.

Searle, Mark. "Infant Baptism Reconsidered." In Maxwell Johnson, *Living Water, Sealing Spirit*, 365-409.

Searle, Mark, and Kenneth W. Stevenson. *Documents of the Marriage Liturgy*. Collegeville, MN: Liturgical Press, 1992.

Seubert, Xavier John. "Ritual Embodiment: Embellishment or Epiphany?" *Worship* 63, no. 6 (1989): 402-16.

Sheerin, Daniel J. *The Eucharist*. Message of the Fathers of the Church 7. Wilmington, DE: Glazier, 1986.

Siegrist, Anthony G. *Participating Witness: An Anabaptist Theology of Baptism and the Sacramental Character of the Church*. Eugene, OR: Pickwick, 2013.

Simons, Menno. "Christian Baptism." In *Complete Writings of Menno Simons*, edited by J. C. Wenger and translated by Leonard Verduin, 229-47. Scottdale, PA: Herald Press, 1956.

Smith, Daniel. *Worship and Remembrance*. Vol. 3. Vancouver: self-published, n.d.

Snoek, Godefridus J. C. "The Process of Independence of the Eucharist." In Fisch, *Primary Readings on the Eucharist*, 37-76.

Sobrino, Jon. *Christology at the Crossroads: A Latin American Approach*. Maryknoll, NY: Orbis, 1985. First published as *Cristología desde américa latina (esbozo a partir del seguimiento del Jesús histórico)*. Río Hondo, Mex.: Centro de Reflexión Teológica, 1976.

Spinks, Bryan D. *Early and Medieval Rituals and Theologies of Baptism: From the New Testament to the Council of Trent*. Burlington, VT: Ashgate, 2006.

Spufford, Margaret. "The Importance of the Lord's Supper to Dissenters." In *The World of Rural Dissenters, 1520–1725*, edited by Margaret Spufford, 86-102. Cambridge: Cambridge University Press, 1995.

Steiner, George. "Nostalgia for the Absolute." CBC Massey Lecture 1974. Toronto: Canadian Broadcasting Corporation, 1974. Audio available at www.cbc.ca/radio/ideas/the-1974-cbc-massey-lectures -nostalgia-for-the-absolute-1.2946821.

———. *Real Presences*. Chicago: University of Chicago Press, 1989.

Stennett, Joseph. *Hymns in Commemoration of the Sufferings of Our Blessed Saviour Jesus Christ, Compos'd for the Celebration of His Holy Supper*. n.p., n.d.

Stoffer, Dale R., ed. *The Lord's Supper: Believers Church Perspectives*. Scottdale, PA: Herald Press, 1997.

Sukarto, Aristarchus. "Witnessing to Christ Through Eucharist: A Proposal for the Java Christian Churches to Contextualize and to Communicate the Gospel to Its Community." ThD diss., Lutheran School of Theology at Chicago, 1994. www.dropbox.com/s/3bu89kkecxqjjfq/Diss_Sukarto_Wit- nessing%20to%20Christ%20to%20Eucharist.pdf?dl=0.

Swartley, Willard M. *John*. Believers Church Bible Commentary. Harrisonburg, VA: Herald Press, 2003.

Tait, Jennifer L. Woodruff. *The Poisoned Chalice: Eucharistic Grape Juice and Common-Sense Realism in Victorian Methodism*. Tuscaloosa: University of Alabama Press, 2011.

Tarnas, Richard. *The Passion of the Western Mind: Understanding the Ideas That Have Shaped Our World View*. New York: Ballantine, 1993.

Taylor, Charles. *A Secular Age*. Cambridge, MA: Harvard University Press, 2007.

Thomas, John Christopher. *Footwashing in John 13 and the Johannine Community*. Cleveland, TN: CPT Press, 2014.

Thompson, Nicholas. "Martin Bucer." In Wandel, *Companion to the Eucharist in the Reformation*, 75-96.

Turrell, James F. "Anglican Theologies of the Eucharist." In Wandel, *Companion to the Eucharist in the Reformation*, 115-38.

Wainwright, Geoffrey. *Doxology: The Praise of God in Worship, Doctrine, and Life*. New York: Oxford University Press, 1980.

———. *Eucharist and Eschatology*. New York: Oxford University Press, 1981.

Walker, Michael. *Baptists at the Table*. Didcot, UK: Baptist Historical Society, 1992.

Walsh, Christopher. "Reservation" in Paul Bradshaw, ed., *The New Westminster Dictionary of Liturgy and Worship*. Louisville, KY: Westminster/John Knox, 2002, 404-6.

Walsh, James, and P. G. Walsh, eds. *Divine Providence & Human Suffering*. Messages of the Fathers of the Church 17. Wilmington, DE: Glazier, 1985.

Walsham, Alexandra. "The Reformation and the 'Disenchantment of the World' Reassessed." *Historical Journal* 51, no. 2 (2008): 497-528. https://doi.org/10.1017/S0018246X08006808.

Wandel, Lee Palmer, ed. *A Companion to the Eucharist in the Reformation*. Brill's Companions to the Christian Tradition 46. Boston: Brill, 2014.

Webber, Robert E. *The Complete Library of Christian Worship*. 8 vols. Nashville: Star Song, 1994.

Weber, Max. *The Sociology of Religion*. Translated from the 4th edition by Ephraim Fischoff. Introduction by Talcott Parsons. Boston: Beacon, 1963. First published in German in 1922.

Wegman, Herman. *Christian Worship in East and West: A Study Guide to Liturgical History*. Translated by Gordon W. Lathrop. Collegeville, MN: Liturgical Press, 1990.

Welker, Michael. *What Happens in Holy Communion?* Translated by John F. Hoffmeyer. Grand Rapids: Eerdmans, 2000.

Whitaker, E. C. *Documents of the Baptismal Liturgy*. London: SPCK, 1970.

White, James F. *John Wesley's Prayerbook*. Akron, OH: Order of St. Luke, 1995.

———. *Protestant Worship: Traditions in Transition*. Louisville, KY: Westminster John Knox, 1989.

———. *Sacraments as God's Self Giving: Sacramental Practice and Faith*. Nashville: Abingdon, 1983.

Wiesel, Elie. *Night*. New York: Avon, 1969.

Williams, D. H. *Evangelicals and Tradition: The Formative Influence of the Early Church*. Grand Rapids: Baker Academic, 2005.

Winter, Stephan. *Eucharistische Gegenwart: liturgische Redehandlung im Spiegel mittelalterlicher und analytischer Sprachtheorie*. Regensburg: Pustet, 2002.

Wolterstorff, Nicholas. "John Calvin." In Wandel, *Companion to the Eucharist in the Reformation*, 97-114.

Wright, Shawn D. "The Reformed View of the Lord's Supper." In *The Lord's Supper: Remembering and Proclaiming Christ Until He Comes*, edited by Thomas R. Schreiner and Matthew R. Crawford, 248-84. Nashville: B&H Academic, 2010.

Wright, Stephen. *The Early English Baptists, 1603-49*. Rochester, NY: Boydell, 2006.

Yoder, John H. *The Royal Priesthood: Essays Ecclesiological and Ecumenical*. Edited by Michael G. Cartwright. Grand Rapids: Eerdmans, 1998.

Zwingli, Ulrich. "On the Lord's Supper." In Bromiley, *Zwingli and Bullinger*, 176-238.

NAME INDEX

Abbott, Walter, 89
Abrams, M. H., 21
Aers, David, 122, 127
Ahlstrom, Sydney E., 8, 158
Aldwinckle, Russell Foster, 13
Ambrose of Milan, 15, 50, 117, 126
Aquinas. *See* Thomas Aquinas
Arendt, Hannah, 58
Arnold, Matthew, 21
Auden, W. H., 13, 16
Augustine of Hippo, 23, 51, 82-83, 90, 92, 117-18, 124-26, 132, 137, 143
Barrett, C. K., 106
Barth, Karl, 14
Baylor, Michael G., 88
Beachy, Alvin, 89, 91, 93, 146
Beasley-Murray, George R., 69, 96, 110, 160
Bebbington, David W., 149
Berdyaev, Nicolas, 190
Berengar of Tours, 125-27, 131, 135, 186
Bernard of Clairveaux, 126
Bernier, Paul, 49
Blough, Neal, 148
Boers, Arthur, 27
Boersma, Hans, 45, 73, 87, 160
Bonhoeffer, Dietrich, 10, 26
Bradshaw, Paul, 73, 80, 105, 129
Brandt, Willy, 57-58
Breidenthal, Thomas, 163, 170
Brilioth, Yngve, 125
Bromiley, G. W., 135, 137
Brookes, Derek R., 154
Brown, David, 45
Brown, Raymond, 101-102, 108
Buc, Philippe, 31
Bucer, Martin, 86-87, 135-36
Buchanan, Colin, 69, 132
Bullard, Scott, 49, 120, 160
Calvin, John, 86-87, 90, 135-37, 145, 150, 155
Campbell, Alexander, 154-55, 158
Campbell, Ted, 149

Cavanaugh, William, 191-92
Chrysostom, John, 79, 121, 132
Clarke, Neville, 160
Coleman, T. W., 160
Collins, Mary, 190
Constantine the Great, 43, 62, 76-77, 119-20
Cooke, Bernard, 19, 130
Cornelius, 71-72
Cortez, Marc, 112
Cranmer, Thomas, 86-87, 122, 136
Crawford, Matthew R., 150
Crockett, William, 49-51, 117, 189
Cross, Anthony R., 48-49, 95
Cullmann, Oscar, 49
Cuming, G. J., 15, 112-14, 116, 120-21
Cummings, Owen F., 126
Cyril of Jerusalem, 79
Daly, Robert, 138
Darby, John Nelson, 155
Dix, Gregory, 114-15, 125
Driver, John, 145
Driver, Tom, 31
Duffy, Eamon, 129
Durnbaugh, Donald, 152
Dussel, Enrique, 190
Dyck, Cornelius J., 89, 93, 146
Dyrness, William A., 166
Egeria, 78
Eire, Carlos, 130
Eliot, T. S., 29
Erdelyi, Gabriella, 129
Euler, Carrie, 135
Fell, Margaret, 152
Felton, Gayle Carlton, 153
Ferguson, Everett, 76, 175
Fiddes, Paul S., 151
Finger, Thomas N., 147
Finley, James, 45
Finn, Thomas, 66, 73, 75
Fisch, Thomas J., 122
Foley, Edward, 175
Fox, George, 152
Francis of Assisi, 126

Funck, Heinrich, 95
Funk, Joseph, 95
Galileo, 5
Ganoczy, Alexander, 81-82
Gardner, W. H., 53, 93
Gilmore, Alec, 81
Gingerich, Barbara Nelson, 27
Goering, Joseph, 128
Goertz, Hans-Jürgen, 149
Goeters, J. F. Gerhard, 142
Grantham, Thomas, 151
Gregory, Brad S., 158
Gregory of Nazianzus, 79
Gregory of Nyssa, 50
Guzie, Tad W., 49
Gwyn, Douglas, 152
Hammett, John, 163
Hancock, Christopher, 132
Hanson, Michele Zelinsky, 145
Hayden, Roger, 150
Heim, S. Mark, 69
Heller, Dagmar, 87
Heschel, Abraham, 58-60
Hildegard of Bingen, 126
Hill, Kat, 130
Holland, Scott, 53
Hopkins, Gerard Manley, 53, 93
Howard, Thomas Albert, 130
Hubmaier, Balthasar, 72, 89, 98, 145, 147
Hunsinger, George, 139
Isaiah, 13
Jasper, R. C. D., 15, 112-14, 116, 120-21, 169
Jeremiah, 27
Jeschke, Marlin, 69
Johns, David, 152
Johnson, Lawrence, 61-62
Johnson, Maxwell E., 69, 74-75, 79, 83, 85, 87
Jones, Joe R., 13
Julian of Norwich, 126
Jung, Carl, 52
Justin Martyr, 15, 75, 81, 113-14, 116
Kalantzis, George, 112
Kant, Immanuel, 24

Kaufman, Gordon D., 20
Keach, Benjamin, 151
Keeney, William E., 89, 93, 146
Klaassen, Walter, 5, 38, 58, 64, 79-80, 82-87, 146-47
Klassen, William, 48, 68, 74, 147, 90-96, 147
Knox, David Broughton, 122
Kreider, Alan, 75, 113
Kreider, Eleanor, 27, 172, 204
LaCugna, Catherine, 13
Lambert, Malcolm, 126
LaVerdiere, Eugene, 164
Lears, Jackson, 21
Leenhardt, Franz Jehan, 49
Leon-Dufour, Xavier, 107
Leppin, Volker, 134
Levering, Matthew, 45, 73, 86-87, 112
Levy, Ian Christopher, 122-23, 128
Lewis, C. S., 13
Lightman, Alan, 3
Lubac, Henri de, 14, 119
Lumpkin, William, 151
Luther, Martin, 5, 86-88, 90-91, 131, 133-36, 140
MacKenzie, N. H., 53, 93
Macy, Gary, 23, 123, 128
Mantel, Hillary, 4
Marpeck, Pilgram, 15, 48-49, 68, 74, 86, 89-96, 137, 143, 146-48
Martos, Joseph, 49
Mary Magdalene, 61, 172
Mary, Mother of Jesus, 102, 114, 123
McCracken, George E., 123-24
McDonnell, Kilian, 75-76, 79
McGinn, Bernard, 86
McNeill, John T., 136
Meyer, Hans, 63
Miles, Sarah, 163
Mitchell, Nathan, 24, 74
Montague, George, 79
Niemöller, Martin, 26
Noll, Mark A., 130
O'Loughlin, Thomas, 177
O'Meara, John J., 82-83
Packull, Werner O., 15, 89-90, 95, 146
Paris, Arthur E., 39

Paul (the apostle), 2, 6, 8-11, 14-15, 17-18, 22, 28, 30, 44, 47, 49-50, 61, 66-69, 71-75, 94-98, 102-9, 112-13, 124, 141, 158, 160, 174, 193, 196
Pelagius, 82-83
Phelan, Owen M., 124
Philips, Dirk, 89, 93, 145-46
Pipkin, H. Wayne, 89, 98, 145
Placher, William, 12
Polanyi, Michael, 52
Polkinghorne, John, 52
Power, David N., 190
Quoist, Michel, 64
Radbertus of Corbie, 123-26
Ratramnus of Corbie, 124-25, 129, 131, 137
Reid, Thomas, 154
Rempel, John D., 15, 27, 37, 49, 66, 88-91, 95, 139, 146, 163, 183, 190-91
Riedemann, Peter, 96, 98
Riggs, Ann K., 149
Riley, Hugh M., 79
Rohr, Richard, 166
Root, Michael, 69
Roy, Kevin, 69
Rubin, Miri, 127
Ruth, Lester, 153
Sattler, Michael, 88
Saxon, Elizabeth, 123
Schertz, Mary, 27, 201
Schillebeeckx, Edward, 49, 105-6
Schlabach, Gerald, 133
Schmemann, Alexander, 108
Schnackenburg, Rudolph, 110
Schreiner, Thomas, 150
Schwenckfeld, Casper 15, 89, 95, 143, 146
Searle, Mark, 17, 61-62, 69
Seubert, Xavuer John, 35
Sheerin, Daniel J., 50, 118
Siegrist, Anthony G., 92, 99
Simons, Menno, 144-45
Smith, Daniel, 155
Smith, Walter, xi
Snoek, Godefridus J. C., 122
Sobrino, Jon, 13
Spinks, Brian D., 76-77, 87
Spufford, Margaret, 63
Stafford, Gilbert W., 149

Steiner, George, 20, 23-24
Stennett, Joseph, 150
Stevenson, Kenneth W., 17
Stoffer, Dale, 49
Streicher, Helene von, 90, 95
Sukarto, Aristarchus, 78
Tait, Jennifer L. Woodruff, 155
Tarnas, Richard, 24
Taylor, Charles, 25, 52
Tertullian, 82, 96
Theodore of Mopsuestia, 73, 79
Thomas à Kempis, 126
Thomas Aquinas, 85-86, 128-29
Thomas, John Christopher, 177
Thompson, Nicholas, 135
Thompson, Philip E., 48-49, 95
Torrance, T. F., 12, 14, 81
Turrell, James F., 137
Van Ausdall, Kristen, 122-23, 128
Vinci, Leonardo da, 5
Wainwright, Geoffrey, 68, 74, 160
Walker, Michael, 150-51
Walsh, James, 25
Walsh, P. G., 25
Walsham, Alexandra, 6
Wandel, Lee Palmer, 130, 132-35, 137-38, 145
Webber, Robert E. 160
Weber, Max, 5
Wegman, Herman, 175
Welker, Michael, 103
Wesley, Charles, xi, 36, 40
Wesley, John, 40, 67, 153, 155
Whitaker, E. C., 77, 80
White, James F., 153-54, 160
Wiesel, Elie, 40
Williams, D. H., 149
Winter, Stephan, 126
Wolterstorff, Nicholas, 135
Worgul, George, 53
Wright, Shawn, 150
Wright, Stephen, 150
Wycliff, John, 122, 126
Yoder, John Howard, 89, 98, 145, 149, 186
Zwingli, Ulrich, 45, 86-87, 133-37, 139, 142-43, 145, 150, 161, 185

SUBJECT INDEX

absence, 105-9. *See also* "real absence"

absence of God, 107, 109, 152

agape meal, 113, 167, 172-73, 199-201. *See also* love feast

Agnus Dei, 175-76

ambiguous interim, 22-23

Amish, 19

Anabaptism, 88-91, 130-31, 135, 140-49

Anabaptists, 4, 27, 42, 88-93, 98, 130-31, 133, 137, 142-49, 176-77, 185

anamnesis, 114, 175

Anglican, 16, 38, 81, 114, 131, 136-38, 140, 152-53, 155, 176, 183, 186

anointing (with oil), 3, 16, 36, 54, 68, 75, 77-78, 81, 85, 90, 97

antisacramental, 75, 78, 96

apostolic tradition, 31, 48, 71, 75, 80, 86, 98, 114, 167, 186

architecture, 84, 115, 122, 123

ascension (of Jesus), 51, 61, 70, 71, 105, 107, 108, 132, 143, 174

atonement, 14, 41, 98, 110, 132, 144-45

Auschwitz, xiii, 21

baptism, xii, xv, 1-4, 7-8, 14-17, 23, 36-37, 43-44, 48-49, 53-54, 66-99, 109, 114, 120, 124, 142, 145-47, 149, 151, 153, 158, 164-66, 168-73, 174-75, 180-81, 184, 199. *See also* believer's baptism; infant baptism; origin of baptism

baptism of desire, 72-73, 166

baptismal regeneration, 49, 95

Baptists, xii, 4, 7, 40, 63, 95, 100, 149-52, 159, 177, 186

believer's baptism, 4, 7-8, 54, 69, 79-80, 82, 84-85, 87, 92, 96, 98-99, 145, 149, 151, 158, 164

believer's church, 99, 146, 147, 149

berekah, 174

bilingual, 70

bishop, 37, 77, 79, 83-85, 88, 117, 132-33, 145, 180-81

bodied souls, 17

body and blood of Christ, 48, 50-51, 75, 105, 114, 116-19, 123-30, 133-34, 137, 141, 151, 175-76, 178, 185-86, 196

bread of justice, xvi, 190

Breaking of Bread, 3, 15, 36, 41, 45-46, 49, 51, 61-62, 71, 100, 104-7, 111, 113, 131-32, 135, 144-55, 163-64, 169-71, 174-80, 183, 185, 189, 193, 202-4. *See also* Communion; Eucharist; Lord's Supper

Britain, xii, 7, 149, 150

British, 82, 140, 151-52

buried with Christ, 1, 88, 95-97

Catholic Church, xii, 6, 7, 9, 49, 52, 86-87, 88, 89, 90, 117, 128, 129, 130, 131, 133, 149, 156, 157, 158, 178-79, 184, 186; Catholic Reformation, 4

ceremony, 3, 16, 35, 37, 42, 75-77, 145, 147

charismatic, 26, 28, 38, 70, 88, 149, 152, 156, 187

Christian: calendar, 62-63; faith, 28, 120, 173; worship, xi, xiii, 26, 73-74, 119, 154, 161, 175, 183, 188

Christology, 134-35, 143-45, 148

chronos, 57, 59, 62

Church of the Brethren, 152, 167

Churches of Christ/Christian Church (Disciples of Christ), 150, 154

cloud of witnesses, 27

common-sense realism, 8, 78, 154-55, 158

Communion, xii, 3, 26, 33, 36, 41, 48-49, 51, 83-85, 100-181, 185, 191, 193-8, 199, 202-4. *See also* Breaking of Bread; Eucharist; Lord's Supper

communion prayer, 48, 100, 174, 195-98

Confession: of faith, xii, 1, 7, 42, 49, 72, 79, 83-84, 87-88, 96, 98-99, 149, 151; of sin, 131, 175-76, 188

confirmation, 33-34, 54, 83-87, 92, 166

consecration, 123, 125-27, 129, 131, 178-79

Constantinian era, 79

consumerism, 64

conversion, 1-2, 4, 67-69, 71-72, 74-75, 77, 79, 81, 83, 88-89, 97-98, 120, 155, 163, 170-71

corpus: christianum, 149; *mysticum*, 14, 119, 191; *verum*, 191

Council: of Chalcedon, 12; of Constantinople, 46; of Nicaea, 12, 46, 81; of Trent, 76, 87, 129, 131, 138

creation, 2, 5, 8-10, 11, 14-15, 17-20, 23, 27-28, 30, 38, 47-48, 55-56, 59-61, 63-65, 81-82, 93-94, 110, 114, 139, 146, 158-59, 175, 184, 188-89, 194-96

cynical, 21, 26

Dachau, 26

deacon, 100, 113, 132, 180, 196-97

death, 2, 18, 23, 28, 47, 53-54, 56, 61-62, 69, 88, 97, 110, 114, 132, 144 88, 97-98, 100, 110-11, 113-14, 132, 144, 145, 149, 151, 158, 196, 202, 203

demons, 22, 52, 107

demythologized cosmos, 20

Didache, 73, 113-14, 169

Didascalia, 87

disenchanted, 5, 7, 8, 19, 52, 130, 131, 156, 158, 160-61; disenchanters, 159; disenchantment, 4-10, 19, 65, 131, 156, 159

divine initiative, 88-99, 149, 187
divinity of Christ, 14, 47, 133-34, 136
Donatists, 82
early Christian worship, 119, 161
early Christianity, 40, 57, 70, 106, 132, 139, 155
early church, 12, 14-15, 27, 69-72, 112, 130, 153, 167-69, 171, 180, 184-86, 189
Early Middle Ages, 78
early patristic era, 73, 75, 83, 116, 176
Easter, 61-62, 78, 167, 176
Eastern Oriental, 42, 69, 84, 121, 133, 155, 161, 178
Eastern Orthodox, 42, 69, 84, 121, 128, 133, 155, 161, 178; Eastern Orthodoxy, 178
ecumenical, xii, 53, 80, 87, 90, 138-39, 151, 183, 199
eighth day of creation, 61
elements, 15, 23, 49-51, 94-95, 97, 100, 103-5, 108, 114, 116-17, 119, 124-28, 131, 134-36, 141, 147, 151, 161, 177, 191-92; elements of creation, 8
emancipation of humanity, 20
embodied, 30, 40, 106, 109, 188
embodiment, 5, 11-19, 23, 49, 67, 90, 93, 108-9, 138
enchanted universe/world, xv, 1-10, 19, 21, 52, 94, 156, 158-59; enchantment, 4-10, 156
encounter, xiii-xv, 2-4, 12, 15, 27-29, 35, 45, 47-48, 51, 53, 59, 61, 71, 76, 97, 102, 105-12, 118, 120, 141, 144, 170-72, 179, 183, 185, 187-89, 192, 204
Enlightenment, xv, 5-8, 20, 24, 52, 78, 131, 156-57, 159
environmental: destruction, 55; justice, 9; projects, 173
epiclesis, 114, 175-77
eschatology, 109-10, 115, 149, 160
ethics, 10, 158
Eucharist, xii, 3, 14, 32, 45, 49-51, 84, 94, 100-181, 184, 186-87, 190-91, 193. See also Breaking of Bread; Communion; Lord's Supper
Eucharistic: liturgies, 112-21;

prayer, 113-15, 119, 174-76; theology, 45, 51, 125-30, 135, 137-40, 146
evangelical, xii, xiv, xvi, 78, 140, 153, 159-60
Evangelicalism, 7, 157
evil, 25-28, 66, 71, 110, 144, 195
evil spirits, 22
ex opere operantis, 125
ex opere operatio, 120, 125
exploitation of nature, 65
Faith, xiv, 4, 7, 21-22, 24-25, 27-28, 30, 40, 43, 46, 48, 53-54, 64, 66-69, 74-76, 78-93, 95-99, 102-3, 120, 123-27, 129, 131, 133-34, 141, 143, 147, 149, 151, 153, 157-58, 160-61, 164, 166, 170, 173, 175, 180, 187. See also Christian faith; confession of faith; sea of faith
Faith: post-critical, 28; pre-critical, 28
fasting, 19, 56, 73-74
flesh and blood, 102, 104-6, 108, 114, 116-17, 123, 146
footwashing, 29, 42, 86, 122, 146-47, 174, 177-78, 197-98, 199-201
Free churches, xii-xiv, 7-9, 49, 84, 94, 98, 140, 149-60, 177
funerals, 23, 38, 54, 56-57, 167
German Brethren, 157
gesture(s), xiv-xv, 2-4, 12, 19, 26, 28, 30-42, 48, 53-54, 57-58, 70, 76-78, 94, 97, 100-3, 108, 111, 115, 168, 172-73, 178, 183, 187-88, 198
gifts: of the Spirit, 70, 79, 88; of tongues and healing, 28, 70
Global South, 28, 52, 78, 150, 186
God's kingdom. See kingdom of God
God's love, xiv, 9, 11-12, 15, 23, 27-28, 59-60, 67, 71, 73, 108, 110, 149, 169, 171, 179-80, 188-89, 195, 203
God's reign, 18, 22, 44-45, 60, 66, 93, 97, 99, 104, 106-12, 115, 171, 201. See also kingdom of God

Good Friday, 23, 56, 62, 180
grace, xvi, 4. 8, 18, 45, 53, 56, 58, 72, 75, 81-82, 86, 89-99, 123, 125, 131, 142, 147-48, 153, 158, 160, 164, 167, 169-72, 176, 180, 184, 187-88, 192, 194-95, 200, 203
Greek, 15, 43, 44, 49, 50, 56, 57, 67, 71, 84, 104, 114, 115; philosophy, 50, 57
Healing, 22, 28, 30, 36, 45, 54, 94, 97, 109, 195, 200
High Middle Ages, 14, 19, 85, 117, 119, 127, 128
Holy Communion. See Communion
Holy Spirit, 1-2, 4, 7, 10, 12, 17, 22, 26, 29, 30, 35, 48, 51, 61, 71-73, 75, 83, 86, 90, 94-95, 108, 112, 116, 127, 135-36, 157, 161, 165, 187
hope, 24, 28, 53, 61-62, 66, 96, 109, 167
host (bread), 105, 108, 123, 129, 131, 176, 178-79
human ends, 25
humanity of Christ, 15, 24, 44, 47, 90, 134, 136, 147
immortality, 28
incarnation, xii, xiv- xvi, 6, 9, 11-18, 22, 29-30, 44, 46-48, 50, 53, 72, 98-99, 103, 106, 108, 114, 116, 118, 123, 127, 139, 143-44, 146-48, 156, 160, 184, 186, 191
incarnational logic, 93-99
infant baptism, 7, 43, 53, 69, 73, 76, 79-85, 87, 89, 90-93, 99, 120, 149, 151, 153, 164, 175
Israel, 25, 27, 55-56, 58-60, 72, 108, 112, 196, 202; Israelites, 27
Jewish, 18, 49-50, 57, 62, 70, 71, 73-74, 104, 106, 112, 115, 174
justice, xiii, xvi, 9, 10, 22, 26, 41, 49, 57, 106, 170, 187, 188, 201
kairos, 57-58, 60
kingdom of God, xiv, 10, 22, 30, 35, 44-45, 60, 68, 99, 106-12, 136, 142, 149, 164, 173, 194, 197. See also upside-down kingdom

Kyrie, 175-76
lament, xiv, 25, 28
language, xiv, xv, 2-3, 9, 11-14, 21, 23-26, 28, 30, 39, 40-41, 42, 44, 45, 50, 52, 68, 70, 76, 81, 95, 96, 100, 101-2, 105-6, 109-12, 116-18, 124, 127, 141, 146-47, 151, 164, 173, 184, 193, 194
Late Middle Ages, 4, 40, 129, 139
Latin, 15, 43
Latin American, 13, 190
lean liturgy, xv-xvi, 31, 45, 96, 141, 149, 156, 160, 179, 183-84
liminal, 21, 52, 108, 185
liturgy, 2, 16, 35, 38, 40, 76, 77, 100, 116, 119, 120-21, 129, 131, 138, 140, 153, 155, 161, 167, 174, 176, 178, 179, 185, 186, 188, 199-201
Lord's Day, 61-63, 155, 174, 178
Lord's Supper, xii, xv, 3, 10, 14, 16, 23, 24, 33, 44, 45, 49, 86, 94, 96, 100, 102, 104, 105, 107-13, 119-20, 123, 126-27, 132-35, 137, 139, 141-48, 150, 152-56, 161, 164, 167, 172, 174-80, 184, 187-88, 190, 193-98, 199. See also Breaking of Bread; Communion; Eucharist
Lord's Table, 22, 26, 33, 87, 113, 116, 118, 122, 151, 164, 155, 164, 166, 169-71, 176, 179, 185, 188, 193-95. See also table
love feast, 143, 153, 167, 172, 199-201. See also agape meal
love of God. See God's love
magic/magical, 4, 6, 16, 31, 43, 79, 130, 131, 159
material realm, 5, 7, 157
mediation(s), 7, 17, 23, 89, 144, 146, 152, 157
memory, 3, 34, 53, 60, 100, 104, 148, 158, 175
Mennonite, xii, xiv, 7, 37, 39, 42, 87, 99, 143, 149, 150, 152, 159, 176, 177, 183, 186, 195
metabolic realism, 50, 51, 117-18, 138, 185-86
metaphor, 44-45, 75, 102, 137, 171, 184

metaphorical, 14, 43, 50, 53, 105, 116, 117, 125, 152
metaphysics, 24, 127
Methodist, 7, 40, 68, 149-50
Middle Ages, 14, 16, 62, 83, 119, 122, 142, 167, 186, 191. See also Early Middle Ages, High Middle Ages, Late Middle Ages
minister, 1, 26, 32, 38, 39, 56, 96, 100, 131, 135, 153, 154, 180, 185, 193-98, 200-201, 202-4
modernity, 5, 7, 21, 148, 157; modernism, 8
monastic, 41, 88, 122, 172, 177; monasticism, 4, 79, 126
mystery, xv, 5, 8, 11-17, 30, 44, 46, 50, 97, 118, 123, 126, 140, 154, 158, 185; of Christ, 11, 15, 20, 29, 117, 140, 196; of God, 9, 19, 98, 109
mystical, 14, 45-46, 48-49, 71, 75, 101-3, 105, 107-9, 118-19, 137, 142-45, 151-52, 185, 191
mysticism, 4, 86, 136
Nazism, 26
Nicaea. See Council of Nicaea
Nicene Creed, 46
nostalgia for the absolute, 20
objective, 7, 53, 78, 81, 125, 127, 140, 149, 157; nature, 125, 127, 140; presence, 45, 103, 129; reality, 33, 129, 141, 150, 179; truth, 53
ordinance, 15, 16, 42, 86, 151, 155
Oriental Orthodoxy, 178
origin of baptism, 69-73
orthodoxy, 139, 148. See also Catholic orthodoxy; Eastern Orthodoxy; Oriental Orthodoxy
paradigm, 44, 59, 62, 104, 108, 109, 112, 144, 149
paradox, 2, 13, 17, 47, 109, 140, 154, 171-72
paradoxical: assertions, 95; figure, 145; language, 9, 116; reality, 67, 107, 112; relationship, 118; thinking, 13, 52, 107, 140
passing the peace, 2, 3, 42, 175, 188

Passover, 56, 59, 100, 101, 109, 167, 168, 174
pastor, 1, 88, 124, 126, 161, 180
pastoral prayer, 36, 129
patristic: age/era, 43, 49, 73-77, 83, 86, 112-16, 118, 131-33, 139, 167, 175, 179, 186; church, 71; liturgies/practice/ritual, 16, 75, 176, 177; teaching/thought, 25, 70, 184, 191; theologians/theology, 13, 50, 79, 81-82, 142, 153
Pentecost, xiv, 27, 62, 70, 169
Pentecostalism, 39, 156, 169, 186-87
personal confession of faith, xii
pietism, 7, 153, 157
Pietists, 153
Plymouth Brethren, 150, 155, 186
post-Protestant, 156, 161, 163, 165
post-Reformation, 5, 8, 150, 156, 177, 184
prayer, 32, 33, 39, 41, 48, 50, 71, 74, 76, 84-84, 113-16, 136, 137, 151, 153, 155, 169, 175, 176, 177, 183, 196-98, 199, 204
presbyter, 74, 82, 113, 114, 115, 119, 132
Presbyterian, 81, 154
presence, xi, xiv, xvi, 6, 10, 12-16, 19, 22, 24, 30, 35, 45-50, 51, 61, 71, 90, 95, 97, 103, 105-9, 111-12, 115, 117-19, 12-29, 134, 136, 139-40, 141, 143, 147, 150-51, 164, 165, 167, 171, 173, 176-80, 183, 185, 187-88, 191-92, 193, 198
priest, 85, 117, 119, 122, 123, 125, 126, 127, 129, 130, 138, 142, 155, 178, 179
priesthood of all believers, 88, 135, 142, 132, 135, 142, 180
promise (as a noun), 3, 19, 22, 27, 30, 44, 45, 46, 53, 54, 58, 59, 97, 103, 134, 173, 185, 194
promise (as a verb), 10, 15, 18, 66, 70, 172, 188, 194, 198
Promised Land, 55
prone, 129

Protestant(s), xiii, 6, 7, 9, 49,
  51-52, 75, 86, 87, 88, 90, 91,
  105, 128, 131, 132, 133, 137, 138,
  139, 141, 142, 149, 154, 156,
  157, 159, 160, 161, 163, 165,
  178, 184, 186. *See also*
  post-Protestant
Protestant liturgy/worship,
  154, 176, 185
Protestant Reformation, 4, 6,
  16, 44, 85, 86, 124, 130, 133,
  138, 143, 152, 156, 186
Protestantism, 5, 7-8, 40, 78,
  96, 130, 131, 134, 135, 141, 156,
  158, 178, 184, 187
Quakers, 39, 143, 150, 152-53
Quest for meaning, 22
radical, 49, 91, 96, 130, 131-32,
  135, 149, 154, 159, 185
Radical Reformation, 143-44,
  129, 152, 186
radical Reformers, 78, 86,
  88-89, 91, 142, 177. *See also*
  Reformers
rational/rationalistic, 3, 7, 8, 11,
  17, 20, 21, 32, 41, 53, 72, 96,
  140, 154, 157-58
rationalism/rationality, 7, 8,
  22, 52-53, 140, 157
"real absence," 177, 185
realism, 50. *See also*
  common-sense realism;
  metabolic realism; symbolic
  realism
reason, xv, 3, 8, 19, 20, 22, 24,
  52, 53, 128, 157
Reformation. *See* Radical
  Reformation; Catholic
  Reformation; Protestant
  Reformation
Reformed, 12, 15, 32, 129, 130,
  131, 135, 139, 140, 150, 157, 161,
  186
Reformers, 44, 85, 86, 87, 89,
  124, 130-34, 138, 141, 143, 144,
  176, 179. *See also* Radical
  Reformation; radical
  Reformers
reign of God. *See* God's reign
religious certitude, 20
remembrance, 3, 114, 116, 136,
  155, 175, 185, 195, 196, 197, 203

Renaissance, 4, 5, 38, 52, 131
renewal movements, 44
resurrection (of Jesus), 14, 19,
  28, 30, 31, 45, 47, 56, 60-62,
  70, 71, 78, 88, 100, 104, 111,
  113, 114, 152, 167, 168, 196
rite(s), 4, 15, 16, 31, 36, 37, 38,
  42, 54, 69, 74, 77, 81, 83, 84,
  85, 87, 121, 122, 164, 177
ritual, xi, xii, xiv, xv, xvi, 2-4,
  7-8, 12, 15, 21, 23, 24, 26,
  30-42, 44-45, 48, 50, 51, 53,
  54, 68, 69, 75, 77, 78, 86, 97,
  101, 109, 111, 112, 115, 117, 132,
  142, 146, 152, 155, 157, 158,
  161, 164, 167, 168, 170, 171,
  172, 177, 180, 183, 187, 188,
  189, 190, 191-92, 198
Sabbath, 56, 58, 59-60, 62, 64
sacrament, xii, xiv-xvi, 8, 11-14,
  17, 19, 22-23, 30, 42-47, 50,
  70, 75-76, 78, 82, 84, 86, 90,
  97, 99, 102, 108-9, 112, 119-20,
  124-25, 127-29, 133-37, 142,
  147, 158, 164, 170, 177, 181
sacramental, xii-xvi, 6, 14-15,
  19, 23, 28, 30-31, 35, 46-48,
  50-53, 55-62, 72, 75, 77,
  80-81, 90, 98-99, 102-3, 105,
  107-9, 115, 117, 123, 125-26,
  130, 137-40, 144, 146, 149,
  151-54, 156-57, 158-62,
  163-64, 183-91
sacramental: body of Christ,
  14, 118-19, 125, 136, 142;
  minimalism, 83; proximity,
  132; universe, xvi, 5-6, 8, 19,
  35, 47, 53, 94, 158-59, 162, 186
sacramentalism, xvi, 48, 97
sacraments, xiii, 3, 7-8, 12,
  14-17, 22, 24-26, 31, 44-47,
  51-53, 72, 78, 86-88, 108, 117,
  119, 125, 147, 150, 152-53,
  157-58, 187
salvation history, 62, 97, 175
science, xiii, xv, 5, 6, 7, 20, 156,
  157, 158, 159
scientific worldview, 20
sea of faith, 21
Second Temple Judaism, 5
secularization of time, 63-65
sign, 19, 23, 28, 33, 35, 36, 42,

  50, 53, 70, 81, 85, 101, 107,
  109, 113, 117, 125, 135, 137, 151,
  167, 170, 172, 173, 185, 188,
  195, 196, 197, 198, 199
skepticism, 26, 154
skeptics, xv, 101-2, 107
spiritual, xvi, 6, 8, 17, 18, 28, 47,
  48, 51, 53, 81, 86, 94, 99, 105,
  107, 113, 123, 124, 125, 126,
  127, 128, 133, 135, 137, 144,
  147, 148, 151, 167, 183, 187,
  189, 190
spiritual: Communion, 134,
  178; life/path, xv, 146, 153;
  meaning, 167; reality, 8, 17,
  18, 28, 70, 75, 78, 109, 143;
  realm(s), 6, 7, 157; world(s),
  xv, 117, 118, 159
spiritualism, xvi, 97, 135, 144,
  146
spiritualistic interpretations, 96
spiritualists, 86, 90, 135, 143
spirituality, xiv, 21, 40, 52, 126,
  131, 146
spiritualize, 89, 152
suffering, xiv, 12, 25, 26, 27, 28,
  114, 148, 150
supernatural, 52, 127, 130, 139
Swiss Anabaptism, 135
symbol(s), xv, 4, 6, 8, 10, 19, 20,
  24, 25, 26, 28, 30, 31, 33, 36,
  42-44, 45, 65, 93-94, 96, 100,
  117-18, 127, 130, 134-35,
  136-37, 141, 157, 168, 170, 172,
  178, 179, 184, 189
symbolic acts/gestures/words,
  4, 19, 30, 32, 33, 39, 43, 76, 96
symbolic realism, 51, 117-18,
  124, 126, 137-38, 150, 184-86
table, 61, 110, 111, 113, 116, 132,
  137, 148, 150, 163-64, 166, 200,
  203. *See also* Lord's Table
table fellowship, 109, 111,
  168-69, 171-73
table ministry, 164, 167, 172
Taizé, 41
tongues, the gift of/speaking
  in, 28, 70, 72, 156
trade unions, 64
transcend/transcendence/
  transcendent, xv, xvi, 3, 16,
  17, 20, 21, 23-24, 28, 30, 35,

46, 47, 48, 54, 57, 59, 112, 146, 161, 183, 187
transignification, 49, 105, 124
transubstantiation, 51, 105, 127-28, 129, 134, 139
Trent, Council of. *See* Council of Trent
trinitarian, 9, 20, 21, 46, 94, 147, 186
trinitarianism, xii, xiii, 46, 148

Trinity, 1, 3, 12, 13, 47, 82
union of church and state, xii
upside-down kingdom, 38, 197
witness, 2, 10, 19, 26, 41-42, 68, 92, 95, 106, 108, 109, 187, 201. *See also* cloud of witnesses
words of institution, 94, 100, 106, 110, 114, 123, 131, 144, 151, 174, 175, 176, 196, 197, 199
worship, xi-xvi, 2, 8, 15, 16, 19,

21, 25, 26, 28, 33, 35-36, 38-39, 41-44, 47, 51, 62, 74, 76, 77, 78, 85, 113, 115, 119, 122, 123, 129, 148, 149, 152, 153, 154, 155, 160-61, 170, 174, 175-80, 183, 187-90, 192. *See also* Christian worship; early Christian worship, Protestant liturgy/worship

SCRIPTURE INDEX

OLD TESTAMENT

Genesis
1:6, *2*
1:14-19, *55*
1:29–2:3, *59*
2:2-3, *55*
2:24, *9, 17*
12:1-3, *55*
28:11-17, *44*

Exodus
3:1-6, *13*
12:1-27, *59*
16:1-8, *27*
20:8-11, *59*

Leviticus
25:1-7, *59*
25:8-17, *59*

Deuteronomy
5:3, *59*
5:12-15, *60*
24:17-22, *166*

Psalms
10:1, *25*
10:14, *25*
78:13-25, *199*

Isaiah
6:1-8, *13*
40–55, *27*

Lamentations
3:22-24, *27*

Amos
5:21, *188*

Micah
6:8, *26*

NEW TESTAMENT

Matthew
3:13-17, *69*
3:16-17, *67*
3:17, *69*
10:32-39, *66*
12:28, *22, 45*
14:19, *174*
19:4-6, *9*
25:31-40, *71*
25:31-46, *103*
26:26-28, *36*
26:26-29, *27, 168*
28:16-20, *89*
28:19, *73*

Mark
1:15, *67*
6:34, *166*
6:42, *167*
9:24, *27*
10:35-40, *35*
10:45, *27*
14:22, *174*

Luke
3:15-22, *69*
7:36-50, *68, 170*
11, *107*
11:14-20, *107*
11:16, *107*
11:20, *107*
15:1-2, *166*
19:1-10, *71*
22:15-16, *109*
22:18, *109*
22:19, *101*
22:19-20, *203*
22:24-30, *168*
22:29-30, *110, 111*
24:1-10, *61*
24:13-32, *61*
24:28-35, *111*
24:30, *111, 174*
24:33-42, *61*
24:35, *111*

John
1, *103*
1:1, *104*
1:1-3, *11*
1:1-17, *197*
1:14, *9, 11, 18, 102, 104*
1:18, *10, 47*
1:51, *44*
3, *69*
3:1-8, *105*
3:1–8, *97*
3:3, *69, 108*
3:5, *68, 69, 95, 98*
3:8, *69*
3:16, *108*
6, *101, 102, 103, 104,*
    105, 124, 144, 145,
    150, 152, 165
6:25-40, *67*
6:25-59, *105*
6:27, *101*
6:32, *101*
6:35, *101, 104*
6:35-50, *102*
6:41, *104*
6:44, *67, 102*
6:48, *104*
6:51, *101, 104*
6:51-58, *102*
6:52, *102*
6:53, *108*
6:53–56, *104*
6:57, *102, 104*
6:60-63, *104*
6:63, *102*
6:65, *102*
9:6-11, *94*
10:17, *196*
10:30, *104*
13, *177*
13:1-17, *174*
13:1-20, *199*
13:3-5, *199*
13:3-17, *35*
13:14, *199*
14:8-17, *67*

14:27, *195*
15:1-8, *200*
15:1-11, *102*
15:16-17, *200*
16:5-15, *48*
16:12-15, *67*
20:16, *18*
20:20, *18*
20:24-29, *61*
21:4-19, *71*
21:7, *18*
21:12, *18*

Acts
1:1-11, *107*
1:6, *112*
1:6-8, *22*
1:8, *112*
2:1-4, *107*
2:1-36, *70*
2:29-42, *169*
2:37-42, *72*
2:38, *70*
2:41-47, *189*
2:43-46, *169*
8–17, *71*
8:12, *98*
8:14-17, *98*
8:25, *71*
8:26-39, *71*
8:35-38, *98*
9:1-22, *68*
10:1–48, *71*
10:44-48, *72, 98, 165*
10:47, *71*
17:1-7, *71*
17:7, *111*
17:16-34, *50*
17:28, *22*
19, *98*
19:1-7, *75*

Romans
2:4, *67, 169*
5, *83*
5:6-11, *71*

5:10, *169*
5:12, *83*
6, 8, 14, *158*
6:1-4, *96*
6:1-11, *75*
6:3, *2, 8, 158*
6:4, *95*
6:10, *138*
6:11, *68*
7:4, *148, 171*
8:9-11, *108*
8:14, *108*
8:15-16, *109*
8:19-23, *94*
8:22-25, *19*
9–11, *196*
10:14-17, *97*
10:17, *96*
12:1, *49, 132*
16:26, *89*

1 Corinthians
6:19-20, *17*
10, *193*
10:14-22, *176*
10:16, *106, 176*

10:16-17, *14, 45, 49, 71, 148, 196*
11:23-26, *14*
11:24, *148*
11:26, *110*
11:27, *148*
12, *10, 14, 49, 66, 106*
12:12, *148*
12:12-13, *67*
12:13, *97, 109*
12:27, *118, 148*
15, *18*
15:20-22, *71*
15:42-55, *104*
15:42-58, *28*

2 Corinthians
1:22, *22*
3:17-18, *61*
4:5, *27*
4:6, *9, 11, 44*
5:1-9, *18*
5:5, *22*
5:14-15, *71*
5:14-19, *30*
5:16, *103*

Galatians
2:20, *49, 70, 103, 109, 160*
4:4, *61*

Ephesians
2:11-18, *110*
2:11-22, *171*
2:11–3:10, *72*
2:13-16, *27*
3, *196*
3:1-12, *15*
3:2-11, *44*
3:4, *29*
5:31-32, *17*

Philippians
2:5-7, *6, 12*
3:7-11, *71*

Colossians
1:15-19, *11*
1:15-20, *19*
1:17, *47*
1:19, *47*
1:24, *191*
2:9-15, *27*

2:11-13, *75*
2:13-15, *110*
3:5-11, *76*

Hebrews
1:2, *47*
2:12-19, *97*
2:14-18, *146*
4:14-16, *47*
6:4, *81*
7:27, *138*
9:24-28, *119*
9:26, *132*
10:2, *132*
11:1–12:2, *27*

1 John
4:2, *103*
4:7-12, *15*
4:7-16, *199*

Revelation
1:10, *61*
2:4, *155*
21, *9*
22:20, *111*

DYNAMICS OF CHRISTIAN WORSHIP

Worship of the triune God stands at the heart of the Christian life, so understanding the many dynamics of Christian worship—including prayer, reading the Bible, preaching, baptism, the Lord's Supper, music, visual art, architecture, and more—is both a perennial and crucial issue for the church. With that in mind, the Dynamics of Christian Worship (DCW) series seeks to enable Christians to grow in their understanding of the many aspects of Christian worship. By harvesting the fruits of biblical, theological, historical, practical, and liturgical scholarship and by drawing from a wide range of worshiping contexts and denominational backgrounds, the DCW series seeks to deepen both the theology and practice of Christian worship for the life of the church.

TITLES INCLUDE

+ John Rempel, *Recapturing an Enchanted World: Ritual and Sacrament in the Free Church Tradition*

+ Glenn Packiam, *Worship and the World to Come: Exploring Christian Hope in Contemporary Worship* (forthcoming)

+ Esther Crookshank, *Christ Our Song: Psalms, Hymns, and Spiritual Songs in the History of Worship from the Early Church to Watts* (forthcoming)